A Nation by Rights

In the series
Queer Politics, Queer Theories,
edited by Shane Phelan

A Nation by Rights

National Cultures,
Sexual Identity Politics, and the
Discourse of Rights

Carl F. Stychin

 Temple University Press
PHILADELPHIA

HQ
76.5
.S79
1998

OCLC # 37987035
Temple University Press, Philadelphia 19122
Copyright © 1998 by Temple University
All rights reserved
Published 1998
Printed in the United States of America

∞ The paper used in this publication meets the requirements of
American National Standard for Information Sciences—Permanence
of Paper for Printed Library Materials, ANSI Z39.48–1984

Library of Congress Cataloging-in-Publication Data

Stychin, Carl F. (Carl Franklin), 1964–
    A nation by rights : national cultures, sexual identity politics, and the discourse
of rights / Carl F. Stychin.
        p.   cm. — (Queer politics, queer theories)
    Includes bibliographical references and index.
    ISBN 1-56639-623-9 (alk. paper). — ISBN 1-56639-624-7 (pbk. : alk. paper)
    1. Gay rights—Cross-cultural studies.   2. Gender identity—Cross-cultural
studies.   3. National characteristics—Cross-cultural studies.   I. Title.
II. Series.
HQ76.5.S79   1988
305.9′0664—dc21   97-32826
                                                                            CIP

Contents

Acknowledgments

I would like to begin by expressing my appreciation to the many activists, politicians, and others who generously granted me interviews for this project. I also want to thank all of those friends (old and new) in the United Kingdom, Canada, South Africa, and Australia, for their support, encouragement, and advice, and especially Shauna Van Praagh and Kate Harrison for finding me places to live in Montreal and Sydney. The institutional support I received from McGill University Faculty of Law while I was a visitor there in 1996 was invaluable in the writing of this book, as was the support of the University of Sydney Faculty of Law, which awarded me a Parsons Fellowship in 1997. The financial support of the British Academy, in the form of a Small Personal Research Grant in 1995, allowed me to travel to South Africa and is gratefully acknowledged.

My former institution, Keele University, has been enormously supportive of this book. I want to thank the Department of Law for granting me a sabbatical semester in 1996 and the university for a Research Award in 1997, both of which allowed me the time to research and write. The Keele University Inter-Library Loan Service has been extremely helpful in gathering materials. Most of all, I want to thank my former colleagues in the Department of Law for creating such a collegial, fun, and supportive place to work. I am convinced that there is no law school quite like it anywhere.

Special thanks are due to those friends and colleagues who read and commented on earlier versions of the manuscript. Kenneth Armstrong generously instructed me on European integration and gave detailed comments on chapter five; Wayne Morgan provided numerous insights on Australia, and critically commented on a draft of chapter six; and Noel Whitty helpfully shared his observations on Irishness and parades, as well as commented on chapter two. Davina Cooper generously read many chapters, and I greatly appreciate the combination of critical insight and encouragement she provided throughout the writing process. I also am enormously appreciative of the support of Didi Herman, who commented faithfully on drafts, encouraged me to further develop my own ideas, and supported my work in innumerable ways. Thanks to my series editor Shane Phelan for her detailed comments and encouraging words, to Doris Braendel at Temple University Press for her unfailing support of this project, and to Yvonne Ramsey for copy editing. I also want to thank my mother Grace Baranyk, not only for her encouragement of my work, and her frequent (and not subtle) inquiries on its progress, but most importantly, for her help with computers. Finally, thanks to Michael Thomson for sharing the exhilaration and hysteria of completing his book at the same moment as this one.

This book has greatly benefited from the comments of audiences at numerous academic gatherings: Queen's University, Kingston, Queer Studies Group seminar (1996); McGill University Faculty of Law Legal Theory, Annie Macdonald Langstaff Workshop (1996); Canadian Law and Society Annual Conference, Brock University (1996); American Law and Society Annual Meetings at Strathclyde University, Glasgow (1996) and St. Louis (1997); Critical Legal Conference, University of East London (1996); staff seminars at the Faculties of Law, University of Sydney and Macquarie University (1997); Socio-Legal Studies Association Annual Conference, Cardiff University (1997); and the "Queering the Nation" Conference, Warwick University (1997).

Finally, I acknowledge permission to reproduce previously published, earlier versions of portions of this book. An earlier version of chapter two appears as "Celebration and Consolidation: National Rituals and the Legal Construction of American Identities" in *Oxford Journal of Legal Studies* (1998), and an earlier version of chapter four appears as "Queer Nations: Nationalism, Sexuality, and the Discourse of Rights in Quebec" in *Feminist Legal Studies* (1997, 5:3). Chapter two appears by permission of Oxford University Press, and chapter four is here reprinted by permission of Deborah Charles Publications.

A Nation by Rights

1 Introduction

This book is about three central themes: national cultures, sexual identities, and the discourse of rights. My interest is in how national identities are constituted in sexual and gendered terms, how groups mobilize around sexual identities and articulate their relationship to the national culture, and how rights discourse informs and constitutes both national *and* sexual identities. The relationship between these identities has intrigued me for a number of years. When I arrive at London's Heathrow Airport, I am immediately confronted by the physical separation of travelers at the immigration checkpoint into two categories: European Union citizens and Others. As a permanent resident of the United Kingdom, I occupy an awkward position that does not easily fit either category. I proceed to the Other line, among those who have no entitlement or right to enter the country. Although many in the line may be subjected to questioning, I know that as a white, male, middle-class academic, my encounter with the authorities will be brief, painless, and perhaps even friendly. I may be sharing the line with others, but I know that, to all outward appearance, I am not the other here.

The construction of some identities as other to the nation makes me think about how English (as opposed to British) national identity has had such an ambiguous and contradictory relationship to sexual identities, particularly the "homosexual" as the nation's other. Official discourse has long sought to constitute homosexuality (or, in contemporary terminology, lesbians and gays) as a threat to the nation and its values. Historically, homosexuality was bound up in the identity of the upper class as decadent and perverse, thereby erasing diverse working-class sexualities. But British popular culture has regularly deployed at least male homosexuality as an integral, and not particularly threatening, element of the national identity, even when the word "homosexuality" could not be spoken on stage or screen. Homosexuality seems to reside both

1

within and outside the nation, defying easy categorization as inside or out.

Moreover, some British gays and lesbians today are arguing for their "right" to join the military and fight for "their" nation state. It seems increasingly likely that they will be victorious, thanks in part to the growing influence of European Union law within the United Kingdom. The arguments presented seem to replicate the American debates, a culture in which rights talk (and litigation) is so much more central to national life. Yet, the process has been facilitated by the Europeanization of constitutional law. Nationality and sexuality thus are dynamic identities, and their openness to reimagination is closely related to the translation of political demands into the language of rights. This book is an attempt to understand this contested relationship.

Identifying Nationally

While the modern nation may be a social construction that emerged at a particular historical moment in Western consciousness, it is a construction that has proven extremely versatile in its capacity for transplantation into different social, geographical, temporal, and political contexts. Although the nation is as Anderson (1991, p. 6) famously termed it an "imagined political community," it is surely one of the most durable political imaginings we encounter. While our collective political consciousness may now be virtually inseparable from the concept of the nation state, Anderson argues that the imagining of nation was made possible by historical changes in the West in the ways in which the world came to be perceived. The emergence of print culture in Europe served to constitute an imagined sameness between authors and audiences, which came to replace religion as the central marker of identity (see also Steedman 1995).[1] In addition, sovereignty depended on the conception of borders as finite and limitable (and therefore capable of being mapped) and on the determination of membership in national collectivities (through, for example, the census). But both the map and the census were the product of a particular comprehension of physical and human geography that first emerged in the sixteenth century (Blomley 1994). The combination of the nation's centrality and its historical specificity must be kept firmly in view, for together they confirm that the nation is "at the same time a fiction and a principle organizing actual social relations" (Laclau and Mouffe 1985, p. 119). The success of "nation," however, rests in large measure on how it has managed to camouflage its constructedness. While all social constructions must be continually reinforced, the nation has been extremely successful in naturalizing itself as a way of managing both people and place. But the nation, like social constructions more generally, never fully masks the fact that it is always in process. Moreover, the boundaries of nations and nation states are rarely identical, but the belief that they *should* be has conveniently served as the basis for dominance by some national groups at the expense of others and for the construction of minorities as outside of the nation *and* the nation state (Yuval-Davis 1997, p. 11).

Anderson (1991, p. 145) observes that the constructedness of nation is apparent in the language used to describe the relationship between the immigrant and the national community. The "foreigner" seeks "naturalization"—to be *made* a part of the community. The term "naturalization" highlights how the language of nation can be deeply essentialist; membership is a product, not of politics, but of nature. At the same time, the individual can be reconstituted as *inside* this imagining; he or she can be remade (or, perhaps, "born again"). Naturalization also suggests that the condition placed on the invitation to the outsider is that inclusion will bring normalization. That is, naturalization implies homogenization—to lose one's difference in the process of gaining membership in the greater "universal" of the national community (Grosz 1993).

The nation thus appears at the same time to be both fixed and porous in its membership. Naturalization means that one need not be born into membership. One's nature can be refashioned. But the nation *state* simultaneously needs borders that are fixed. After all, membership has its privileges and is both finite and limited. Not just *anyone* is capable of being naturalized. How those conditions of membership are understood is central to the construction of nation.

There have been three principal meanings of nation (Jackson and Penrose 1994). In the thirteenth century, nation was first used in the English language to connote a racial or religious group, thus creating the relationship between *ethnos* and nation. The second meaning of nation emerged in the eighteenth century, when nation was increasingly employed to define smaller groups, each constituting a separate people that in turn came to be essentialized as fundamental human divisions. But, with this usage, the connections between nation and race became more tenuous. Rousseau is credited with the idea of political nationalism, the third meaning of nation as a product of political agreement between individuals (the *demos* of nation) rather than as coterminous with a racially defined people. Thus, the politically defined nation has come to have a spatial dimension through which its legitimacy *qua* nation state is greatly enhanced.

Despite its redefinition as an agreement between members who are its citizens, the nation has remained a primary arena for the articulation of racist ideologies (see, e.g., Preuss 1994). It continues to resonate with the belief in a common blood bond shared by its members, which constitutes them as an essential group. Through the implicit and often explicit connections between race and nation, a biologically and culturally based essentialism is reinforced and the social constructedness of nation further disguised.

The connections between race and nation have been developed by Fitzpatrick (1995), who argues that because the nation is constitutively finite, it is through the articulation of its limits that the nation defines itself. But, in a seemingly contradictory maneuver, the nation is constructed as the universal in opposition to what appears other to it, an other that is defined in terms of particularity. Thus, universalism and particularism, rather than being opposing concepts, are in fact both implicated in the constitution of national identity (see also Chow 1993). The universal of nation must incorporate that which it simultaneously excludes. That is, if the nation is universalized by virtue of defining itself oppositionally against the other, then the other resides within the very concept of nation. For the modern Western nation, the other is represented as that which is opposed to "civilization"—"the possibility of reversion to a savage and barbaric past" against which the nation must guard itself (Fitzpatrick 1995, p. 15).

The mode of organizing people and place through which the modern nation was imagined may be altering in the face of economic and cultural globalization. The term globalization signifies a range of economic, political, and technological shifts that have weakened the capacity of the nation state (particularly in the Third World) to control those processes that historically were considered to be central to national governance (see, e.g., Fitzpatrick 1995, Maurer 1995, Coombe 1995, Calhoun 1994). Central to globalization has been the increasingly free movement of capital and the integration of states into a world economy where the economic levers are no longer controlled by national governments. Thus, economic borders are becoming historical artifacts as capital flows more freely and flexibly (see Maurer 1995). The economic impact includes the further separation of production and consumption, with the former centered in low wage Third World economies. The flexible movement of capital also means that the ability of national governments to control tax and fiscal policies, particularly in developing economies, is severely limited. Policies are now designed to facilitate investment by multinational corporations, which remain ready to "pack up" and move should those policies become comparatively less attractive (see Maurer 1995, Coombe 1995).

The free movement of capital is closely connected to the mobility of persons. Instantaneous communication and global travel have resulted in widespread economic migration and new diasporic communities (although both phenomena have histories that long predate current movements). These communities increasingly have the ability to mobilize transnationally, which further challenges the coherence and homogeneity of national identity (Rattansi 1995). National borders now are being conceived by both financial and, to a lesser extent, human capital as fluid, porous, and open to free movement. With respect to the movement of people, this is actively resisted in many cases by governments through tightened immigration laws.

Corporate managers are well aware of the power of capital to foreclose assertions of economic nationalism by governments. Ohmae (1995) provides managers and policy makers with a blueprint documenting the decline of the nation state in terms of its economic impact. He outlines how the power of instantaneous shifts of capital, made possible by the rapid development of information technology, means that trade now only constitutes a small percentage of international economic activity. In addition, global capital markets have ensured that nation states can no longer effectively control their exchange rates or protect their currencies against market forces. The nation becomes a "nostalgic fiction," a "bit actor" (p. 12), and an *"unnatural,* even dysfunctional unit in terms of which to think about or organize economic activity" (p. 42, emphasis added).

The relationship between the national and the global, however, is multidimensional. The conditions of globalization do distort the balance between universality and particularity that was central to the constitution of the modern nation state. For example, Darian-Smith (1995a) has illustrated how the globalization of law through transnational political and economic arrangements such as the European Union has created the conditions under which some individuals and groups in the United Kingdom now appeal to a "plurality" of legal systems—at the local, national, and transnational levels.[2] The relationship between the national and the global operates along other trajectories as well. While globalization may undermine the claims to universality of nation, the nation state also responds to the global (see Calhoun 1994). Nationalism can serve to resist the universalizing strategies of international capital through, for example, the increasing emphasis on the closing of national borders to immigration. Moreover, as has become so tragically apparent, the political terrain in which globalization is occurring has seen "the recreation of the political frontier" through dangerously reinvigorated nationalisms (Mouffe 1994, p. 105). As Darian-Smith (1995b, p. 86) argues, "nationalism and transnationalism are distinct but aligned processes."

Globalization, in fact, positively encourages the production of nationalism, but only in those ways that reinforce the free market. The nation continues to provide an important site for individual identity and "belonging," and national identities increasingly have been severed from a critique of capital. For example, Maurer (1995) has shown how in the British Virgin Islands (BVI) national identity is substantially constituted through laws aimed at enhancing the "marketability" of the BVI to offshore capital investment.[3] National identity comes to depend on the commodification of nation for the benefit of capital. In this way, "transnationalism can be interpreted as a neo-imperialist process, requiring as much as any form of nationalism an abstracted other through which to define itself as a coherent force" (Darian-Smith 1995b, p. 87).

The free movement of capital is tied to the mobility of persons engaged in economic migration across national borders. The movement of persons also undermines the historic claims of national homogeneity. Migration flows have allowed those who historically were constituted as other to the Western nation to occupy those national spaces, which may have transformative potential for how national identity is conceived (Coombe 1995). At the least, the palpable *fear* within the West that "occupation" by the other will prove negatively transformative contributes to an emphasis on closed borders. These challenges, combined with claims by indigenous peoples grounded in the language of national rights, can further decenter the "nebulous mythological concept" of nation (Bowman 1994, p. 144).

Social movements also deploy the language of nation as a means of constituting and reinforcing their own identities. In this way, movements can appropriate and redeploy nationalism for their own ends, using the discourse that has often been employed against them. An example is the Black Nationalist movement in the United States, which existed parallel to the Civil Rights movement during the 1960s. The critique offered by black nationalism grounded racial differences, not within a model based on individual and state discrimination and segregation, but as the outcome of an ongoing history of colonialism imposed on an African diaspora (see Peller 1990, Clark 1991). In this sense, the language of nationalism can be contrasted to integrationism, offering an alternative account (and a critique of the liberal narrative of the nation) that was relegated to a secondary role in race relations (Peller 1990; see also Chang 1992, Alfred 1995).

The politics of appropriating nationalism remains politically volatile. Nations have been historically constituted in gendered and sexualized terms, and oppositional appropriations of nationalism frequently replicate, for example, a gendered understanding of politics. Black nationalism was subject to critique for employing a highly masculinized and sexist conception of the nation (although some of that critique may well be tainted by racism). So, too, Quebec nationalism traditionally was informed by a strategy centered on the "revenge of the cradle," wherein women's bodies were the front line of a nationalist struggle that encouraged high reproductive rates.[4] Nationalism in that context depended on the reduction of women to agents of reproduction in the name of national survival. Thus, while oppositional deployments of nation can prove strategically useful, they may also reinforce relations of domination along other vectors.

Gendering and Sexualizing the Nation

One of the historically central relations of domination in the construction of national identity has been gender. Recent feminist interventions have provided an important corrective to the literature on nationalism and national identity in this regard (see, e.g., Yuval-Davies 1997; Eisenstein 1996; West 1997; McClintock 1995, 1996). Yuval-Davies (1997, p. 3), for example, has described "a gendered understanding of nations and nationalisms, by examining systematically the crucial contribution of gender relations into several major dimensions of nationalist projects." She finds three key aspects to the relationship. First, women have been constructed as the biological reproducers of the nation. Demands have been placed on them to have more children, fewer children, and to "improve the quality of the national stock," all in the service of the nation (p. 22). Second, gender symbols have played an important role in the cultural reproduction of the nation. That is, specific national codes define and constitute appropriate gender roles. Third, the discourse of citizenship—the basis of membership in nation states—is gendered in its construction of the public and private spheres and through the notion of active (male) and passive (female) citizenship. Active citizenship includes the duty of defending the nation militarily (and defending women and children in the process).

Eisenstein (1996, p. 43) refers to this dynamic as "the gender exclusivity of nation," whereby "the symbolised woman, as mother of us all, psychically attaches the nation to family and nature, with their racialized meanings." Similarly, McClintock (1995, p. 357) has shown how "nations are symbolically figured as domestic genealogies," wherein familial discourse becomes crucial to relationships centering on the nation:

> The metaphoric depiction of social hierarchy as natural and familial—the "national family," the global "family of nations," the colony as a "family of black children ruled over by a white father"—depended in this way on the prior naturalizing of the social subordination of women and children within the domestic sphere. (McClintock 1995, p. 358)[5]

Thus, national identities clearly have been bound up with gender and race within the Western imaginary. My focus in this book—the sexuality of nation—is closely related. I will argue, following Beriss (1996, p. 191), that "sexuality appears to be a volatile symbol in debates about the character of national identity." In its sexual dimension, European nationalisms historically were closely connected to bourgeois morality and a concomitant aesthetic of respectability (Mosse 1985, p. 9). Central to that aesthetic was the constitution of "normality," which was deployed as the basis for new national stereotypes as well as the reinforcement of middle class morality. Fixed and unchanging sex and gender roles were of prime importance, and anything that could be construed as undermining that fixity was constructed as the nation's other. In this way, sex role confusion was ascribed to those most clearly defined as outside the nation, namely othered races. So, too, the homosexual, an historically specific construct, symbolized the confusion of the sexes and a sexual excess, which also was other to the nation's self-constitution.[6]

It is important, however, to avoid claiming a single dynamic of sexuality that has operated cross-culturally and trans-historically—of arguing that there is some essence in the relationship of national, and sexual, acts and identities (see generally Herdt 1997). To do so is likely to impose a specifically Eurocentric construction under the guise of universality.[7] At the same time, it does seem clear that when the nation state perceives a threat to its existence, that danger is frequently translated into sexualized terms. Same sex sexuality is deployed as the alien other, linked to conspiracy, recruitment, opposition to the nation, and ultimately a threat to civilization.[8] This phenomenon has been largely, but not exclusively, examined in terms of the maleness of the state and the othering of male same-sex sexual practices, as well as in the construction of some homo-social activity in a nonsexual fashion so as to absorb it within the national character (see Mosse 1985, Harper 1994).

Moran (1991), for example, has examined the association of ho-mosexuality and "security risk" in 1950s Britain, finding that ho-mosexuality was deployed oppositionally to the nation state. In this context, homosexuality served to consolidate the nation and pro-mote international relations. The British crackdown on homosexu-als in this period was partly the product of American pressure and reflected Britain's increased dependence on the United States in a new postcolonial era of superpower domination. Britain's dimin-ished international role coincided with the reconstruction of the homosexual as a threat within its borders. The effect was to deflect attention onto (male) homosexuality as the cause of national de-cline. The homosexual was the potential (and actual) spy, who had to be identified and excluded from national space:

> The sexual boundary justifies not the establishment of a defence against foreign invasion or the initiation of foreign wars, but the establish-ment of a regime of national surveillance, and a form of civil war waged through domestic repression, domination and eradication. (Moran 1991, p. 167)[9]

In Moran's analysis, it is the male homosexual body that is alien, a threat, and "embodied." In this sense, the national subject and the masculine subject are similarly constructed as abstract, in contrast to the feminine, embodied subject. Yingling (1994) argued, in the context of discourses surrounding HIV, that AIDS is inscribed as foreign to the national imaginary of the United States. Disease itself demands an embodied subject (for it signifies the limits of the body and its transcendence). Embodied subjectivity is rejected in the constitution of the Western nation as abstract, universal, and mas-culine (see also Manalansan 1993). The subject who transcends the body is the full member of the body politic, which reinforces the primacy of the white male as the emblematic Western citizen (see Berlant 1991a).[10]

The relationship between sexuality, gender, and nation "cannot be understood apart from their position in relation to local and global political processes" (Murray 1996, p. 251). These processes have been examined by Alexander (1991, 1994) in her analysis of sexuality and nationalism in the postcolonial state. She has linked the impact of globalization to race, gender, sexuality, and nationhood in Trinidad and Tobago and the Bahamas. Alexander examines the criminalization of nonprocreative sexual activity, particularly lesbian sexuality. Heterosexuality has been nationalized, and some sexualities constituted as perils to the postcolonial state, as "the effects of political and economic international processes provoke a legitimation crisis for the state which moves to restore its legitimacy by recouping heterosexuality through legislation" (Alexander 1994, p. 7). The movement of global capital is not coded as dangerously undermining the national identity or destructive of the state's ability to control the economic levers. Rather, lesbianism and gay male sexuality become the threats to national identity.

The sexualization of the postcolonial state, however, is complicated by the role of "a political economy of desire in tourism that relies upon the sexualization and commodification of women's bodies" (Alexander 1994, p. 6). But the sexualization of black bodies for white tourists is not constructed as imperiling the nation through a neocolonial fetishizing of race. Indeed, the combination of events that signal globalization — capital flows, large scale north to south tourism, the separation of production and consumption across continents — are not interpreted as destructive of nation, but rather as central to its continuing existence: "in this equation, tourism, foreign multi-national capital production and imperialism are as integral and as necessary to the natural order as heterosexuality" (p. 11).

The heterosexuality of national identity underscores how oppositional (in this case, postcolonial) deployments of nationalism can reinforce domination and inferiority along new dimensions. As Murray (1996, p. 252) argues, the postcolonial state "must overcome the racialized and sexualized predispositions of national models of identity that were built out of and against colonized populations." One means by which this is attempted is through the discourse of colonial contamination, wherein homosexuality is attributed to the white colonizer and has served as a means to exploit the colonized sexually (a theme that emerges in many of my case studies). Part of the postcolonial project of nation building, according to Alexander (1994, p. 13), has been the need for a "Black nationalist masculinity" to demonstrate that it was "ready" to govern by replicating (and reifying) those norms of Western nationalist respectability. This appropriation of nationalism is exacerbated by the acid bath operating on national borders through economic globalization, in which the postcolonial state seeks to conform to international definitions of respectable morality and order. In this context, "homosexuality is crucial both for the maintenance of state cultural authority and the popular ethic of hypermasculinity" (Murray 1996, p. 252). If the colonial relationship was constructed as parental, "the aggressive heterosexual male combats this infantilization, yet in doing so perpetuates colonial nationalism's racial construction of the passionate, uncontrollable 'other'" (p. 259).

To characterize national identity as masculine, abstract, universal, and disembodied is an oversimplification. We must also account for "the iconography of interstate relations" (Cooper 1995, p. 72). The relationship between states displays a homosociality, and, in addition, the sovereign Western state "represents the fantasy of a certain kind of heterosexual masculinity . . . impermeable, bounded, separate and Other to the chaotic world that surrounds it" (Orford 1996, pp. 75–76; see also Yack 1995). This construction reflects the threat of the effeminized non-Western state that still claims the status of nationhood. The fear of the other is compounded by the effects of globalization, in which borders are perceived as becoming more porous and boundaries less rigid, and diasporic communities threaten to infiltrate and cause "ruptures within the contingent coherence of the masculine state's corporate identity" (Cooper 1995, p. 72).

The relationship between the disembodied, universal, abstract Western nation state and its other is exemplified by the post–cold war relationship between East and West Germany. Sieg (1995) argues that the East German state was constituted sexually through homophobia. Lesbians and gay men were other to a Communist asexual national identity, reinforced by the national myth of "a Nazi-homosexual conspiracy against the oppositional left" (p. 95). It is ironic that the power differentials today between East and West have resulted in "the inscription of heterosexual power structures into inter-German relations" (p. 105), characterized, in particular, by a sexualized relationship of domination and submission. The former East has become the feminized other to the paradigm of the post–cold war disembodied, masculinist nation: West Germany.

Sexualizing Citizenship

I have argued up to this point that modern nations and nation states constitute themselves through the construction of others, who are located outside of the national imaginary. My focus now shifts to the relationship between sexual "minorities" and the dominant discourses of nation and citizenship—the ways in which social movements around sexuality articulate their claims for inclusion within the national imaginary.

"Deviant" sexual identities exemplify this process of othering. Not surprisingly, those who take up *identities* that have been inscribed in this way often respond by seeking inclusion within the national imaginary. They argue, generally through social movements, that deviance from the heterosexual norm should not be a bar to full membership (or citizenship) in the nation. Thus, lesbians, gays, and bisexuals attempt in various ways to construct themselves as "good" citizens; in the United States, for example, they are capable of being good soldiers and good CIA agents—that is, "normal" citizens (see Stychin 1996c).

These issues have given rise to vociferous disagreements within sexual identity communities about the implications of such strategies. Debates are frequently framed in terms of a division between assimilationist and anti-assimilationist politics. The latter aspires to the transformation of heterosexual institutions, including the nation itself, rather than incorporation within them and is sometimes described, in the United States particularly, as "queer politics" (see, e.g., Stein 1993; Warner 1993; Butler 1993; Sedgwick 1993; Derbyshire 1994; Duggan 1992, 1994; McIntosh 1993; Bower 1994). Such a binary division is problematic, however, because it erases both the cultural politics of lesbian feminism[11] and the nuances of all of these social movements.[12]

A more accurate approach might be to characterize activism along a continuum between ethnic/essentialist understandings of social groups and a more deconstructionist orientation:

> Gay and lesbian social movements have built a quasi-ethnicity. . . . Underlying that ethnicity is typically the notion that what gays and lesbians share—the anchor of minority status and minority rights claims—is the same fixed, natural essence, a self with same-sex desires. . . . In this ethnic/essentialist politic, clear categories of collective identity are necessary for successful resistance and political gain. Yet this impulse to build a collective identity with distinct group boundaries has been met by a directly opposing logic, often contained in queer activism (and in the newly anointed "queer theory"): to take apart the identity categories and blur group boundaries. . . . It is socially produced binaries (gay/straight, man/woman) that are the basis of oppression; fluid, unstable experiences of self become fixed primarily in the service of social control. (Gamson 1995, p. 391)

Despite the differences between ethnic/essentialist and queer/deconstructionist approaches, both are frequently articulated to rights claims and citizenship within the Western nation state (although queer activism less so). In that sense, they share a politics of interest where a broadening of the national imaginary is demanded to include sexual "minorities." But, as Sinfield (1996, p. 272) notes, "it is not that existing categories of gay men and lesbians have come forward to claim their rights, but that we have become constituted *as gay* in terms of a discourse of ethnicity-and-rights." And the discourse of equality has assumed a centrality in these calls for full membership and citizenship. A politics of rights can also facilitate the division between the assimilable and the non-assimilable into a national imaginary constituted around citizenship (see Smith 1994, Eaton 1994). This effect is hardly surprising. As Sinfield (1996, p. 273) observes, while the "ethnicity-and-rights model" holds out the promise of democratic citizenship, the concept of citizenship has been constituted through exclusions:

> "Citizen" has never meant "inhabitant." It always counterposes some others who are present but not full citizens—at best, visitors, but usually also racial, ethnic and sexual minorities, slaves, criminals, the lower classes, women, children, the elderly. In our Enlightenment inheritance, the nation is an unstable construct, and ideas of citizenship

are deployed, typically, in a hegemonic process whereby outsiders are
stigmatized and potential deviants jostled into place.

Citizenship discourse, although intuitively attractive, may well reproduce rather than resolve many of the exclusions from national
identity that outsiders seek to correct.

Aspirations to full national citizenship for gays and lesbians are
not limited to the terrain of rights discourse and claims to legal
equality. Some have argued that the modern Western citizen is increasingly a product of his or her constitution as a consumer (see,
e.g., Cooper 1993). Rather than problematizing that conjunction,
financially well-off gays and lesbians sometimes embrace citizenship in this form. Historically, consumer consumption was fairly
central to the constitution of a Western gay male subjectivity (see
Bronski 1984). However, it has considerable negative implications.
A focus on consumption alone erases the role of labor and also
reinforces class-based divisions within lesbian and gay movements.
Thus, as Hennessy (1995, p. 161) argues, the "fetishization of the
commodity" may well be a limited resistance strategy (see also Herman 1994b; Adam 1995, p. 164; Evans 1993).[13] A model of national
citizenship constructed around the citizen as consumer thus seems
an inadequate basis for reimagining national identity for lesbians
and gays. Other strategies might better serve that project.

Reforming Rights, Reenvisioning the Nation

Throughout this book, I return to the potential and pitfalls of the
deployment of nationhood discourse by lesbians and gays. There
are competing views about the likelihood that struggles around
sexuality might serve as a way in which to reimagine national identity in a less exclusionary fashion. Many feminists, for example, are
skeptical about whether nationhood as a concept can be invoked in
a more open, anti-essentialist way (see, e.g., Phelan 1994, p. 154).
Others describe their feminism as constituted through nationalist
struggles in which they are actively engaged (see generally West
1997). A central issue in my case studies is whether national identity, and identity more generally, can be reconceived in a contingent and flexible fashion that does not depend on the construction
of the other (or, at a minimum, resists such rigid exclusions).

Phelan (1994, p. 154) has argued that such a reimagining of national identity would require "a conscious weaving of threads between tattered fabrics." However, I look to the possibility of such a tapestry woven through the discourse of nationhood, one that is actively engaged in struggling against fixed identity borders.

It is not surprising that Phelan expresses reservations about the discourse of nationalism. Feminist theory and practice have long grappled with the difficulty of both asserting a group identity around gender and recognizing the costs of fixed nation-like borders to identity and membership. Differences within the group too often come to be assimilated or exiled. In this regard, Mohanty (1995, p. 75) has focused on the importance of recognizing the meaningfulness of categories while avoiding the assertion of "groups with *already constituted* experiences as groups," such as universalizing claims about the category "woman." Rather, the group must be understood as composed of a plethora of experiences that stem from differences in material and ideological power.

The attempt to both mobilize and de-essentialize categories also is exemplified by the work of Young (1995), in which she has somewhat revised her earlier (1990) deployment of "city life" as a vision of social relations where group difference is affirmed. While the affirmation of groups remains a central tenet for Young, she now recognizes that groups cannot be understood as possessing a predetermined essential nation-like composition. Instead, membership ebbs and flows and is open textured, with blurred boundaries and shifting unities. In this regard, Young's conception of groups is related to Butler's (1990) claim that gender identity is subject to ongoing conflict and is never essentially fixed. In the task of reconceiving national identity and revising the concept of citizenship, feminist theory is invaluable. The issue many feminist theorists have analyzed is, given that any political community is in some sense *bounded,* how do we learn to live with boundaries and to reconfigure them so as to challenge their exclusionary power?[14] In other words, can the solid line that marks out national boundaries on the map be reimagined in alternative forms?

Rights discourse is one site for the engagement in that dialogue. However, many have argued that historically the achievement of rights claims by the disempowered has often resulted in the "normalization" of more radical claims aimed at social transformation. "Minorities" thus become absorbed and validated in terms of prevailing national norms (see, e.g., Herman 1990, Brown 1995, Cheah 1997). Difference from that norm becomes a deviation, although one that can be privatized and thereby overlooked in the monocultural liberal state (Slaughter 1994). But the power of rights discourse lies in its claim to universality, and there are no inherent limits on who can make rights claims, potentially broadening the horizon of citizenship in the process. For example, I examine the deployment of rights around sexual orientation in the language of *universal* human rights in chapter six, a case in which rights appear to "trump" claims grounded in the language of democracy and even national sovereignty.[15]

While normalization is one side of the rights equation, the norm itself may become "troubled" and possibly destabilized through the articulation of rights (Herman 1994a, p. 147). Thus, as the dominant background norms of national identity must continually be reconstituted, rights claims are one means by which groups and individuals can play an active role in altering how the nation is imagined. In fact, given the centrality of rights discourse in the Western national imaginary, it seems an obvious arena in which to engage in that struggle.

There is, however, nothing inevitably progressive about rights (Brown 1995). Rather, the outcomes of rights discourse are a result of political, legal, and historical context, and the power of rights discourse is culturally specific. Not only is this discussion heavily Western in its focus, but, in addition, the role of rights varies between Western cultures (Weeks 1995, p. 119). Awareness of this cultural variability must be combined with an appreciation that the function of rights can shift over time within cultures. I examine these points in greater depth throughout this book.

The reimagination of nation through the deployment of rights raises interesting and difficult questions. Although history is replete with examples of nationalist-inspired violations of individual and group rights of the most egregious sort, nationalism, and individual and group rights, are not inherently irreconcilable. As Kiss

(1995, p. 369) argues, the universal norms of rights and the particular allegiances of nation can be brought together, for "a commitment to respecting human rights can be a constitutive element of some forms of nationalism, and, conversely, the contemporary human rights ideal seeks to guarantee respect for many of the demands voiced by nationalism." We might ask, though, to what extent are constitutional regimes within which claims to rights are embedded *actually* open to reimagination? Does any nation not depend constitutively on a particular, essentialized notion of identity against which difference is defined and excluded? In fact, systems of constitutional rights have been described as reflecting tension between national identity and "difference." That is, to deviate from the nation is to *need* the protection accorded by rights (Rosenfeld 1994). But Preuss (1994, p. 163) has questioned "whether the constitutional state presupposes some minimum degree of prepolitical sameness and homogeneity." In other words, at issue in this book is whether the constitutional state is capable of defining itself constitutively *in terms of* difference and rights to differ.

In the end, the relationship between rights and national identity is a two-way street, in that each informs the other (see Fletcher 1994, Teitel 1994). An investigation of the ways in which sexual identities fit within that conjunction can, I believe, usefully illuminate this relationship.

In the case studies that make up this book, I look at particular intersections of national cultures, sexuality, and rights. Each study illustrates a particular dynamic in that relationship, but there are also common threads that run through all of them.

Chapter two examines a case in American constitutional law concerning the right of lesbians, gays, and bisexuals to march in Boston's St. Patrick's Day Parade. I argue that the dispute provides a prism through which to analyze the place of identity politics in American life, the constitutive role of rights discourse in shaping an American national identity, and the construction of sexual identities within public space.

The focus of chapter three remains with a culture in which the language of rights is now central to national identity: South Africa. As South Africa engages in a process of reconstruction and reconciliation, *all* identities are open to reimagination, and space now exists for the inclusion of self-identified lesbians, gays, and bisexuals in public life and within the constitutional discourse of rights. In a society in which identity categories were so egregiously deployed by the state, the ways in which identities and rights are now invoked proves to be both continuous with and a radical break from the past.

From a culture in which previously divided groups are being brought together to forge a reimagined national identity, I turn in chapter four to a national culture located within an increasingly fragmenting nation state: Quebec. Interestingly, Quebec was the first jurisdiction in North America to make "sexual orientation" a legally prohibited basis of discrimination, a law enacted by a newly elected nationalist government in 1976. My interest here is in how sexual identities have been discursively deployed so as to consolidate national identities in a culture where a disjunction exists between nation and nation state. I also consider how sexual identity politics might serve as a model for reconceiving national identity in a social order in which the nation state is in turmoil.

While the relationship of Quebec and the rest of Canada exhibits all of the signs of national breakup, in Europe, by contrast, the focus of attention is on a "supranational" European identity. This provides the basis of chapter five, which examines the extent to which rights discourse serves as a bond of commonality within the European Union, forming the basis of European citizenship. I use rights struggles involving lesbian and gay sexualities to illustrate both the potential and the limits of rights as a means of reimagining this evolving legal and political order.

Reimagining the nation is also central to chapter six, which looks at how an Australian national identity has been reinvented through the state in recent years. I argue that in Australia, sexual identities have been an important part of that process. Struggles surrounding lesbian and gay rights have served to enhance the legitimacy of rights discourse as a constitutive element of national identity. They have also been important in the articulation of national identity within an increasingly globalized context, one shaped by the language of international human rights.

In chapter seven, I draw some conclusions from the case studies and highlight some of the directions in which future analysis might be most productive.

My choice of which national identities to study is a result of a number of factors. Personal contacts, linguistic barriers, research funding, and areas of expertise all contributed to the way in which this book was written. That leaves it very much a Western collection, although South Africa can be seen as a national culture that troubles simple east/west–south/north binaries. Given my central focus on rights discourse and sexual identities, the range of geographic options was further limited. However, I believe that these chapters—specific as they are—may contribute to the development of a set of analytical tools that can assist in the study of other national cultures, especially those outside of the west, where sexual identity categories are being articulated in distinctive ways which combine local experience and the universality of rights. As I hope to show, while the case studies are distinct, they are also overlapping and often mutually constructed.

Research for this book has involved many travels, both physical and intellectual. I have tried to convey this sense of "journey" in all of the case studies. In that regard, this could be considered as much a travel book as anything else. In these travels I have met many people who are politically engaged with the questions I raise here. I hope that I have managed to convey their voices and express their efforts to take control of how their sexualities are imagined nationally.

2 The Nation's Rights and National Rites

This first case study of national cultures, sexual identity politics, and the discourse of rights begins with a national culture frequently described as the paradigmatic culture of rights: the United States. I start with the United States with some hesitation. In commencing with "America"—the world's only remaining superpower, a nation state whose rights culture at times has assumed imperialist dimensions—I am aware of the danger of reinforcing such a dominant position. In the remainder of this book, I will argue that the construction of rights in the United States represents a particular balance of interests, one that is not necessarily replicated in other rights cultures. However, I give the United States a central place in this study because, without doubt, rights have assumed a vital role in the constitution of national identity. Moreover, sexuality and sexual identities have proven a central site of American political struggle in recent years, which has been articulated through rights rhetoric as well as claims regarding the meaning of the national culture. Those disputes have also entered into the international consciousness (which will be apparent in my other case studies), although perhaps not to the extent that Americans frequently assume.

Given the tremendous amount of attention that issues of sexuality, rights, and nation receive in the United States—in academic, political, and popular discourses—it is difficult to draw attention to the United States as simply one of a series of studies. The voluminous literature and range of issues currently the subject of debate and struggle can (and do) give rise to several books in themselves. Consequently, in this chapter I focus primarily on a single judicial decision to illustrate a number of different themes that connect the three central trajectories of this book: nations, sexualities, and rights. The case I have chosen involves that most quintessential ritual of American national identity: the parade. In *Hurley v. Irish-American Gay, Lesbian and Bisexual Group of Boston* (1995), the issue was whether a lesbian, gay, and bisexual group could be prevented from marching in Boston's St. Patrick's Day Parade.

I have chosen this dispute as the basis of my analysis for a number of reasons. First, the issue seems so uniquely American. It is hard to imagine the ferocity of this particular debate arising elsewhere, and it is nearly impossible to conceive of it being translated into rights discourse before the highest court in the land in any other country. Thus, the case underscores the centrality of rights in political struggles in general and the particular way in which identity politics is frequently "legalized" in the United States. Furthermore, it is significant that the parade, as a spectacle, has historically been a central site for the constitution of the national identity. The case exemplifies the role of "ethnicity" as a feature of American national life and the ways in which ethnicity serves as a locus of tension between assimilationism and pluralism within American culture. The St. Patrick's Day Parade in particular shows how the national community leaves space for some forms of group identification and does not read them as threats to nation, provided those identities operate within fairly narrow, depoliticized, and disciplined confines. I will use the parade dispute to explore the importance of constitutional rights struggles as themselves constitutive of national identity. In particular, rights of expression and equality, both of which are central to national identity, interact in this instance in a plethora of conflicting ways, thereby suggesting that national identities often may be constructed through contradictory discourses.

Finally, I examine Boston's St. Patrick's Day Parade, not simply as a site for the constitution of national identity, but also as a *metaphor* for the nation, in which physical space is filled by a panoply of different groups to which citizens pay allegiance. In this regard, the St. Patrick's Day Parade was interpreted by the litigants in two competing ways: one in which national identity is devoid of any essential feature other than a faith in the power of rights discourse to resolve disputes, and the other—representing a more assimilationist, potentially exclusionary vision—in which an American national identity is conceived in terms of the unity and shared values of an underlying group from which lesbians and gays are excluded. Thus, the specific dispute underscores a range of more general tensions at the heart of the national culture of the United States. It is not surprising that these issues come together in the context of a struggle over the expression of sexual identities and are translated into the language of rights.

I explore these diverse claims by beginning with some historical background on the construction of the American national identity. My focus here is on the centrality of a liberal constitutional rights discourse and its emphasis on equality and speech as core values. I also look at the relationship between national and constitutional identities and interrogate how a national identity can be based on faith in the power of rights. I then examine a particular "rite" of national identity—the parade—and how it serves as a narrative and performative space for the nation. The changing ways in which the parade has helped constitute the nation speak to a diversity, and a tension, in how national and group identities are conceived in the American polity. As a consequence, the parade continues to be a useful vantage point from which to interrogate national identity. I attempt to connect this discussion to a more general examination of how national identities construct exclusions and "threats" to nation (be they racial, ethnic, sexual or otherwise), and how parades can function as a response by those groups to their construction as other to the nation.

I then turn to the particular parade that gave rise to the deployment of rights discourse in litigation: the Boston St. Patrick's Day Parade. I briefly review the facts, legal reasoning, and implications of the decision. But my primary interest is in what the case suggests about an American national identity—how this parade functions symbolically as a spectacle of nation. The question of who gets to march and what their marching signifies serves therefore as a microcosm for who is incorporated (and how) in the constitution of the American nation itself.

National Rights

Throughout the world, both in admiration and derision, the United States is perceived as a culture founded on a deep-seated belief in rights. To the outsider, a faith in the power of rights seems central to what it means to be an American, and the irony (frequently lost on many Americans) is how such a culture could deny the most fundamental rights, in such an egregious way, to so many for so long through the institution of slavery and its aftermath. But that historical contradiction also underscores the political indeterminacy of rights, and does not in itself refute the proposition that "nothing is more deeply rooted in the American political tradition than the vocabulary of rights" (Lacey and Haakonssen 1991, p. 1). Rights serve as "potent symbols of nationhood" (p. 3), are central to the "foundational myth" (p. 6) of the United States, and thus serve to nourish the national imaginary.

The power of rights in the American psyche can be traced back to the founding revolutionary moment. Rights discourse was not itself an innovation of the American Revolution. Rather, at that time, the language of rights was "pervasive in Anglo-American political culture" as well as in the rhetorical basis of the French Revolution (Rakove 1991, p. 106). The American Revolution, however, sought to resolve the tension within English constitutional thought between the inherent rights of "Englishmen" [sic], secured through timeless custom, and the doctrine of parliamentary supremacy, whereby those inherent rights were vulnerable to any statute duly enacted by Parliament (p. 106). For revolutionary Americans, one of the results of independence was the recovery and security of their rights as English subjects, rights which over time were increasingly grounded in nature. Madison called these "pre-existent rights" (Hutson 1991, pp. 76–77). In that respect, the constitutional theory of the American Revolution was continuous with English constitutionalism, in which rights discourse has also played a powerful role (see generally Stychin 1993, Reid 1986) and the subsequent entrenchment of the Bill of Rights was a logical outcome of the process. By 1787, it was widely held that bills of rights served as "repositories of reserved natural rights" (Hutson 1991, p. 76).

The inalienability of certain rights has been central to American thought. Rights were grounded in natural law and natural duty, and "if certain basic rights were to be the moral touchstone by means of which the conduct of all instituted authority was to be checked, such rights must exist on a basis that made them transcend all institutions of authority" (Haakonssen 1991, p. 47). Thus, the institutions of society would serve "primarily as safeguards for such rights" (p. 47). But, if rights were inalienable, then the content and scope of those rights constructed as "natural" had to be limited (p. 50). Life, liberty, and the pursuit of happiness were the inalienable, natural rights precisely because they could be framed simultaneously in the language of duties: "since life, liberty, and the pursuit of happiness are equally duties for all, they are equally rights for all, and accordingly there is a duty on everyone not to disturb this equality" (p. 51).

To a large extent, natural rights also came to be associated with rights to property, and a symbiotic relationship was constructed between property, liberty, security, and the rule of law (Stychin 1993). The threat to property and liberty stemmed from the potential for arbitrary power, which could be controlled only through restraints upon government. Common law had protected these natural rights, and their entrenchment in a written constitution subject to judicial review was a "natural" outgrowth of that tradition. As Nedelsky (1990b, p. 2) observes, concerns for the protection of property rights shaped the American Constitution, "and then hardened into a notion of rights as judicially enforced boundaries dividing the legitimate scope of government from the protected sphere of individual liberty." But this emphasis on property rights, which were to be safeguarded from majoritarian power through the principle of limited government, by definition placed substantive "*inequality* at the center of American constitutionalism" (p. 2, emphasis added). Yet, at the same time, civil rights were to be enjoyed equally by all citizens.

This constitutional theory faced enormous problems of self-justification given the political realities of the American Revolutionary War period, the most obvious being the institution of slavery (see Wald 1995). The apparent contradiction eventually forced a reconsideration of the relationship between rights, constitutionalism, and national identity. Rights served as a means for the delineation of membership in the national community, secured through the Bill of Rights. Inclusion within the national identity thus was inextricably tied to the enjoyment of rights, and that depended on the law's acknowledgement of the individual as a holder of rights. Furthermore, the recognition of the individual as citizen was dependent on how the national founding myth was articulated. In other words, "the law constitutes a 'we' through an official story beginning with a founding moment that generates a code of laws and principles expressive of the spirit of the 'we'" (p. 16). Exclusions from "we the people," such as slaves, proved difficult in terms of the theory and practice of American natural rights. That problem centered on "how to keep claims of rights violations made by British colonists leading to the rebellion from extending to those groups not included among their ranks" (p. 18). After all, the nation had to explain why some groups could be denied the rights that had served to justify revolution in the first place. But, of course, the exclusions also underscored that rights were not natural, but were instead the product of government, precisely the point which natural rights theory seeks to disguise (p. 39).

It was this gap between constitutional theory and practice, in combination with underlying economic reasons, that led to the Civil War, the abolition of slavery, and the enactment of the Reconstruction Amendments to the Constitution, which guaranteed among other things, the "equal protection" of the laws.[1] The central figure in this reconstruction of the national identity was Lincoln, whose task was no less than to create a new national narrative based on equal rights (Wald 1995, p. 51). Indeed, the Civil War has been described as a second American Revolution, one which was waged over moral ideals and national identity (Richards 1993, p. 109). It was a challenge to the idea of "a racial conception of American national identity as constitutionally compelled" (Richards 1994, p. 103). The Civil War thus made necessary a reexamination of the meaning of nation, and constitutional change was the outcome of that process. Richards (1994, p. 141) argues that the Reconstruction Amendments provided the basis for a "rights based political theory of American constitutionalism," and their role was to fulfill the initial promise of the first American Revolution, namely, the idea that political power must be justified and contained by guarantees of rights. A revolutionary tradition grounded in a belief in liberal rights is thereby central to the constitution of the American national identity (see also Ackerman 1995).

The Reconstruction Amendments are a manifestation of a theory of rights and national identity and, specifically, the idea of the racial equality of all citizens. Richards (1993, p. 146) suggests that as a consequence of the amendments, a theory of modern constitutionalism must turn on the centrality of equality more generally to the national identity and its manifestation, constitutional law: "rights-based contemporary egalitarian political theory must . . . play a central role in the interpretation of the requirements of the Reconstruction Amendments in contemporary circumstances." Those amendments provide the foundation for the modern American constitutional law of legal equality. They have served as the basis for civil rights struggles by disempowered *groups,* particularly African Americans, and play a central role in the American national imaginary. As Herrell (1996, p. 276) observes, "while the rhetoric of civil rights derives from the individualistic language of Enlightenment political philosophy, its American elaboration in the nineteenth and twentieth centuries speaks the collectivist language of subnational, often overlapping identities." In this way, constitutional theory has a symbiotic relationship with national identity: "the Reconstruction Amendments stood for an ethical vision of *national* identity based on respect for the human rights of all persons" (Richards 1993, p. 154).[2] In other words, constitutional/national identity might be understood as officially based on the idea of "a group of individuals who ought to relate to one another as moral equals" (Rosenfeld 1994, p. 7).[3]

If a theory of equality represents one central strand of the American national identity, freedom of speech—as protected by the First Amendment to the American Bill of Rights—represents another (see Fletcher 1994, Shiffrin 1995, Passavant 1996). Not infrequently, however, the exercise of the right of free speech has been constituted within American culture as threatening to the nation and its identity.[4] The Supreme Court's holding that the burning of the American flag is constitutionally protected "speech" provides a graphic example of how an act that is speech within American constitutional discourse is, in a fairly obvious way, read by many as threatening to the nation's identity and values (*Texas v. Johnson* 1989, *United States v. Eichman* 1990). Shiffrin (1995) argues, in the specific context of flag burning, that such disputes represent a clash over the meaning of American culture. His thesis is that dissenting speech must be read as central to the American national identity and as crucial to any theory of the First Amendment (see also Fletcher 1994). Protection of dissent is thus a common bond and, in this way, nationalism *might* serve to strengthen the right to dissent from what are widely perceived to be shared national ideals and symbols. That right of dissenting speech becomes a fundamental ideal.

The centrality of the protection of dissenting speech in the United States, however, is paradoxical. As Shiffrin (1995, p. 337) recognizes, while constitutional discourse stresses the importance of upholding the right of unorthodox or dissenting speech free from governmental interference (although historically there certainly have been "exceptions" to that protection, such as speech labeled "Communist ideology" in the 1950s), the right "masks the extent to which free speech is marginalized, discouraged and repressed" today. Indeed, the frequent *reaction* to dissenting speech among the general public is the best evidence for this argument, which again underscores the political indeterminacy of rights rhetoric.

These two threads of the American constitutional tapestry— speech and equality—will prove central to this chapter. Each has frequently served as the basis for mobilization by historically marginalized groups and dissident individuals. Their very capacity for deployment, however, is often read, not as the fulfillment of the promise held out by the American founding myth, but as divisive and sometimes subversive to the nation.[5] In this respect, the centrality of rights discourse has a paradoxical quality. While rights are deployed by the marginalized, and read by some as socially fragmenting, the very resort to the language of national rights "constitutes in a profound sense a willingness to join the dominant community" (Minow 1995, p. 355). Indeed, "participation in rights talk may be one of the few mechanisms for symbolizing and securing unity in multicultural, polyglot communities" such as the United States (p. 356). Yet such claims to rights often produce a backlash, with arguments that the group is seeking, for example, "special rights" to be treated differently, rights not enjoyed by the "ordinary" American (on special rights discourse, see generally Herman 1997, Currah 1997).[6]

The many-sided character of rights is also underscored by the ways in which the language of rights is often mobilized by all sides in a political dispute, with the state constructed as arbiter between rights claimants. In this situation, rights may be articulated to competing visions of community and national identity. That will prove to be the case in *Hurley v. Irish-American Gay, Lesbian and Bisexual Group of Boston*, wherein the two central strands of rights discourse in the United States today—equality and speech—come to be deployed along a range of different registers. Before proceeding to the judgment, though, I want to sketch in some background on the ways in which the disputed performative space—the parade—has been central to the construction of national identity. This discussion, I believe, can more fully illuminate the constitutional context of the controversy.

The Spectacle of Nation

To understand how rights discourse is mobilized by both sides in the *Hurley* case, it is important to recognize the centrality of the parade as a ritual, constitutive feature of American national identity. The parade is an organized movement of a mass of people through public space, and it is that movement which serves as the "ritualized element . . . raised to consciousness" in the public's mind (Da Matta 1984, p. 216). Parades have been described as "richly symbolic activities" that historically played a "crucial part in the invention of American nationhood" in the post–Revolutionary War era (Waldstreicher 1995, p. 37), giving "the abstractions of nationalist ideology a practical sense" (p. 38). The parade was a tradition *invented* to fit a new nation, and it served as one of the important "practices of nationalism" (p. 38).[7]

Ryan (1989) has provided evidence of the central role of the parade in the construction of national identity, particularly in the nineteenth-century United States, in her description of a transition in terms of the relationship of parade to nation. The "classic American parade" was a product of the period 1825 to 1850 (p. 136). At that historical moment:

> The genius of the parade was that it allowed the many contending constituencies of the city to line up and move through the streets without ever encountering one another face to face, much less stopping to play specified roles in one coordinated pageant. . . . Like a civic omnibus, the

parade offered admission to almost any group with sufficient energy,
determination, organizational ability, and internal coherence to board
it. (p. 137)

Ryan (1989, p. 138) characterizes this parade as "an exercise in
popular sovereignty," and she analogizes it to a "street railway on
which a panoply of different social groups mounted and occupied
a string of cars, with each car embodying cultural and historical
meaning and giving ceremonial definition to some component of
the urban social structure." I will return to this interpretation of the
parade in the specific context of the *Hurley* case. Such a parade
might be understood less as the organized procession of a social
group than as a *series* of different individuals and groups, connected only by their common pursuit of the objective of physical
movement through a route within the public space of the city.

By contrast, in the second half of the nineteenth century, "ethnicity had begun to erode the public and inclusive character of parading" (Ryan 1989, p. 145). The consolidation of the St. Patrick's
Day Parade in this period symbolized the switch in the form of the
ritual from civic to ethnic, and it was no longer a "vehicle" through
which a series of different groups could participate. Instead, it had
come to serve as "the first of many examples of independent parading whereby distinctive social groups imprinted their identity on
the public mind" (p. 153) and, in the process, those groups sought
acknowledgement as equal participants in the polity, with equal
rights of membership. The parade thus became a means for the
mobilization of those who had been denied many of the privileges
of American citizenship.

The *Hurley* case also shows how the discourse of equality became a motivation for group organization, realized *physically*
through parading. The Irish Americans served to change the character of the parade into an exercise in group mobilization, wherein
the marchers shared more than simply public space for the day. In
this way, parades "both presuppose and, especially, create 'community,' 'ethnicity,' and 'culture'" (Herrell 1992, p. 228). An analogy
might also be drawn here to the historic marches on Washington—
mass mobilizations aimed at securing, for example, civil rights for
African Americans and, later, for women and lesbians, gays, and

bisexuals—which vividly demonstrates the relationship between the performativity of marching and the struggle for rights.[8]

In the twentieth century, the character of the St. Patrick's Day Parade shifted again, coming to replicate the civic parades that had been central to the consolidation of national identity in an earlier period: "the distinctive ethnic nature of the event gave way to a mixture of Irish and non-Irish participants and a blend of ethnic and dominant American symbols" (Bodnar 1992, p. 68). The parade represented the "mainstreaming" (or assimilation) of the Irish in the United States and the "Americanization" of the parade, in which Irishness melted into an overarching American national identity. The parade graphically portrayed the "melting pot" interpretation of the United States, wherein the achievement of some measure of substantive social equality occurs alongside the normalization of the group such that they form just another ingredient in a melting pot. As the ethnic basis of the parade diminished in importance, it was replaced by a *series* of diverse groups and individuals who share little more than public space and physical movement—thereby replicating the civic parades of an earlier historical period. Indeed, in recent times, the "[Boston] Parade boasted 20,000 participants and one million spectators" (Van Ness 1996, p. 631), making it difficult—given the numbers and diversity of people involved—to realistically characterize the parade as a vehicle for the political mobilization of a group.

In using the language of group and series to describe the parade, I do not want to overgeneralize the historical transitions in parading. However, the parade might best be understood as a site for both the celebration *and* the constitution of an American national identity. Moreover, the *way* in which the parade is interpreted serves as a metaphor for how the polity is conceived. The parade as series—which may best characterize the current form— is composed of groups who may be proud of their ethnic and other identities, but for whom most of those identities have ceased to be sufficiently politically charged to raise questions of divided loyalties in the mind of the "general public." By contrast, the group-based parade on the "ethnic" model serves as a vehicle for displaying, performing, and constituting the group; criteria for participation can legitimately be based on *perceived* essential characteristics of the group (on the group-series distinction, see Young 1995). The parade in those cases may also act as a site for mobilization and, in that form, "the performance comments, implicitly or explicitly, on the structural conflicts between national and subnational allegiances and identities" (MacAloon 1982, p. 266). Tensions between national ("American") and subnational (racial, ethnic, or other) identities may well be played out through parades. The respective "loyalties" of the individual to nations and groups are manifested in the very space of the spectacle. In a parade characterized in terms of civic pride, wherein the group marching represents the polity as a whole, the individual is connected directly and immediately to the nation state. In the case of a parade by a more narrowly defined group, the individual might be read as "communing" with the nation derivatively, mediated by the group that is parading (Calhoun 1994, p. 315).[9]

The group-based parade can give rise to the same questions of membership, rights of inclusion, and essential attributes of identity that characterize national identities (see generally Berlant and Freeman 1993). Indeed, within the lesbian and gay communities, issues of membership and inclusion are probably as prevalent as in ethnic and national communities. These tensions frequently manifest themselves in a series of well-worn political disputes, often in the context of the "right" to use group space (such as the parade route): Are "straights" to be included? sadomasochists? transgendered persons? Can anyone (and, it seems, everyone) sometimes be "queer"?[10] In these moments, communities founded on sexual identities replicate national and other groupings. In the United States, they all have parades. In fact, the parade brings these tensions into sharp relief because of its visual, spectacular, spatial quality.

It is the presence of lesbians, gays, and bisexuals seeking to "come out" in "other" parades that has given rise to contestations over claims to membership in various ethnic/national communities. At such times the parade quickly becomes less serial, where the only thing that participants may seem to share is space, and instead is more group based, where one of the primary conditions of membership in the nation/group is an ostensibly heterosexual orientation. For example, Montero (1993, p. 23) has described how Latina/Latino lesbians and gays are "excluded or pushed to the edges of parades of national affirmation" and are forced to carry "a portable closet" within a national imaginary in diaspora as it is being affirmed publicly in American space. The community emphasizes sexual sameness, rather than heterogeneity, and that unity is translated into essential (and essentially heterosexual) terms (see generally Minow 1995).

The parade is a microcosm for struggles around identity because it is a spectacle for the performance of the national or group imaginary. It operates along a spectrum between group and series, depending on the extent to which the participants conceive of themselves as sharing a common, homogeneous identity (national, sexual, or otherwise). The articulation of a shared identity can then give rise to conditions of group membership, which have served in the past to construct lesbians and gays as undermining the group's respectability and pride. But just as the parade serves to display (and constitute) an array of groups in the United States, it also provides a spectacle of the American national identity and a ritual of national culture. In this fashion, the ethnic otherness of the group based parade gives way to a celebration of national identity in "diversity." Such parades symbolize the normalization of a range of groups into the American culture, overcoming the "fear of balkanization" that nonassimilation holds in the American psyche (Brody 1995, p. 152). In other words, while the United States may be a nation of immigrants, they can and should assimilate such that they no longer pose an implicit threat to the nation and "we the people." Their loyalties should become undivided and "their" parades "ours" to enjoy. This is one of the messages of parades of *American* national celebration, such as the St. Patrick's Day Parade today. Everyone can join in the fun because, while the group is rightfully proud of its past, its loyalties have now been transferred to the United States. The individual communes directly with America, and "hyphenation" in these circumstances does not signify a threat to nation (see generally Brody 1995, Slaughter 1995). The superficial diversity of the parade masks an underlying conformity that characterizes so much of American public life.

If one of the meanings of the parade ritual is a celebration of American national culture and identity, then the ambivalence expressed towards the participation of "out" lesbians and gays by some groups can be reinterpreted. The experience Montero (1993, p. 23)

describes as being required to carry a portable closet in public space
speaks not only to the way a national identity in exile constructs itself *per se,* but also might say something about what groups perceive
is demanded by the dominant culture as a condition for full inclusion in the United States today. In this regard, there is considerable historical evidence to suggest that American ideology has long
connected homosexuality, foreignness, and threats to nation (on
U.S. government policy, see generally Herrell 1996, p. 278). In the
immediate post–World War II era, for example, "Communism"
served as the central signifier for the construction of a threat to
nation and national identity. But, as Epstein (1994) and others have
argued persuasively, the fear of a Communist conspiracy *within*
American society—a conspiracy of individuals with foreign allegiances and connections to foreign powers (which also implicated
immigrants)—was constructed in an analogous fashion to the fear
of the "homosexual." In the 1940s and 1950s, the dominant discourses of both anti-Communism and anti-homosexuality emphasized threats to "national security and national welfare," emanating
from both within and outside the nation (p. 39). Moreover, the two
conspiracies reinforced each other, as "many homosexuals, from
being enemies of society in general, became enemies of capitalism
in particular" (p. 40). So too, Epstein argues, an analogy can be
drawn to anti-Semitic discourse (p. 41).[11] In all three cases, "loyalty to the U.S. was seen as questionable at best," and individuals
were apt to be members of conspiracies (p. 41). These figures—
the Communist, the homosexual, the recent immigrant, the Jew—
served as dangers to the nation because their *essential* foreignness
was not immediately apparent (p. 41). As Edelman (1994) observes, the homosexual in the 1950s United States threatened a
"suburban national-cultural identity" (p. 157), and the American
values of industriousness and loyalty (p. 163). As a consequence,
homophobia was "metonymically anti-Communist" (p. 157).

My argument is that as social groups strive for acceptance, as
well as social and political equality and rights, a rejection of the
homosexual as other to their group identity is comprehensible and
predictable. Homosexuality, after all, has long been "un-American"
(see also Harper 1994). While this construction may be modifying gradually, Yingling (1994) argued that *both* homosexuality and

a nonassimilationist multiculturalism are frequently constructed within dominant discourses today as foreign agents that have invaded the American body politic (especially the universities, along with that other contaminant, feminism). A "healthy national ideology" demands the rejection of all of them (p. 109).[12]

The American constitutional identity continues to reinforce this historical construction of nation. In *Bowers v. Hardwick* (1986), the decision of the majority of the Supreme Court—that criminal laws which prohibit homosexual sodomy are constitutionally permissible in terms of a right to privacy—was grounded explicitly in national tradition (see generally Teitel 1994, Thomas 1993). On this point, Edelman (1994, p. 137) argues that sodomy carries an important signification in the American national imaginary because of the way in which it is read as a threat to the sexual/national identity of heterosexual American men. Once again, it is gay sexuality—now reduced and essentialized to male sodomy—that becomes "an unnatural because un-American practice" (p. 158) and therefore not an appropriate subject for constitutional protection.[13]

Thus, a discourse of rights has been central to the nation and precipitated what has been called a second American Revolution. The promise of that revolution—equal rights—has been and continues to be the basis for social movement mobilization by a range of groups. At the same time, many such groups (including lesbians and gays) are discursively constructed as the nation's others, which justifies social, political, and even constitutional marginalization. Rights claims made by those groups are constructed as threats to nation, underscoring the extent to which rights—even in a rights based culture such as the United States—may be politically indeterminate. Opposing litigious parties both make political claims—with each side pulling on a strand of the American national tradition and identity—that have been translated into the language of rights.

The Private on Parade

The parade in American culture functions as a signifier of both national identity composed of diverse but assimilated groups and ethnic, racial, and other cultural "difference" from the norm. This tension between the sameness and difference of groups is apparent within the factual background of *Hurley v. Irish-American Gay, Lesbian and Bisexual Group of Boston*. The dispute concerned Boston's annual St. Patrick's Day Parade held on March 17, a celebration dating back to 1737 in Boston (*Hurley* 1995, p. 2341). The parade ritual has two histories. First, the public, civic celebration of "Evacuation Day" marked "the evacuation of royal troops and Loyalists from the city" (p. 2341). This commemoration has a clear national, militaristic pedigree and might be labeled a "classic" civic/national celebration, marking "the first major victory of the Revolutionary War" (Van Ness 1996, p. 629). Evacuation Day was officially made a holiday in 1938 (p. 629).

Over time, however, the parade assumed a second celebratory purpose: to mark St. Patrick's Day (*Hurley* 1995, p. 2341). It thus became characterized by a procession of Irish Americans in South Boston, a group that had gained considerable political power in the city (Van Ness 1996, p. 630). In this respect, it has featured both sides of the parade ritual: civic/national and ethnic performance. Moreover, as an Irish identity came to be assimilated in the American national culture, the celebration of ethnic identity became de-essentialized. As one commentator has noted, on St. Patrick's Day—and in the parade—"everyone is Irish" (p. 632).

In recent years, the parade has been conducted under the auspices of the South Boston Allied War Veterans Council, "an unincorporated association of individuals selected from various South Boston veterans groups" (*Hurley* 1995, p. 2341). Each year it has received a permit to conduct the parade, and the format was determined through the granting of permission to groups to march as contingents of the parade through South Boston (p. 2341). In 1992, for the first time, "a number of gay, lesbian, and bisexual descendants of the Irish immigrants joined together *with other supporters*" (emphasis added) to create the "Irish-American Gay, Lesbian and Bisexual Group of Boston" (GLIB), formed chiefly for the purpose of marching as a unit in the parade (p. 2341).[14] The Veterans Council eventually sought to refuse them permission to march, and the issue, over a period of years, wound its way through the courts.[15]

The legal issue in the case can be framed as a clash between two of the central rights that inform the American national identity: the right of a "minority" group not to be discriminated against by parade organizers versus the right of those organizers to conduct a march that "speaks" (or does not "speak") a particular statement, without being legally coerced into expressing a message that conflicts with their viewpoint. Thus, speech and equality *seem* to collide directly.

The argument advanced by GLIB was that the parade constituted a place of "public accommodation." The lower courts decided against GLIB, holding that the parade lacked sufficient nexus to the municipal government to constitute "state action." This finding severely limited the scope of GLIB's legal argument, for "private" actors are not normally subject to constitutional review. Consequently, GLIB turned to the Massachusetts state antidiscrimination law, which does apply to the activities of private citizens and forbids discrimination on the basis of sexual orientation (among other grounds).[16] GLIB argued that the actions of the Veterans Council contravened the law. The State Trial Court and a majority of the Supreme Judicial Court of Massachusetts agreed, ordering the inclusion of GLIB in the parade. As a consequence, the Veterans Council canceled the 1994 parade pending an appeal to the United States Supreme Court, which decided against GLIB in June 1995.

Justice Souter, for a unanimous Court, framed the issue as "whether Massachusetts may require private citizens who organize a parade to include among the marchers a group imparting a message the organizers do not wish to convey" (*Hurley* 1995, pp. 2340–2341). The question thus became one of "free speech" (the First Amendment), rather than equality, and framed in this way, it was almost inevitable given American constitutional doctrine that the Veterans Council would win. The Supreme Court held that "the requirement to admit a parade contingent expressing a message not of the private organizers' own choosing violates the First Amendment" (p. 2343). A parade, Justice Souter reasoned, by definition consists of people seeking to make "some sort of collective point," and the "inherent expressiveness" of marching does not require "a narrow, succinctly articulable message" to give rise to constitutional protection (p. 2345). The choice to exclude the *message* put forward by GLIB (which the Court distinguished from the alleged nonexclusion of homosexuals *per se*), was central to the right of the "speaker" (the Veterans Council) "to choose the content of his own message" (p. 2347). Speech is therefore exempt, for constitutional reasons, from the state public accommodation law. Otherwise, "the communications produced by the private organizers would be shaped by all those protected by the law who wished to join in with some expressive demonstration of their own" (p. 2347).

The Court analogized the Veterans Council to a composer, who produces a score from "the expressive units of the parade" (p. 2348). Consequently, "each contingents' expression in the Council's eyes comports with what merits celebration on that day" (p. 2348). As a speaker, the council has the constitutional right to choose the point of view it will (and will not) articulate, and each unit of the parade contributes to a "common theme" (p. 2349). To rule differently would be to "limit speech in the service of orthodox expression" (p. 2350). In this way, the case becomes a "classic" American free speech case.

My interest in the *Hurley* decision is not so much for the doctrinal maneuvers of constitutional law which the Supreme Court undertakes. In fact, one commentator sympathetic to GLIB's position has suggested that, given the focus on GLIB's message rather than its lesbian, gay, bisexual, and straight members, "there is some substance to the claim that the exclusion of gay and lesbian *groups,* as opposed to individual homosexuals marching with other units, is not discrimination on the basis of sexual orientation at all" (Yackle 1993, p. 851). Rather, my interest is in how the decision, and the parade itself, function metaphorically for national identities—of "Irish,"[17] "Irish American," and "American."

Whichever national identity it is said to represent, the dispute between the Veterans Council and GLIB underscores how the parade, like national culture and identity, is "a contentious, performative space" (Bhabha 1990, p. 307), wherein alternative narratives of nationhood (and belonging) can serve to challenge the dominant narrative of, in this instance, the heterosexualized national identity. Thus, national space can be shown to be "*internally marked by cultural difference*" (p. 299). That difference highlights how the nation constitutes itself through a process of "hybridity" in which new members are incorporated into the nation (or parade), generating "new sites of antagonism" along the way (Coombe 1993, p. 418; see also Pease 1992). Ultimately, in *Hurley,* at issue is the ongoing consolidation of national and group identities, and "the extent to which discourse involving the notion of public or the identity of nation recognizes or represses the plurality of identities that shape the lives of individuals and the constitution of communities, societies, and even civilizations" (Calhoun 1995, p. 240).

The facts in *Hurley* demonstrate how this process operates along a series of different trajectories of incorporation or abjection. The early St. Patrick's Day parades, in which the "ethnicity" of the ritual superseded the previously "civic" spirit of parading, met with a hostile reaction from within the dominant American culture. In 1873, for example:

> the *New York Times* expressed great disdain for the Irish and the ritual of the parade. Commenting on the procession of some twenty-five thousand marchers, it opined: "It is difficult in the extreme for the American mind to understand." Parading, if we are to believe the *Times,* had become an ethnic rather than a civic ritual, and the particular avocation of the Irish. (Ryan 1989, p. 146)

In this period, then, the ethnic group identity of the parade was read in opposition to, and therefore as threatening to, an American national identity that did not "understand" the ritual. Bodnar (1992, p. 69) suggests that over time the parade became "Americanized," as Irishness came to be incorporated in the process of hybridity symptomatic of national identity. The American "mind" had come to accept a *version* of Irishness as reconcilable with the national imaginary and, in turn, the symbols of the parade became increasingly evacuated of an essential Irishness. Everyone could be Irish for a day (simply by wearing green).

The acceptance of an ethnic march as sufficiently "American" within the dominant culture, so as to become a national ritual, depended on how the marchers were perceived every other day of the year. Early hostility to the parade may have reflected not simply outright bigotry (although that was probably the predominant factor), but it also demonstrated how nationalist ideologies often demand an unmediated relationship between individual and national identity. An ideology of nation "typically rejects claims to the quasi-autonomy of subnational discourses or movements as divisive" (Calhoun 1995, p. 242; see also Brody 1995). The Americanization of St. Patrick's Day served to quell those concerns and helped de-essentialize, normalize, and assimilate an Irish American identity.

My claim is not that Irishness in the United States has become an empty signifier devoid of political meaning. Although Irishness may not now carry with it the threat of balkanization implicit in the backlash against multiculturalism in the United States, it *has* come to be read almost exclusively as a Catholic, anti-British, anti-colonial identity. The sectarian conflicts of Northern Ireland— where marching of a highly politicized character that often incites violence is a *Protestant* phenomenon—have not entered the American consciousness to a significant degree.[18] This may be because Irishness has been constructed in the United States as having an essential religious character, namely, Roman Catholic (see, e.g., Duncan 1996). In this regard, the Irish American case exemplifies how national identities in diaspora become frozen in time, given that a conservative Catholicism may well more centrally inform an Irish American identity than it does an increasingly securalized and pluralistic Irish identity in the Republic of Ireland, as I will explore in chapter five (see also Rose 1994).[19]

The St. Patrick's Day Parade signifies a particularly *American* conception of Irish group identification, one that is highly culturally specific. As Herrell (1992, p. 236) observes, the Dublin parade historically was a small, religious affair. Its expansion in the last quarter-century has been the product of intervention by the national tourist bureau, which "remade the procession on the model of an American parade" (p. 236), in part to satisfy American tourists searching for their "roots." Thus, it is the meaning of Irishness in the United States that goes on parade, even in Dublin. Irishness is therefore constituted and reflected through American spectacles, which celebrate a mythical past that then must be replicated in the "old country" and performed for an American audience seeking an "authentic" display of their own histories.[20]

The dispute in *Hurley* centers directly on the *sexuality* of national identities and speaks to *both* the construction of the sexuality of an Irish American and to an American identity. In this regard, Calhoun (1995, p. 245) has argued that the determination of "whose speech is more properly public is itself a site of political contestation." The determination of public speech is political in that it may serve to consolidate not only group identities but national identities as well. But by framing the dispute in *Hurley* as centering on the speech *rights* of the parade organizers, the political character of the dispute is obscured. Rather, the free speech right "trumps" other considerations because it is constructed as so firmly anchored in the American political tradition. The right to exclude GLIB becomes foundational to the meaning of free speech in the United States, at the same time that the exclusion is an attempt to consolidate an essential, heterosexual character to the Irish American identity.[21]

It is here that the cultural centrality of the constitutional protection of dissenting speech assumes a particular importance. By deploying this discourse, the Court in *Hurley* is easily able to characterize the value at stake as central to the American identity. As a consequence, it becomes an easy case. As Justice Souter concludes:

> The very idea that a noncommercial speech restriction be used to produce thoughts and statements acceptable to some groups or, indeed, all people, grates on the First Amendment, for it amounts to nothing less than a proposal to limit speech in the service of orthodox expression. The Speech Clause has no more certain antithesis. (*Hurley* 1995, p. 2350)

The Bill of Rights thus has, at its bedrock, the protection of "nonpolitically correct" speech. Recognition of the right of the Veterans Council to exclude GLIB is transformed into protection of dissenting speech from being silenced by the majority. To fail to protect that right would be "un-American." In fact, counsel for the Veterans Council described their motivations with candor:

> The Veterans group . . . was loathe to serve as a vehicle for "gay pride" messages. Part of the reason was social. South Boston is a conservative,

family-oriented neighborhood. Part was religious. "Southie" is heavily
Catholic, and St. Patrick is the patron Saint of Boston's Catholic Arch-
diocese. (Duncan 1996, p. 666)

That rationale raises the question of whether the Supreme Court
was upholding the right of dissent or, on the contrary, whether it
was vindicating the sentiments of the majority, or at least a sizeable
segment of the population.

Importantly, in locating free speech at the center of the American national identity, Shiffrin (1995, p. 343) has argued that this
value must be reconciled and read together with that of equality.
This recognition might serve as the basis for reformulating the issue in *Hurley*. The case can be understood, not as a clash between
orthodoxy and dissent (a rather counterintuitive interpretation),
but as representing a tension between two messages or, alternatively, as a conflict between the values of speech and equality (see
Van Ness 1996, p. 627). In this way, *Hurley* underscores the contingency and malleability of rights categories. Ultimately, the decision is made to appear inevitable because of the *construction* of the
parade as "private" rather than "public" by the courts.[22] After all,
"no right of freedom of expression exists against private actors"
(Hunter 1995, p. 140). Consequently, the "expression" of the Veterans Council trumps the competing claims of expression and nondiscrimination, namely, the equal rights of lesbians, gays, and bisexuals to *speak* as a group within the seemingly public space that
has been legally constituted as private. The *public* meaning of the
narrative of national identity is kept under the control of the Veterans Council, control that is legitimized through both the privatization of space and the "propertization of free speech" (Sunder
1996, p. 144).[23] This construction of difference as properly outside of public space is often understood "as necessary for the
maintenance and reproduction of a common national citizenship"
(Cooper 1996, p. 538). That control over the narrative of national
identity ensures that dissident or ironic readings of the nation are
foreclosed from entering the public sphere.

By characterizing the parade as a private activity, the value of
GLIB's speech is lost sight of, just as it was erased from the public
space of the streets of Boston. Further, the relationship between

that speech and the substantive right of equality was a central part of GLIB's message. Not only did GLIB seek to speak to the public, it sought to enter national public space and to rewrite a national spectacle through participation. A legal finding in its favor might have helped facilitate "the deconstruction of the compulsory privatization of homosexual preference" (Richards 1993, p. 197), which Richards argues is a legitimate interpretation of the equality rights-based national identity he ascribes to the United States.

The relationship between identity, speech, and equality thus is fundamental to this dispute. As Hunter (1995, p. 140) has explained:

> Self-identifying speech does not merely reflect or communicate one's identity; it is a major factor in constructing identity. Identity cannot exist without it. That is even more true when the distinguishing group characteristics are not visible, as is typically true of sexual orientation.

In this context, identity constituting speech in the public sphere not only enhances the value of equality, it furthers the protection of *dissenting* speech, which is supposedly at the core of the American national identity:

> The collective communal impact of forced silence amounts to more than an accumulation of violations of individual integrity. *It creates a form of state orthodoxy.* If speaking identity can communicate ideas and viewpoints that dissent from majoritarian norms, then the selective silencing of certain identities has the opposite, totalitarian, effect of enforcing conformity. In that sense, homosexuality is not merely, or either, status or conduct. It is also, independently, an idea. (p. 141)[24]

While this argument may suggest that there are compelling reasons for judicially imposing a space for GLIB and its message, reasons that might be translated into the language of a right to "*public accommodation*," the malleability of rights is demonstrated by how the argument actually "backfired" on GLIB. By highlighting the political *significance* of gay identity-constituting speech (through, for example, lesbian and gay legal theory), the Veterans Council was supplied with the reasons it should not be forced to "speak" that *political* message in its constitutionally protected discourse. As its legal counsel explained, "far from being a matter of self-identification, then, the expression of one's sexual orientation was fairly teeming with significance. At the very least, it was a significant message" (Duncan 1996, p. 685). Thus, the Veterans Council ostensibly objected, not to the presence of homosexuals in the parade, but to the political message GLIB conveyed.[25]

These arguments also serve to highlight the constructedness of the public/private distinction. The argument implicitly made by the Veterans Council is that lesbians and gays can march, so long as their sexuality is sufficiently "privatized"—that is, their sexual identities do not translate into gay acts (see Yalda 1997). The parade thus becomes a "spectacle of heterosexual performative identity" (Yalda 1997). To participate as part of the class of heterosexuals, lesbians and gays would be required to *identify* with, and be accepted by, some other marching group, since the parade is organized as a *series* of *groups,* rather than as a number of individuals (Van Ness 1996, p. 655). The paradox of the public/private distinction lies in the fact that the articulation of identity is such an inherently public and political act that the Veterans Council is not obliged to include it. Its own act—organizing the parade—is constructed as a *private* act of speech, despite the fact that the parade proceeds through public space and, by virtue of the purpose of marching, constitutively *demands* such space.[26] The applicability of a "public accommodation" statute therefore seems intuitive. By unscrambling the public/private dichotomy, the issue can be framed as:

> whether a group of *private* citizens who help a city administer a *public* event commemorating a *public* holiday, an event first established by the City which has received *public* funding and support throughout its long history and which takes place on the *public* streets of that city, can exclude a group of city residents because of the sexual orientation of the group's members. (Van Ness, 1996, pp. 649–650)

Moreover, the Veterans Council "claim[s] a special purchase" to the public space on a particular day:

> permanent warrant to conduct massive, annual processions over traditional routes—which turn out to be major thoroughfares through the heart of each city. They attach vital significance to the time and place they march and refuse to step aside or even to moderate their demands in order to accommodate competing groups. (Yackle 1993, p. 863)[27]

Dictum from a majority judgment of the U.S. Supreme Court, in the context of the regulation of cable television, seems directly on point:

> The First Amendment's command that government not impede the freedom of speech does not disable the government from taking steps to ensure that private interests not restrict, through physical control of a critical pathway of communication, the free flow of information and ideas. (Justice Kennedy, *Turner Broadcasting v. FCC* 1994, p. 657)

By shifting to the speech interest of GLIB, and in emphasizing the physical control of the (literal) pathway held by the Veterans Council, precedent now provides strong authority for GLIB's claim that the speech rights of the holder of the pathway of communication are not absolute, a move the Supreme Court is unwilling to make in this context.

The Court also manipulates acts and identities, in addition to the public and private, to secure the desired result. Homosexual acts and identities are discursively separated, unlike the Court's judgment in *Bowers v. Hardwick* (1986) in which a set of sexual acts (sodomy) was *assumed* to be the defining characteristic of a homosexual identity, practiced exclusively by homosexuals (see Yalda 1997). The Court in *Hurley,* by contrast, constructs the *right* of the Veterans Council to prohibit only the *act* of GLIB—namely, being "out" marching in the St. Patrick's Day Parade. At the same time that homosexual acts are judicially separated from identities, a heterosexual identity is inscribed on the parade participants, and their act of marching is conflated with that identity. As Yalda (1997) argues, *Hurley* implicitly raises the question of what it "takes" to homosexualize an act, as opposed to an identity. Is the Veterans Council's decision limited to that most homosexual of acts—coming out—or could a gay identity "spill over" into other acts that might be read by the Veterans Council as "too gay"? After all, when is a self-*identified* lesbian or gay not sending out a "message" that might be read as such?

It is this manipulation of act and identity, as well as public and private, that serves to silence lesbians and gays in the space of national identity constitution. Such an effect, as I have argued, violates those supposedly "core" values of the national identity— equality and dissenting speech—but the parade also serves as a space for acts of national identification. While the Veterans Council has sought to silence acts of sexual identification that challenge the parade as a spectacle of heterosexuality, the parade equally serves as a site for the consolidation of nations as heterosexual. The act of parading consolidates Irish American and American national identities simultaneously and, importantly, in such a way that they are constructed as complementary, rather than in a competition giving rise to divided allegiances.

In an analogous fashion, lesbian and gay Pride Parades seek, often uneasily, to consolidate an overarching identity wherein multiply-identified individuals and groups can coexist harmoniously (under the rainbow flag). At least to some extent, ethnicity becomes the model for the Pride Parade, with the parade serving to reflect and constitute a social group, and as a means to appropriate public space (Herrell 1992). Whether the Pride Parade will (or ought to) evolve into a more series based performance is an interesting question, which goes to the heart of sexual identity politics today. Must there be identity "conditions" for participation, or is the parade open to anyone (and any group) who wishes to express "pride" on parade day? Despite the challenge of a queer (non)identity position in the 1990s, the Pride Parade still seems much closer to the ethnic model, rather than to a series. Should the parade ritual come to approximate a series, then exclusion of groups that might be judged offensive (or, for that matter, "inauthentic" in terms of the identities being celebrated) would be increasingly difficult as a normative matter. This point underscores one of the advantages that the "certainties" of a relatively fixed group-identity politics provides.

A harmonious concert of identities is far from simple to orchestrate, and it inevitably gives rise to questions regarding the parameters of the identity, which are resolved either through inclusion or closure. In the case of the Veterans Council, that dialogue is closed off through the translation of the debate into the language of rights (a discourse first deployed by GLIB). The history and outcome of the case further Minow's (1995, p. 363) argument that "complex intragroup and intergroup relationships are not well expressed through the language of rights" because of the way conflicts tend to be framed as individuals against the group. In the case of the Veterans Council and GLIB, this was articulated in terms of what constitutes the "authentic" expression of the group. In other words, are Irish American gays simply "part of the Irish family" (Van Ness 1996, p. 639), which was GLIB's claim, or does a lesbian, gay, or bisexual identity operate to undermine the immediacy between the individual and the group? The Veterans Council implicitly assumed the latter, treating "sexual orientation and ethnicity as two discrete categories" (Yalda 1997).[28]

Simultaneously, the parade serves as a ritual of American national identification and the construction of an overarching American national identity. In that respect, interesting comparisons again can be made to Pride Parades. As Herrell (1992) argues, the St. Patrick's Day Parade represents the assertion of (white) ethnic difference through "indexes" of community (shamrocks, green, etc.). Such emblems are deployed "to assert dissimilarity where very little exists" today (p. 245) and also serve to constitute the "internal homogeneity" of the group (p. 241). Difference is celebrated because, in the Irish American context, that difference has been reduced to a (depoliticized) "romantic past" (p. 243). By contrast, in the Pride Parade the construction of community is often a contested issue and, at least to some extent, the focus seems to be the assertion of an "everyday sameness" to the national community in the face of perceived difference (p. 245). In both cases, then, the parade becomes a celebration of "Americanness," and the interesting question turns on whether that has any essential meaning. For example, organizers of the New York St. Patrick's Day Parade claim that it celebrates "the proposition that all Americans, native and immigrant alike, enjoy the freedom of the City on the streets of New York and, by implication, throughout our land" (Yackle 1993, p. 815).[29] In this moment, the parade becomes a site for the articulation of an American *sameness* that unites diverse marching groups, serving to manage and orchestrate that diversity. Through this interpretation, it seems that the parade should have no essential conditions of membership other than, perhaps, an identification that unites the group identities as part of a larger series, called "America," possibly defined in terms of a faith in rights.

If this is an apt description of what the St. Patrick's Day Parade signifies today, then the problematic character of the decision in *Hurley* becomes apparent. If the parade serves as a space for the performative of an American national identity, which consists simply of individuals who identify with a multiplicity of groups marching in linear fashion, then there is no basis for excluding GLIB or any other group on the grounds of its (non)representativeness of an authentic national identity, nor because it violates some core set of values held by the organizers.[30] Rather, the character of the parade is such that individuals must identify with, and be accepted by, groups that mediate between the individual and the national symbolic of the parade (see generally Herrell 1996, pp. 287–292).

Thus, while the decision in *Hurley* may be doctrinally "correct" given the privatization of the parade by the judiciary, the Supreme Court's decision also resists the recognition of "out" gays and lesbians as constituting a group accepted within, and making up part of, an overarching American identity. The assumption, instead, is that ethnic/national identities can have an essential (heterosexual) meaning. More generally, the decision might be read as a refusal of the idea that national identity can be interpreted as a series, composed of politicized identities out of which groups have been formed. This approach can be characterized in terms of Young's (1995) spectrum of series and groups. An American national identity today might be more productively described as a series, of which the performative of the parade constitutes a manifestation. While the groups from which the nation is composed are made up of members who "undertake a common project" (p. 198), the series (national identity) is a more "amorphous collective":

> To be said to be part of the same series it is not necessary to identify a set of common attributes that every member has, because their membership is defined not by something they are but rather by the fact that in their diverse existences and actions they are oriented around the same objects or practico-inert structures. (pp. 202–203)

The series is composed of "self-conscious groups" that "arise from and on the basis of serialized existence" (p. 203). The St. Patrick's Day Parade, on this reading, ideally could serve as a metaphor for serialized national life, wherein participating groups share simply a space and a set of rules which regulate that space for their collective coexistence. Yet, at the same time, they are all differently positioned in terms of what the parade means to them and how they identify with it.

If American national life and the St. Patrick's Day Parade are more usefully understood today as closer to a series rather than a group, then the metaphor Justice Souter deploys to describe the parade and the position of the Veterans Council is dubious. In Justice Souter's reasons, the Veterans Council is likened to a symphony composer (*Hurley* 1995, p. 2348). The parade, like the nation, is constructed as a social group, wherein the Veterans Council serves to coordinate and determine the conditions of membership to create an authentic message.

By contrast, if the parade is envisioned as a series, then the better analogy in American law might be to a common carrier, such as the operator of a railroad, telephone, or telegraph company. A common carrier "undertakes to carry for all people indifferently" (provided that they pay for the service) and will be required by law to do so, based on the "quasi-public character of the activity involved" (*National Association of Regulatory Utility Commissioners v. FCC* 1976, p. 611). The Veterans Council becomes, not a composer of original speech, but a conduit or common carrier, delivering the messages of a diverse range of groups forming a series. Thus, national identity and culture might also be reconceived, not as based on a common purpose or project, but as providing a space for the performance of a wide range of different projects, with no single, authentic way of relating to that national space.[31]

Pursuant to this analysis, membership in the nation turns, not on the voicing of an authentic message, but on respect for the space being utilized by other groups.[32] Although a series may "speak" something as a whole, the meaning of that communication is beyond the control of any one entity. The message might be described as cacophony rather than harmony. Of course, an argument could be made by religious groups that GLIB's participation in the parade impacts on their enjoyment of space and the articulation of their group identities. An analysis of that claim would require, not the invocation of rights discourse, but a careful analysis of the relations of power that might exist between the groups and, ideally, a solution could be sought to accommodate them. For example, can the space be manipulated so that the conflicting groups need not be within close proximity of each other? That is a very different approach to the one pursued by the Veterans Council, which sought to "circumscribe the Irish community" (Yackle 1993, p. 866) by claiming a right to, in their legal counsel's words, "select groups that are consistent with what they perceive to be their version of a celebration of St. Patrick in their neighborhood" (Duncan 1996, p. 688).[33]

In response to this attempt to construct a parade reflecting and constituting an *authentic* national identity, the Supreme Court upheld the Veteran Council's claim and recognized it as a right. This process underscores a final feature of American national identity—namely, the legalization of politics and, more specifically, the translation of politics into the language of competing rights. The observation of de Tocqueville (1958) on the American national character in the early nineteenth century seems equally appropriate to this dispute:

> Scarcely any political question arises . . . that is not resolved, sooner or later, into a judicial question. Hence all parties are obliged to borrow, in their daily controversies, the ideas and even the language, peculiar to judicial proceedings. (p. 290)

For those situated outside of the American tradition, this is perhaps the most extraordinary, yet obvious, facet of the *Hurley* case. The legalization of politics is widely perceived to be central to the public sphere in the United States. As de Tocqueville recognized, this feature of American life is deeply rooted in the national identity.

In this chapter, I have interrogated a particular political struggle around the expression of sexual and national identities and explored how the dispute came to be articulated through the language of American constitutional rights as well as how it was resolved by the judiciary on that basis. By first tracing the central role of rights in the American national imaginary, I attempted to situate the factual background to the case more broadly by exploring how the ritual at the center of the dispute—a parade—is crucial to an understanding of the controversy.

The parade has a particular historical significance in the panoply of American celebratory rituals. In its current manifestation, it acts as a complex metaphor for competing approaches in under-standing a particularly American politics of identity in the late twentieth century. Where sexual identities (other than heterosexu-ality) fit within that politics, and the extent to which the public discursive space is open to them, continues to be tested in the United States today. How these questions come to be resolved no doubt "speaks" to the way in which an American national culture continues to be constituted and reflected, and to how space is regu-lated and deployed in the construction of identity.

3 Righting Wrongs

The summer of 1995 in South Africa was a time of unprecedented change, when unpredictable events never ceased to provide
for fascinating juxtapositions. Lesbian and gay activists vigorously
lobbied Parliament for the retention of "sexual orientation" as a
prohibited basis of discrimination in the guarantee of equality in
the Constitution, in the lead-up to the drafting of a permanent Bill
of Rights for South Africa.[1] At the same time, in neighboring Zimbabwe, President Robert Mugabe instigated the exclusion of the
group Gays and Lesbians of Zimbabwe from an international book
fair, and he described homosexuality as a Western corruption imported to Africa through colonization. National Women's Day became an official holiday on August 9, commemorating the fortieth
anniversary of the march on the union buildings in Pretoria by
twenty thousand women protesting the extension of the "pass laws"
to women, which regulated movement by nonwhite South Africans. At the celebrations, women of all races addressed the crowds
with statues of Boer heroes looking on stonily. But calls for law
reform to allow abortion on demand were met throughout the
country by conservative Christian opposition (matched by their
opposition to homosexuality). This series of contrasts (and every
day in South Africa provides a spate of new ones) illustrates the
extraordinary times in which South Africans are living.

This chapter focuses on how this national identity is in a process of being reimagined. The construction of race and its relationship to nation has an overwhelming centrality, and I will examine
the relationship of nationalism to race in some detail. Gender, too,
has been of crucial importance to national identity. Furthermore,
the regulation of sexual acts and identities was also connected to
the system of apartheid that continually worked to constitute and
separate racial groups. Thus, this chapter will interrogate the ways
in which national identity is bound up with race, gender, and especially sexual identity in South Africa today.

In the process of reconstituting a South African identity, a discourse of constitutionalism and rights is crucially important. This is exemplified by the ways in which lesbians, gays, and bisexuals are being reimagined as within (rather than radically outside) the South African nation. Their struggle illustrates the ways in which rights can help refashion national identity in a time of radical change. A blending of the "foreign" and the "indigenous" is deployed as the basis for the construction of identities, and for how South Africa now grounds itself within a cultural context of "human rights." In this time of change, voices of conservatism can also be heard calling for the maintenance of "traditions." In a country in which so much tradition is irredeemably tainted and scarred by an ignoble past, a turn to tradition can only be credible when it is selectively (and imaginatively) appropriated, and then brought into the present as the basis on which national identity is molded. Thus, appeals to history and tradition are made both by conservative actors, and in the name of progressive social change.

From Essential Categories to a Rainbow Nation

> The election not only reaffirmed that which the West desired but also, and perhaps more importantly, it instituted a new imaginary, a horizon within which for the first time, a fluid, open South African identity became a possibility for all those denied it before. (Norval 1994a, p. 157)

The constitution of national identity in South Africa occurred over a historical period of exploration, colonialism, and capitalist expansion. Exploration and white settlement caused the gradual dispossession of an array of African peoples of the region (see generally Pomeroy 1988, Thompson 1995). Through this process, a racially segregated society came into being long before the system of "grand apartheid" was introduced after World War II. In the nineteenth century, the colonial order sought to manage the African population, first through an "incorporationist strategy" where a minority might be brought into the governing order (Marks and Trapido 1987, p. 5). By the late nineteenth century, however, social Darwinism and scientific racism "provided a convenient rationalisation for denying political rights to the allegedly biologically 'inferior' black proletariat" (p. 7). That ideology informed the development of an English-speaking South African identity, wherein non-English white settlers were also constructed as an "inferior race" (p. 7). The British colonial system was unsuccessfully challenged in the Boer War (1899–1902), one of the signal events in the formation of an Afrikaner national consciousness and a precursor to South African union in 1910. But the formation of the nation state did not lead to the articulation of a single South African national identity. Rather, postwar South Africa saw the consolidation of a segregationist policy to control the urbanization of Africans, along with a manipulation of the authority of "traditional" chiefs as a means of maintaining social control (p. 8).

The emergence of Afrikaner nationalism was a response to the dominance of English speakers in the government and economy. By the late 1930s a race-based ethnic identity became mobilized, centered on the development of Afrikaner business and culture and the standardization of the Afrikaans language. This identity was infused with a combination of Christian nationalism and belief in an Afrikaner destiny. As Dubow (1992) argues, Christian nationalism provided apartheid (a term that became widely used during this period) with an essentialist rationale for racial segregation. A combination of several factors in this decade contributed to the way in which the relationship of individual and group came to be articulated. Poverty among Afrikaners facilitated the linking of anti-black sentiment to a critique of English and Jewish capital.

Christian nationalist ideology was based on the *volk:* the nation as an organic entity with a soul and subject to historical mission. God had ordained that nations were all different and, moreover, each was composed of a different people. Cultural difference and national diversity were anathema, and that construction was combined with an essentialist understanding of culture that stressed racial difference (and purity).

Afrikaner ideology arose, not only from an interpretation of scripture, but also from the discourses of "practical experience" and the "science" of eugenics (Dubow 1992, p. 215). The latter combined environmental and biological determinism, both of which played important roles in the nationalist movement. Afrikaners saw themselves as a distinct biological race, uniquely suited to the environment of South Africa. This claim provided a particular basis for the prohibition of miscegenation—that this divinely created race must not be tampered with. But Afrikaner "ethnicity" is a melange of diverse European groups and, therefore, could be construed as the product of, if not interracial sex, at least interethnic sexual intercourse.

For Africans, political identities were a response to this historical trajectory. The incorporationist strategy of the nineteenth century fostered an expectation by some of their eventual "incorporation in the colonial order" (Marks and Trapido 1987, p. 6). This belief was undermined by subsequent ideological shifts, which were fostered in part by the emergence of a mining-based capitalist order. The union of 1910, which brought together colonial white interests, also led to the consolidation of a formal oppositional movement—the African National Congress (ANC)—formed in 1912, which developed a nonracial national identity centered on the discourse of equality and freedom (see generally Norval 1995).

The National Party—the political manifestation of the Afrikaner nationalist movement—came to power in 1948 and remained in power until the democratic elections of 1994. The government quickly introduced the system of "grand apartheid" in South African law. This outcome of nationalist ideology helped consolidate an oppositional national imaginary on the part of the ANC. The ANC's demands were articulated to a discourse of nonracialism in the Freedom Charter, adopted in 1955 (Thompson 1995, p. 208). It states, for example, that "South Africa belongs to all who live in it, black and white, and that no government can justly claim authority unless it is based on the will of all the people." Nonracialism, as opposed to pan-Africanist nationalism, was the dominant discourse through which apartheid would be opposed. The Freedom Charter speaks from a position of heterogeneity and plurality, rather than the singularity usually associated with the manifestos of nationalist movements (see Norval 1995, pp. 41–43). It was partly because of the diversity of voices that made up this umbrella coalition of resistance to apartheid that the discourse could be framed in terms of universality: freedom and equality for all on the basis of personhood.

Apartheid ideology was also grounded in universalism, but in this case the discourse of equality was invoked at the level of race and ethnic *groups*. This required the ongoing constitution of a plethora of population categories. The "native" of colonial discourse (a category that could be reappropriated and deployed oppositionally as a basis for unity) was broken up into a number of different ethnic groups, which then became *the* central markers of identity: "the imaginary that came to structure the whole of South African society" (Norval 1995, p. 36).

From the 1950s onward, this process of constructing ethnicity by the state was fostered through the "Bantustan" policy in which "homelands" were constituted as ethnic nation states to which all blacks were allocated, a process "designed to fragment and diffuse pan-South African black nationalism" through "a massive programme of social engineering" (Marks and Trapido 1987, p. 22). Traditional tribal structures were bolstered and supported as a means of governing the homelands: "a political ideology which was designed to legitimate the Bantustans as nation-states and to co-opt a new collaborative class of 'tribal chiefs'" (p. 53).

The signifier "African" has been complex within the Afrikaner national imagination. It conjures up not only a "false" nationalism, but the image of the Christian "civilizing" mission of the other, a Communist threat, as well as images of "black on black" violence. The last was strategically deployed to maximum effect with the message that violence was the *inevitable* result of "intercourse" between ethnic groups. Nonracialist nationalism was undermined by the claim that "'culture contact' had internal limits which, if breached, could lead only to destruction, not only of 'national communities' but of 'western civilization'" (Norval 1995, pp. 40–41).

Furthermore, white nationalists have tried to connect black nationalism to "foreign" influence, particularly Marxism (Holiday 1988). At the same time, white South Africans have a highly contradictory relationship to Africa and, for that matter, to Europe, as geographically based identities:

> They claim European roots and a history embedded in European civilization, yet renounce these roots and that history in favour of their present situation whenever European norms threaten the South African status quo. They lay claim to African roots and an African past, but renounce both in favour of 'Western Civilization' whenever the African

majority attempt, by whatever means, to make them comply with African norms of political and economic justice. (p. 82)

Central to apartheid discourse was the belief, whether as a result of nature or nurture (or both), that there are *essential* differences between groups (however described). The discourse of equality was invoked at the level of groups to encourage their "separate" development. Thus race, ethnicity, culture, and nation could be employed selectively. The irony is that:

> despite the rhetoric, ethnic categories in South Africa are neither natural or immutable. The boundaries of ethnic identity are fluid, and have constantly shifted in response to political, social and economic circumstance. For much of this century, the state has actively intervened to shape this ethnic identification. (Marks and Trapido 1987, p. 61)

The "achievement" of apartheid, then, was to construct ethnicity and then to attempt to discredit "African" as a form of ethnic nationalism. The majority were reconstructed as a series of minorities within a white national logic of identity. Central to this imaginary was the belief in the "*a priori* impossibility of the inclusive management of the interests of all subjects of a multinational state" (Pretorius 1991, p. 7). Therefore, the destiny of ethnicity is nationhood, realized in the form of a political state and "only in the form of a state does the nation attain meaningfulness" (p. 7). As Pretorius suggests, such an imagining of natural destiny gives rise to a "survivalist" mentality in which multiculturalism is a threat to identity. Moreover, ethnic conflict is the logical, inevitable and *natural* outcome of the multicultural state. Consequently, a policy of "denationalization" of nonwhites from South Africa into the Bantustans could be justified on the basis of the survival of the white (or Afrikaner) race/ethnicity.

The undermining of apartheid ideology necessitated problematizing its categorical discourse (see Norval 1994b). For resistance movements, the universality of the Freedom Charter achieved a hegemony that marginalized black nationalism as an anticolonial discourse of resistance (Norval 1995, pp. 41–42). Instead, a multiracial coalition—the African National Congress—was central to resistance politics. The logic of apartheid was confronted by an opposing logic grounded in terms of universal rights, which revealed the particularism of apartheid—the contingency and constructedness of its categorical discourse and its perversion of equality and freedom.

This history has led to the current possibilities for constructing a reimagined, fluid, open, and inclusive South African national identity. What might be the basis for such a new national imaginary? How might it be conceived and constituted, given that this national identity must accommodate the competing demands of national "reconciliation" and "reconstruction"?

Given South Africa's past, the discourse of nonracialism remains in tension with the obvious continued *meaningfulness* of race and ethnicity as categories, for they are still central markers of identity. In this regard, the new political order is often perceived as a "compact" between groups—especially Africans and whites— that in turn may marginalize those for whom the logic of identity is not captured by that binary (the Indian and "colored" communities, for example) (see Goldin 1987, Swan 1987).

To the extent that the creation of a "new" South Africa is the product of an agreement to share power between racial and ethnic *groups* (combined with a federal system where the identities of states are sometimes closely tied to those of ethnicity), it is extremely difficult to avoid the assumption of essential group difference. Yet, that essentialism reproduces the construction of groups engaged in by the state under apartheid. While South Africa is now officially nonracial, decades of cultural essentialism cannot simply be "transcended," particularly when the new order is in large measure the product of power sharing between racially and ethnically defined groups.

This current tension reproduces what Comaroff (1995) has described as a central paradox in South African history, which is grounded in the deployment of rights. Colonial evangelists contrived for indigenous southern Africans "an entire ethnology, dividing them into 'tribes' and ascribing to them a primordial identity based on common ancestors and origins, language and lore, culture and customs, sentiments and interests" (pp. 214–215). Tribal politics thus was a product of the colonial encounter, shaping collective identities that could then be the basis for claims within the language of rights. But, for the colonial and later the apartheid state, the fact that rights were consequential upon membership in tribal groups facilitated the disenfranchisement of the majority. That is, Africans were assumed to be ineluctably tied to tradition, customary law, and the "premodern," which was "invoked to deny them the kind of personhood to which they were exhorted to aspire" (p. 231). In resistance, the ANC articulated its demands in the "language of rights and universal citizenship," evidencing "a continuing commitment to a classically European form of nationalism" and to modernity itself (p. 233).

The creation of a new legal and political order provides the opportunity for a newly imagined national identity characterized by the dereification of identity categories, and by an ongoing contestation over the meaning of ethnicity, culture, race, nation, and other markers of identity. Dubow (1994, p. 369), for example, wonders whether it is possible within this new order to try to reimagine ethnicity "as a malleable, historically conditioned process" (p. 370). South Africa may be particularly suited to such a challenge because the *construction* of difference as essential has been both historically central and, now, officially repudiated. As a response to that history, could a South African identity based on an antagonistic relationship to essentialism emerge?

There continue to be divergent interpretations of what nonracialism signifies in South Africa. The conundrum remains how to build a South African identity from a history of separateness and the continued meaningfulness of group identity. Indeed, that identity was inscribed within the Interim Constitution, with "the right to self-determination" by groups included as a basic principle.[2] Thus, the founding document of the new order both recognized the meaningfulness of group identity and provides a discourse through which it could be invoked, even by Afrikaners (see Kymlicka 1989, pp. 246–251). This is but one example of the continuing role of ethnicity; others abound. The Zulu people of KwaZulu-Natal province exhibit strong ethnic national impulses that have served to resist the universalism of ANC discourse, impulses delivered through "the politics of primal sovereignty" by the Inkatha Freedom Party (Comaroff 1995, p. 233).

To the extent that South Africa is imagined as the bringing together of groups without the transformation of identity, the logic of group self-determination may be an inevitable consequence. As Comaroff (1995) has demonstrated, the politics of primal sovereignty has been in tension with the language of universal citizenship throughout South Africa's history, and it stems from the contradictions embedded within the colonial discourse of rights. As a political matter today, that tension is most often resolved through pragmatism, ongoing negotiation, and compromises—strategies that may well prove central to the meaning of a new South African national identity. However, Norval (1994a) argues that an alternative understanding of a new South Africa could involve the reworking of group identities. Such a reimagining seeks to avoid the further reification of race as a basis upon which society is ordered (or disordered). Rather, it demands "the problematisation of the racial as an ordering principle" (p. 164). In that sense, a "post-apartheid" society would retain apartheid as its other (Norval 1995, p. 44). Apartheid, as signifying the essential fixity of identity, becomes that which must be resisted, and is at the heart of the inscription of a new national self. In other words, the very idea of an essential, biological, fixed identity as a political logic becomes "foreign" to the "new" nation. That national imagining would be characterized by "the principle of openness and the need for continuous self-creation, resisting forms of closure characteristic of the onto-theological principles of apartheid discourse" (pp. 43–44).

While racial identity has had an overwhelming centrality within the South African imaginary, I now turn to the constitution of sexuality as closely related to racial categorization within both dominant and oppositional discourses.

Sexuality and Nationalism in South Africa

> . . . homosexuality is un-African. It is part of the spin-off of the capitalist system. We should not take the European Leftist position on the matter. It should be looked at in its total perspective from our own Afrocentric position. (Bennie Alexander, Secretary General of the Pan-African Congress, quoted in Gevisser 1995, p. 71)

In the summer of 1995, a major news story in the southern African region concerned the unlikely event of the Zimbabwean International Book Fair. The theme of the fair that year was "human rights," and the fair was to feature a presence by the organization Gays and Lesbians of Zimbabwe (GALZ). On the eve of the opening, a letter from the state director of information advised the book fair trustees that the government strongly objected to the presence of GALZ. The trustees, claiming that they had been placed in an impossible position, canceled GALZ's registration. A storm of protest ensued, much of it emanating from South Africa. At the book fair opening, President Robert Mugabe stated that he found it "extremely outrageous and repugnant that such immoral and repulsive organisations like those of homosexuals . . . should have any advocates in our midst" (quoted in Wetherell 1995, p. 15). Previously, Mugabe had equated homosexuality with immorality, condemning it as an abhorrent Western import (see generally Dunton and Palmberg 1996, pp. 8–17; Phillips 1997).

The Zimbabwean International Book Fair episode exemplifies the many issues that I consider in this section. On one level, it might be dismissed as an isolated outburst from a virulently homophobic national leader, and there are plenty of those throughout all parts of the world. It might also be interpreted as an attempt by Mugabe to reassert political leadership in the region in the face of a declining international role for Zimbabwe with the election of Nelson Mandela as president of South Africa. On another level, the episode exemplifies a particular discursive deployment of homosexuality that links it to the degeneration of an indigenous African (hetero)sexuality caused by colonialism, capitalism, and the sexual exploitation of Africans by white men. In that way, attacks on sexual perversion reproduce tensions around ongoing racially-based economic inequalities in Zimbabwe (Phillips 1997, pp. 482–483). Black nationalism is deployed to resist a history of exploitation, which then demands the physical expulsion of homosexuals from the public sphere—such as GALZ from the book fair. This expulsion becomes metaphorically equated with the erasure of the white colonizer and, with him, his degenerate influence on a mythologized precolonial African sexuality.

The following sections explore a range of connections between discourses of nationalism, race, and sexuality in the specific context of South Africa—analyzing both African and Afrikaner nationalism and their constructions of race, nation, and sexuality. The focus then shifts to the rise of lesbian and gay political activism in

South Africa with an examination of the relationship of that activism to discourses of nation and sexuality and an interrogation of the ways in which lesbian and gay political actors, and their opponents, negotiate the dynamics of race in South Africa today.

Homosex is Un-African

The Zimbabwean International Book Fair episode provides a useful introduction to a broader theme: the relationship of an Afrocentric national imaginary to same-sex acts and identities. At a theoretical level, this conjunction was described by Fanon (1967), who argued that there was a fundamental connection between homosexuality, colonialism, and race. Racism is articulated with homosexuality through the figure of the "Negrophobic" white (pp. 154–159). For Fanon, the Negrophobic white woman's fear of the black man reflects her endowment of him "with powers that other men (husbands, transient lovers) did not have" (p. 158). In the imaginary of the Negrophobic woman, then, the black man is a "putative sexual partner" (p. 156) and, in a parallel logic, the "Negrophobic man is a repressed homosexual" (p. 156) who yields to his own "feeling of impotence or of sexual inferiority" (p. 159). That inferiority comes to be remedied through the castration of black male sexuality within the colonial imaginary. Edelman (1994, p. 55) succinctly underlines the false syllogism of this logic:

> Where it is "given" that white racism equals castration and "given" that homosexuality equals castration, then it is proper to conclude that white racism equals (or expresses through displacement) homosexuality and, by the same token, in a reversal of devastating import for lesbians and gay men of color, homosexuality equals white racism.

Fanon (1967, p. 180) asserts that male homosexuality is not indigenous to Martinique, the focus of his attention, which is explainable by "the absence of the Oedipus complex in the Antilles." Rather, Martinican men are susceptible to (passive) male homosexual acts only because of economic necessity in Europe. In this way, homosexuality is further constructed as a colonial exploitation and a metaphorical castration of the colonized.

Fuss (1995) has argued that Fanon's concern with the econom-

ics of sexual exchange between colonizer and colonized is not without considerable validity—central to colonial discourse *was* the
desire for the exotic black body, the institutionalization of a system of sexual exploitation, and a castrating representation of black
male sexuality. Moreover, the effect of white racism on the colonized manifested itself in the sexual exploitation, not only of black
women, but also of black men. However, Fuss claims that the
central problem with Fanon's analysis is the articulation of homosexuality with racism. Although the connections between colonialism, homosexuality, and sexual exploitation certainly can be
documented, "Fanon's theory of sexuality offers little to anyone
committed to both an anti-imperialist and an antihomophobic politics" (p. 158). That is, Fanon did "not think *beyond* the presupposi-
tions of colonial discourse in order to examine how colonial domination itself works partially through the social institutionalization
of misogyny and homophobia" (p. 160). Instead, Fanon constructs
the colonial encounter "within exclusively masculine parameters;
the colonial other remains an undifferentiated, homogenized male,
and subjectivity is ultimately claimed for men alone" (p. 160). Furthermore, the colonial other is an undifferentiated, essentially heterosexual, colonized, and sexually exploited male subject.

Fanon's theoretical stance has been given expression most recently in the GALZ case. More famously, it was articulated in the
Winnie Mandela trial for kidnapping, assault, and intent to do
grievous bodily harm in 1991, in which supporters carried placards
outside the courthouse that read "homosex is not in black culture"
(see generally Holmes 1995). Importantly, her defense strategically
deployed the logic of colonial contamination. Homosexuality manifests itself as the exploitation of an essentially heterosexual black
culture and becomes another form of white masculinist colonial
defilement. The defense described Mandela's actions as an attempt
to save young black men from the alleged homosexual advances
of a white Methodist minister. Within this anticolonial discourse,
as Holmes argues, white homosexual men are politically suspect
(p. 289). Moreover, homosexual practices among Africans not only
are a product of colonial exploitation, but also are infantilized
through their construction as the activities of wayward children.
This renders the alleged "victims" devoid of political agency, with

Mandela constructed as the "mother" to her nation, fighting to save her children (p. 292). An ideological model of the family is employed, where the alleged violence carried out by Mandela and her followers is necessary to preserve the heterosexual African family. In this family structure, homosexuality is other and Winnie Mandela is mother.[3]

The colonial contamination model has been furthered by a very different analysis, centering on the impact of capitalism on the displacement of African men. This example focuses particularly (although not exclusively) on the development of the gold mining industry in South Africa that began in the late nineteenth century. The industry demanded the mass dislocation of men, who were forced to live in single-sex hostels often miles away from their families, and underscores how thoroughly colonialism, apartheid, and capitalism are implicated both in damaging the African family and in economically exploiting black labor. One aspect of the industry was the presence of "situational homosexuality" in the mining hostels (see generally Moodie with Ndatshe and Sibuyi 1988, Harries 1990). This phenomenon was thoroughly documented by colonial administrators and was well known within African communities. It has often been interpreted exclusively in terms of the impact of economic exploitation—homosexuality is *produced* by the conjunction of capitalism and colonialism, which "perverted" the miners: "[M]en sleep with men in the hostels, this interpretation goes, because the hostels are unnatural prisons in which they have been wrenched away and cordoned off from their families and communities to work as slaves for the white economy" (Gevisser 1995, p. 71).

This reductivist reading of same-sex sexual acts in the mines has been shown to be problematic (see generally McLean and Ngcobo 1995, Ndatshe 1993, wa Sibuyi 1993). Achmat (1993, p. 104) has argued that the colonial/capitalist exploitation model "serves as an historical apology for male homosexuality in institutions with a preponderance of African men." He posits that while same-sex practices did occur in precolonial societies (as did prohibitions), colonialism and capitalism "helped establish a new constellation of power relations," which separated the bodies and desires of African men from purely reproductive functions (p. 105). As de Vos (1996, p. 274) reiterates:

> The central role of missionaries in the process of colonial conquest, the rise of the colonial state as the new sovereign power on the subcontinent, and the interests of the mining houses sometimes contested but mostly colluded in the formation of institutions to regulate the distribution of discipline on the bodies of all its subjects.

These examples illustrate why the colonial contamination model is an insufficient account of the role of same-sex practices and identities in South Africa. However, the argument that homosexuality is "un-African" does have a ring of truth, but for reasons different from those usually offered. In resistance to the discourses that deploy African nationalism in conjunction with a defense of heterosexuality, it has become commonplace not only to document same-sex practices within African communities, but to speak of "lesbians," "gays," and "bisexuals" in universal terms—the "we are everywhere in the world and throughout history" argument. In one sense, this is attractive. What "we" would construe as same-sex sexual acts have a habit of turning up in most societies historically in an array of different forms, carrying with them a multiplicity of culturally diverse significations. Documentation of these practices tends to focus on men, but this may say more about the erasure of female sexuality transculturally and transhistorically (and by ethnographers) than it does about the existence of what would be perceived today in the West as female same-sex sexual practices (see Blackwood 1986, Gay 1986).

Social constructionists have convincingly shown that homosexuality as an identity is an historically and culturally specific term, a product largely of medical and legal discourses in Europe. In that sense, homosexuality is a European social construction, and:

> there may be some truth in the assertion that homosexuality in South Africa is a white European imposition. While same-sex desire is a transcultural phenomenon . . . it would be missing the point of constructivism not to be careful about universalizing conditions which go to the making of a gay identity. (Pantazis 1996, p. 299)

Furthermore, the European national imaginary has invested homosexuality with a good many racial features (and vice versa). The
identities "lesbian," "gay," and "bisexual" are even more culturally
specific and temporally recent. It would be hard to say that "gayness" and "lesbianness" as political identities are not products of
European culture and, especially, of Anglo-American culture (see
Fuss 1995, p. 159).

A Eurocentric analysis of sexuality has tended to interpret same-
sex practices that clearly did occur in many societies through the
prism of European sexual identity categories. It has been documented in a number of cultural locations, for example, that same-
sex practices occurred without the inscription of an identity, be
it "sodomite," "homosexual," or anything else (see generally Bleys
1996). Thus, our categorical discourses of sexuality clearly do not
apply universally. The imposition of a colonial system, on this reading, does not necessarily introduce the colonized to same-sex practices. Rather, colonial discourse names and forbids practices that
may have been accepted in some cultural contexts (and forbidden
or ignored in others) while, at the same time, frequently exploiting
the colonized sexually. And one of the exploitative effects of colonialism was to construct the "native" as sexually depraved.

In the southern African region, that project was undertaken
largely by the Methodist missions, which carried on the "civilizing"
role during the nineteenth century. As Comaroff and Comaroff
(1992) demonstrate in their ethnography of the Tswana people of
southern Africa, the colonial encounter between "Protestant imperialism and Africa" (p. 160), in which each "culture" came to define
itself in relation to the other, was dynamic (p. 162). The distinction between systems of native "tradition" and European ways was
constituted and consolidated in the process. The "ideological on-
slaught on the part of Christian missionaries" (p. 258) intervened
in all areas of life, especially Tswana sexuality. The polygamous
family and matricentric unit were central sites for missionary attention, and they sought to reform conjugal relations through
Christian marriage, nuclear families, fixed gender roles centering
on public and private spheres, and European property relations.
Women were to be confined to the private sphere (losing control of

agricultural production in the process), and a model of "domesticity" was imposed. At the same time, "in seeking to cultivate the 'savage' . . . British imperialists were actively engaged in transforming their own society as well, most explicitly in domesticating that part of the metropole that had previously eluded bourgeois control" (p. 293).

The constitution of African "tradition" and identities thus, in no small measure, was a product of the colonial encounter, which "contrived for them an entire ethnology, dividing them into 'tribes' and ascribing to them a primordial identity based on common ancestors and origins, language and lore, culture and customs, sentiments and interests" (Comaroff and Comaroff 1992, p. 214). In the domain of sexuality, that tradition was constructed as immoderate, undomesticated, and improper in terms of gender roles, domestic arrangements, and relationships to private property.[4]

Some South Africans have drawn on the colonial construction of sexuality and have sought to redeploy the signifier "African," resisting discourses of antihomosexual Africanism, through a "Gay Africanist" subject position (see Gevisser 1995, pp. 72–73). African homophobia is read as an appropriation of a colonial discourse: the "censure of homosexuality is a colonial import . . . and there is irony to the fact that latter-day Africanists have assimilated this Judeo-Christian biblical propaganda and reconstructed it as precolonial African purity" (p. 73).

The deployment of "Africa" by black nationalists through homophobic discourse leaves the "colored" community in an indeterminate position. Caught between Afrikaner and African nationalism, the colored—a separate racial/ethnic category constructed and regulated under apartheid—can also be read as an aporia or excess to essentialist categorization. Interestingly, the colored community of Cape Town has a long, documented, and fascinating history of male homosexual expression and identity within fairly public discourse (see generally Chetty 1995, Gevisser 1995, Lewis and Loots 1995).

More generally, this strain of African antihomosexual nationalist discourse is problematic in that it denies the agency of Africans who may now have appropriated, and perhaps reworked through a discourse of Afrocentrism, the identities "lesbian," "gay," or "bisexual." It serves "to misrepresent Africa as statically monocultural, to ignore the richness of differing cultural constructions of desire, and in suggesting such a totalized notion of African culture, one simply replicates much of the colonial discourse on African sexuality" (Phillips 1997, p. 474). But antihomophobic discourse, too, must be wary of framing homosexuality as a universal category of identity, without recognizing its historical and cultural specificity. Thus, "just as the notion of a singular 'African' culture dangerously misrepresents the wide variety of a multiplicity of African cultures, so it is misguided to assume that the same behaviour will be construed as 'sexual' within different locales" (p. 474). Such universalizing interventions can act as a form of neocolonialism, ignoring how Africa has its own histories of sexuality—shaped inevitably by the colonial experience and capitalist exploitation. It is not, however, necessarily the history that some black nationalists might claim. Rather, as Phillips argues, "the corruption that has been 'imported' is not the homosexual act, but rather the growth of the bourgeois notion of sexuality as constitutive of social truths, and the concomitant need to declare and control these truths through such categorical mechanisms as a hetero/homosexual dichotomy" (p. 483). In South Africa, however, a heterosexually informed nationalism is not limited to African nationalist ideology.

Corrupting Our Sons: Afrikaner Nationalism and Homosexuality

Afrikaner nationalists subscribed to the essential categorization of groups as divinely inspired and ordered. Maintaining the purity of those categories had sexual implications, particularly in terms of the need for strict sanctions (legal and otherwise) against miscegenation. That prohibition was undermined by the very existence of the offspring of interracial sex, who then had to be fitted into the racial categorization scheme. Thus, the regulation of sexuality was intricately related to race, both of which were key to Afrikaner nationalism. Although this section focuses specifically on the ways in which Afrikaner discourse deployed sexuality (often in an oppositional fashion to other whites), white racial unity has also been frequently invoked *vis à vis* the majority population.

While the prohibition against miscegenation is easily understandable ideologically, the construction of heterosexuality also
was central to this nationalist discourse. First, Afrikaner ideology
erased the sexual agency of white women, whose importance to the
nation lay in their reproductive capacity; in the resistance movement as well, the role of African women historically was as "mothers" to the struggle. As McClintock (1996, pp. 275–276) argues, "a
racial and gendered division of national creation prevailed whereby
white men were seen to embody the political and economic agency
of the *volk*, while women were the (unpaid) keepers of tradition
and the volk's moral and spiritual mission" (see also Mangaliso
1997). Within official discourse, the importance of maintaining
high birth rates among whites has long been emphasized. Population was crucial to survival, and women played *the* central role in
preserving the nation (Retief 1995, p. 102). Related to this point
was the way in which homosexual men were discursively constructed, first, as white and male within Afrikaner nationalist discourse. As a consequence, the homosexual was a threat to survival
because he undermined the "sexual purity and moral solidarity" of
the nation—and would not propagate the race (p. 109). In this
way, Afrikaner constructions of homosexuality are similar to some
black nationalist constructions of precolonial Africa as morally and
sexually pure. Both deploy a "tradition," thereby obviating the degree to which Afrikaner tradition is a recent invention and, conversely, the extent to which African cultural traditions are a product of the colonial imagination.

This reading of homosexuality as white and male (and middle
class) does reflect most gay subculture that existed throughout
much of South Africa's history (see generally Gevisser 1995). However, as one activist suggested to me, this reading may be problematic in the way in which it defines subculture, in that it tends to
erase informal, undocumented communities that may well have existed outside of the white, male, and middle class context (Achmat
1995). But, in any event, there clearly was no lesbian or gay political movement historically in South Africa. The one event that did
mobilize certain segments of the population was the Forest Town
Raid of 1966 (see generally Retief 1995). This police raid on a home
in a wealthy Johannesburg suburb found a party of some three

hundred men dancing, in the words of the South African police, "to the strains of music, kissing and cuddling each other in the most vulgar fashion imaginable" (Retief 1995, p. 101).

The Forest Town Raid was extremely significant in the public consciousness and was deployed within official discourse as a threat to nation and social order. After deliberation in Parliamentary Select Committee (with representations on behalf of lesbians and gays), and following parliamentary debate, amendments to the *Immorality Act* were enacted, whereby "[a]ny sexual acts between men at a party were to be banned; the age of consent for male homosexual acts was to be raised from 16 years to 19; and the manufacture or distribution of any article intended to be used to perform an unnatural sexual act was to be prohibited" (Retief 1995, p. 103).[5]

The articulation of homosexuality within public, parliamentary discourse provided the opportunity for a section of gays—white, largely male, and middle class—to organize and make representations that ultimately may have contained the degree of legal restrictiveness. The focus of this campaign was on maintaining some safe social space within the existing system. It was a conservative strategy aimed at parliamentarians, and not at organizing any kind of movement within South African society (let alone a movement connected to broader social struggles). The episode underscored the conservatism of the gay, white, male community and the way in which it conceived itself within the social order.

The homosexual was also under construction within the dominant ideological framework of Afrikaner nationalism and apartheid discourse. Gevisser (1995, p. 31) argues that at the time of the Forest Town Raid, "Afrikaans cultural and religious organizations were agitating about the fact that wealthier Jewish and English men were corrupting their youths." The discourse of colonial contamination thus has a history in Afrikaner nationalism, in which homosexuality was a corrupting influence on an invented "pure" racial group.

Many of the ideas that have animated Afrikaner nationalist ideology continue to resonate within conservative discourse in South Africa today, but they are now shaped by the changed political context. In fact, in a climate characterized by the successful invocation of the universalist discourse of human rights for lesbians and gays, conservative positions on homosexuality assume the stance of backlash, a phenomenon which I will examine shortly.

Resisting Homophobic Nationalism: The Rise of a Movement?

The ways in which movement politics is developing within South Africa today and its relationship to discourses of national identity form a complex relationship. Such complexity stems from the fact that many "different homosexual identities were and still are produced by a unique set of power relations and apparatus in the context of colonialism, capitalist development and racial domination" (de Vos 1996, p. 274; see also Pantazis 1996).

The 1960s were noteworthy for the conservatism of a white, homosexual, largely male and middle class subcultural community. The gender imbalance within this subculture is related both to the sexism of the society and the class basis of subcultural life. Gender economic inequality meant that many white lesbians, to the extent that they were self-supporting, inhabited a lower socioeconomic rung. Gay political organization, such as it was, also was racially based. The conservatism of gay whites was reflected in a history of suspicion regarding the deployment of rights discourse—no doubt because of the way in which that discourse of rights has had an overwhelmingly racial inflection, tied to the rights-based tradition of the ANC (see generally Gevisser 1995).

This conservatism is exemplified by the emergence in 1981 of the organization Lambda, an activist organization aimed at protecting the "rights" of homosexuals. In this context, rights turned exclusively on the criminal law and its focus on male same-sex acts, and the organization explicitly sought to remain "apolitical" in its pursuit of rights (an interesting conception of the politics of rights struggles!) (Gevisser 1995, p. 47).[6]

It is hardly surprising, given this attitude, that gay rights struggles lacked any legitimacy within, or connection to, the anti-apartheid movement in this period. Within the liberation struggle, 1976 proved to be a watershed with the rise of student protests in the townships. It has been argued that the student protest movement was important in part because of the way it signaled a change in attitude among township youth (McLean and Ngcobo 1995).

Political mobilization and rights discourse became central, and "split young people from their roots and conventions of their elders" (p. 180). In that context, the discourse of rights tentatively began to be appropriated by young township gays and lesbians. While it cannot be claimed that this was the beginning of a gay rights movement, the period marked a change among those youth who came to identify as lesbian or gay, but whose central political identity stemmed from anti-apartheid struggles.

The impact of one person on the shaping of lesbian and gay consciousness among young black South Africans cannot be underestimated. Simon Nkoli emerged as a central figure in the convergence of anti-apartheid and lesbian and gay politics in the 1980s. Nkoli, with a group of twenty-one others, was tried for murder and treason in the Delmas trial of 1986—a signal event in anti-apartheid mobilization (see Nkoli 1995). The articulation of Nkoli's gay sexuality while awaiting trial in prison served in no small measure to mobilize liberationist lesbian and gay organizations abroad in support of the struggle against apartheid. Nkoli's "coming out" was also immensely important to youth within South Africa in the forging of a sexual identity (Achmat 1995, Mtetwa 1995a).

Nkoli was extremely threatening, however, to the "apolitical" rights struggles being pursued by some white gays. GASA (Gay Association of South Africa), for example, did not actively support Nkoli nor, for that matter, did the majority of gay whites necessarily support the anti-apartheid struggle (Gevisser 1995, p. 56). As one of the Delmas defense lawyers explained to me, lawyers representing the defendants found Nkoli's gayness a problematic diversion that threatened to upset their litigation strategy (Satchwell 1995).

Upon his acquittal, Nkoli helped found in Johannesburg in 1988 the Gay and Lesbian Organisation of the Witwatersrand (GLOW), which attempted to bring lesbian and gay rights struggles into the broader human rights agenda and develop a gay rights movement through multiracial organization (and continues to do so today). The presence of Nkoli and other anti-apartheid activists provided GLOW with credibility within wider anti-apartheid struggles. Along with the Cape Town based Association of Bisexuals, Gays, and Lesbians (ABIGALE), formed in 1992, and a range of different individuals and groups, a new awareness developed during this period in which many lesbians and gays of all racial and ethnic groups aligned themselves with the ANC Freedom Charter (see Fine and Nicol 1995).

The dismantling of official apartheid in South Africa has created space for a previously unthinkable range of sexual expression including, but certainly not exclusively, lesbian and gay organizing (see Keller 1994). This was exemplified by the inauguration of an annual Gay Pride march in 1990, which at that time included a substantial (although not majority) black presence. In fact, it was perceived by some whites as "too political" precisely because of that interracial configuration (Gevisser 1995, p. 82).

Of overwhelming significance during this period was the unbanning of the ANC in 1990 and the return from exile of many of its leaders. In terms of the deployment of rights discourse within lesbian and gay activism, these larger events are of great importance. ANC Constitutional Committee members Kader Asmal and Albie Sachs were largely responsible for the ANC's 1991 Bill of Rights. Both were influenced by identity politics in Europe and the United States, which included the deployment of "sexual orientation" within a discourse of human rights. In returning from exile, Asmal and Sachs (and numerous other ANC architects) brought back a rights consciousness that extended to lesbians and gays (Cameron 1995a, Botha 1995). In drafting the ANC Bill of Rights, then, equality discourse came to be shaped significantly by international political and legal developments. More generally, it has been argued that "South Africa's new constitutional order was shaped by and reflects the post–cold war hegemony of an American-style constitutionalism" (Klug 1996, p. 25). The ANC draft included reference to sexual orientation in a clause dealing with gender rights, although it was not included in the main equality provisions. The ANC Policy Conference in May 1992, however, expressly endorsed the principle of nondiscrimination on the basis of sexual orientation (see Cameron 1995b, pp. 96–97).[7] Also important in the early 1990s was the articulation of lesbian and gay rights claims as part of a broader human rights struggle by anti-apartheid activists within South Africa, particularly Edwin Cameron, then a professor of law at the University of the Witwatersrand. Because of his involvement in the anti-apartheid legal network, Cameron could influence ANC constitutional architects and strategists (see Cameron 1993).

The informal connections between constitutional "players" and advocates for lesbian and gay equality rights was crucial in the process of drafting the equality provisions of the national Bill of Rights in the 1994 Interim Constitution. This document has been the fundamental law until the operation of the final Constitution, which has now been adopted by the Constitutional Assembly (Thompson 1995, p. 269). The content of the Interim Constitution was the outcome of a compact between political parties representing different racial and ethnic communities in South Africa. It was drafted by a small group of lawyers and academics, one of whom acknowledged, in an interview with me, the influence of gay rights activists (Corder 1995). The equality provisions, as one of a series of enumerated bases of nondiscrimination, expressly includes protection against discrimination on the grounds of sexual orientation (see endnote 1). It was the first constitution anywhere to expressly include such a prohibition. As Klug (1996, p. 20) argues, through the constitution-making process, as they came to mobilize around gender, social class, and sexual orientation so as to exert organized influence on the constitution drafters, "South Africans discovered that political participation is built on a far more complex, fluid set of identities and interests than those privileged by apartheid."

The election of the Government of National Unity and the beginning of a new constitutional order also saw a period of public discourse and debate on the content of the final Constitution. Lesbians, gays, and bisexuals participated actively in that conversation, through a carefully managed and orchestrated campaign to retain sexual orientation in the equality provisions. A "grassroots" campaign was eschewed in favor of a high level lobbying approach aimed at members of Parliament and sponsored by a coalition of activist groups from across South Africa: the National Coalition for Gay and Lesbian Equality ("the Coalition").[8] A full time lobbyist, Kevan Botha, was employed by the Coalition in the run up to the final Constitution. The Constitution was again drafted by teams of experts, but this time with broader public input. On October 10, 1995, the Constitutional Committee of the Constitutional Assembly accepted the retention of sexual orientation in the

Bill of Rights, thereby ensuring its inclusion as part of the final Constitution.

It would be erroneous to suggest that the inclusion of sexual orientation in the Constitution was the product of a broadly based campaign organized by a lesbian, gay, and bisexual rights movement (in the way in which those from the Euro-American tradition would understand it). The unique circumstance of South Africa is that the space within which to successfully articulate demands for constitutional equality rights opened up at a particular historical juncture. Activists recognized that this moment could be exploited for its potential, and they chose the strategy that would have the highest likelihood of success (Botha 1995). Thus, from the outside, the South African experience is rather inverted. As Kevan Botha explained it to me, rather than rights guarantees following from demands expressed through a movement, one of the goals of activists is to deploy the inclusion of sexual orientation in the Constitution so as to foster a broad-based interracial lesbian and gay identity politics (Botha 1995). For activists in North America and Europe, lessons can be learned here concerning the importance of rights as a tool for coalition building and inclusivity, rather than viewing rights as an end in themselves.

The impact of the sexual orientation provision remains to be seen. On a strictly legal level, activists have formulated a long-term strategy whereby less controversial claims will be put forward initially, followed by the politically tougher cases. That strategy likely will include both lobbying Parliament for legislative changes and litigation. Cameron (1995b, p. 97) suggests that constitutional protection would impact upon decriminalization of same-sex sexual activity; "legislative enforcement of non-discrimination"; "rights of free speech, association and conduct"; and legal recognition of "permanent domestic partnerships." Because of the protests it would generate, strategists consistently argue that the "right to marry" is at the bottom of the list (Botha 1995).[9]

The inclusion of sexual orientation in the Constitution is of interest, not only for its strictly legal ramifications, nor for the political implications of the strategies adopted by gay rights advocates, but also for the broader impact of the equality provisions on identity—at the level of individual, group, and nation. At a general level, lesbians and gays unquestionably express a strong conviction that the inclusion of sexual orientation means *something* (perhaps something inchoate) beyond the law. It has provided many, especially in the townships, with a sense of approval and legitimacy that continues to be woefully lacking in many communities. In that sense, the success of rights discourse is in the feeling of inclusion within the polity. That inclusivity is being translated into a right to participate as openly lesbian, gay, or bisexual within the public sphere and to bring that perspective to an ongoing dialogue over what it means to be a South African citizen.

In dramatic contrast to the past, there is currently space in which claims for inclusion in a national dialogue usually can be successfully made by anyone. For example, in the process of constitution making, Parliament asked all South Africans to participate in a national dialogue. Exclusions could not be justified on the basis of "tradition" in a nation where tradition is so thoroughly discredited. Although the participation of lesbians and gays has been carefully orchestrated by strategists, their participation proved to be an opportunity to articulate, for example, connections between racial and gender oppression and homophobia. They have argued that the regulation of sexuality was central to apartheid ideology (Botha 1995). Furthermore, activist organizations recognize the importance of rectifying the wrongs of gay rights organizations of the past, in terms of inclusivity and cultivating a diverse leadership for the future.[10] The extent to which an emerging lesbian and gay rights movement will be successful in this regard remains to be seen.

The agenda of lesbian and gay rights cannot be divorced from the task of national reconstruction. Issues of housing, jobs, and safety assume an overwhelming centrality to those many South Africans who historically were denied all three. Not surprisingly, the majority of lesbians, gays, and bisexuals are also making demands for reparation centered on past injustices stemming from the conjunction of racial, gender, and sexual oppression. Activists, too, are aware that rights must be connected to socioeconomic transformation. That is, constitutional protection must mean *more* than rights that appear trivial by comparison to the social problems facing South Africa. In this regard, one of the central goals in the deployment of a rights-based strategy is to secure a right to participate in the development of a new South Africa from the perspective of being openly lesbian, gay, or bisexual. It may well be that a right of participation—of engaging in a dialogue of national identity and reconstruction—is one of the most powerful offshoots to constitutional rights protection (Botha 1995).[11]

A lesbian or gay identity politics might operate to resist the heterosexual exclusivity that historically characterized nationalist struggles. Lesbian and gay activism could contest the very idea of fixed and essentialized borders to sexual (and other) identities, which so centrally informed apartheid discourse. That is, a lesbian, gay, or bisexual identity might challenge—or "queer"—the rigidity of categorization and further a "post-apartheid" national identity of openness and fluidity. Sexual inclusivity could undermine essentialist notions of identity more broadly:

> The idea of colour-coding sexuality is as ludicrous as the notion of
> separate development itself. It is not homosexuality, but the insistence
> on fixed and unhistorical categories of "essential" racial and sexual
> identity which causes violence, sexual policing and the subsequent
> alienation of sexual radicals from the democratic process. (Holmes
> 1995, p. 294)

Claims of incorporation into the national imaginary might be made with the recognition that *who* is being incorporated and *into what* is left ambiguous.

The tension between a conception of national identity as fluid and contingent and the competing position that the newness of South Africa resides in the bringing together of sovereign groups with preexisting homogeneous and essential identities is apparent in the context of sexual identification. In terms of rights struggles around sexual orientation, the strategy adopted by the Coalition would be difficult to describe in terms of fluidity or openness. Instead, the way in which sexuality was articulated was heavily influenced by essentialist arguments about sexual identity, which are invested with the rhetoric of immutability (see National Coalition for Gay and Lesbian Equality 1995). This strategy deployed an analogy between race and sexuality, making the powerful claim that it is illegitimate to discriminate based on an identity over which one has no "control."

To some extent, the radical potential of rights struggles was neutralized by more sexually conservative notions of identity that focus on the "naturalness" of categories. Within gay rights discourse, sexual identity is largely abstracted from sexual acts as a means to distinguish a normalizable lesbian, gay, or bisexual identity (which is not "chosen") from those persons who engage in "deviant" sexual practices (bestiality, pedophilia) that do not and *cannot* constitute sexual identities. In this way, activists replicate categorical discourse rather than challenge it. The problem of legitimizing categories through an appeal to essential (but invented) natures is all too apparent from apartheid discourse, and the tension between the reification and deconstruction of sexual identity categories mirrors the same essential/contingent dynamic of identity unfolding within South Africa more generally.

The relationship of nationalisms and sexualities operates in a multiplicity of ways. Within lesbian and gay organizations in South Africa, difficult questions about the meaning of nonracialism reproduce broader public debates. On the one hand, the dominant theme is "unity" across the races, with an emphasis on inclusiveness and the development of a truly interracial national movement. On the other hand, given the history of racial oppression, "separate development" might be required by lesbians and gays of color, at least in the shorter term. Not surprisingly, a call for racial separateness meets strong resistance but also has its advocates:

> Maybe some of the reasons for fear of a separate Black movement is deeper than meets the eye. Black people in this country are still suffering from a lack of self-esteem, of Black Pride, or rather Black Consciousness. You can see it in the way we seek approval from White people in doing things right—for fear of being either classified stupid or uncivilised, or many of the other terms used to deride us. Our whole existence has always been based on pleasing and serving, and these things have manifested themselves in many ways. . . . It is time to stop seeking approval and being apologetic. Only we know what our needs are. White people may help us achieve but they can't help us name our pain. We need to name it for ourselves. (Ditsie 1995, p. 14)

   The tension between unity and separatism may ultimately be resolved by a balance between the two. Lesbian and gay activism in
South Africa also lacks the material resources of the West and, given
the history of coalition politics (as evidenced in anti-apartheid activism), a nonracial national movement likely will predominate.

Reproducing Tradition, Reconstituting the Nation

As lesbians, gays, and bisexuals consolidate a new-found space
within the South African national imaginary, others seek to mold
that imaginary along radically different lines. For example, African
nationalist discourses of homophobia continue to have some resonance within the public sphere, although official political discourse
has marginalized it. More troubling, in the view of many, is the
possibility of conservative Christian backlash that draws on the
conservative and religious character of large segments of South African society. The potential for backlash is taken seriously by lesbian and gay activists, who monitor these opponents (Botha 1995).
Just as nonracial progressive coalitions require ongoing work so as
to dampen the potential for fragmentation and separatism, within
any Christian coalition the maintenance of an interracial social
movement will be a considerable challenge. Because of its importance within the conservative Christian agenda, sexuality figures
centrally in the ways in which a South African national identity is
imagined by some conservatives in resistance to progressive discourses of inclusivity. Two examples will serve to support this
claim: the political response that emanates from the African Christian Democratic Party and conservative legal academic discourses
on human rights.

From Adam and Eve to Madam and Steve:
Reshaping Christian Nationalism

> I wish to remind those of us who have forgotten that in the beginning God
> created Adam and Eve, and not Adam and Steve. To build a family, Adam
> needed Eve, and not Steve! Even today, Eve needs Adam, and not Madam,
> to build a family. Nation-building cannot be possible while we try to legally
> destroy family values and the moral fibre of our society with clauses in the

Constitution that promote a lifestyle that is an embarrassment even to our ancestors. [*Hansard* (S.A.), January 24, 1995, p. 30, Rev. Meshoe]

The centrality of religion to politics is not restricted to the history of apartheid. In South Africa today, Christianity continues to inform politics explicitly through the African Christian Democratic Party (ACDP). Formed in 1993 to bring Christian views to the political arena, many of its founding members had been active within anti-apartheid politics. ACDP membership consists largely of evangelical Christians who became disenchanted, following the dismantling of apartheid, with the response of the ANC to other issues on the political agenda—such as abortion, homosexuality, and crime (Green 1995).

According to the ACDP, "mainline" Christian churches, in addition to the Dutch Reform Church, have lost their way politically in terms of a Christian moral agenda. The ACDP founding document stresses Christian principles, an open market economy, education based on the Bible, and a strong regional and local government structure. It sees itself connected with neither the extreme right nor left (unlike American evangelical politics), but rather espouses a politics based on the word of God as discerned from an evangelical perspective. As one of its two members of Parliament explained to me, democracy itself is valid only to a point, for "you cannot democratize the word of God" (Green 1995).

In the 1993 elections, the ACDP captured two seats in Parliament through the system of proportional representation. While such a result might suggest its insignificance politically, the ACDP's particular site of resistance to dominant political discourses gives it a public forum far exceeding its electoral base. Moreover, the ACDP articulates a set of views widely thought to be supported by many more of the electorate than actually voted for the party.

The ACDP envisions a national identity in Christian evangelical terms: the nation must be based upon its conception of the Christian family. So too, the Constitution, and its deployment of rights, ought to reflect that foundation by protecting "not only the rights of individuals, but also those of unborn children" [*Hansard* (S.A.), January 24, 1995, p. 32, Rev. Meshoe]. The issue of whether sexual orientation was to be included in the equality provisions of the final Constitution was central for the ACDP. It was the only party actively opposed to the inclusion (although party discipline prevented many others from voicing similar views). The ACDP justification oscillated between biblical teaching and its own reading of public opinion.

In terms of how sexuality is conceived, here again the national identity is defined in exclusionary terms. The ACDP draws upon a mix of evangelical Christian discourse and African nationalism in its rejection of the inclusion of sexual orientation. On the one hand, rights must be tested against the word of God (the limits of democracy). On the other hand, homosexuality is described in terms of the colonial contamination model—as "Eurocentric"— and homosexuals are drawn from a professional, upper class elite. South African lesbians and gays are said to have imported their ideas from rights movements in Europe and North America. Homosexuals thus have not simply co-opted Africans into their sexual practices. In being part of an elite, they have managed to co-opt the political process into accepting them into the constitutional order. Democracy is also invoked: "Does democracy mean promoting the interests of an elitist two per cent movement?" (Green 1995).

The ACDP also manipulates the sexual act-identity binary in a way that inverts its deployment by gay rights advocates. Homosexuality is characterized as an artificial category of identity, as "African" was within apartheid discourse. It represents a choice to engage in a set of sinful and criminal sexual acts. To protect homosexuality as an identity would be analogous to protecting pedophiles, practitioners of bestiality, or, for that matter, common criminals. In any of these cases, "identity" is essentially based on a chosen practice.

A focus on political elites is central to the ACDP discourse, and with considerable justification. The success of lesbian and gay activists in South Africa has come from their manipulation of the elite in the drafting of the original Constitution. Gay rights advocates *were* in some cases close personal friends with members of the Technical Committee that drafted the equality clause in the Interim Constitution. In addition, the ACDP argues that the gay rights movement has aligned itself with the ANC, pushing the ANC into recognizing sexual orientation. This, too, is correct. In the late

1980s and early 1990s, some activists began articulating a relationship between sexual orientation and broader rights struggles within South Africa. The fact that many of those activists have impeccable anti-apartheid credentials (and ANC membership) has been important in establishing their credibility. In adopting a sophisticated lobbying strategy, and in deliberately avoiding a grassroots campaign, lesbian and gay activists left themselves open to counterarguments framed in the language of anti-elitism and democracy. The argument thereby runs that black lesbians and gays have been co-opted so as to put a black face on an essentially white movement.

In this way, the ACDP constructs itself as shut out of elitist decisionmaking and, moreover, it deploys a strategy of marches and protests to stress its democratic character. It also relied on letter writing campaigns to the Technical Committee drafting the equality provisions. While the gay rights movement took a deliberate decision not to pursue that strategy (so as to avoid a numbers game with their opponents), the ACDP and its supporters flooded the committee with letters that emphasized their opposition to forcing churches to marry people of the same-sex.[12] In that respect, the strategies of the Coalition and the ACDP differed. But, in other ways, their discursive deployments were similar.

Apartheid discourse relied heavily on the construction of conspiracies of various kinds that threatened the nation. The discourse of conspiracy still retains a good deal of power within the new South Africa and has been deployed both by the ACDP and gay rights advocates. The ACDP asserts a conspiracy among those who take the "politically correct" position on issues the ACDP would answer in terms of Christian theology—homosexuality, abortion, pornography, and prostitution being high on the list. The conspiracy includes gay rights advocates who have co-opted not only African lesbians and gays (whom they also converted), but also the ANC, the South African Council of Churches, universities, the media, and no doubt many others.

Gay rights advocates also use the rhetoric of conspiracy to strengthen their demonization of the ACDP. In this conspiracy, the ACDP becomes something of a reincarnation of the demons of the past. For example, in his interview with me, Kevan Botha accused the ACDP of having connections to politically right-wing organizations (Botha 1995). One of its founding members was linked to military intelligence under the former regime and was forced to leave the party (Luow 1994). The ACDP is also thought by some to be connected to the American Christian Right movement. The ACDP thus becomes a central player in a conspiracy that threatens the new South African nation; it is an enemy within. Both of these deployments of conspiracy—by the ACDP and its opponents— have resonances in past discursive uses of internal threats to the survival of the nation, financed by foreign capital and influenced by foreign ideas.

Another similarity is at work in the way in which "tradition" is employed to bolster a political position. Members of the ACDP stress their anti-apartheid credentials and, in that sense, they reject a discredited political history. But the ACDP attempts to selectively choose from tradition as a basis for the constitution of a new national imaginary. Appeals to what would be morally acceptable to "our ancestors" and "traditional values" that "have stood and passed the test of time" are strongly made [Hansard (S.A.), January 24, 1995, p. 32, Rev. Meshoe]. This grounding of politics in tradition relies on a language of ancestry suggesting a distant past, long before the African family was subject to the corrupting influences of colonialism, apartheid, and homosexuality (and before a systematic "native" tradition was constructed through the colonial encounter). That past serves as the basis for the creation of a national identity, becoming the founding myth.[13]

Gay rights advocates also appeal to tradition, but in a less obvious way. In this case, apartheid is conjured up. Military intelligence, white Rhodesian right-wing funding, and, more generally, intolerance, sexual regulation, and Christian politics are invoked and attributed to the ACDP, which becomes emblematic of a return to an inglorious past threatening the new nation. The claims of nonracialism by the ACDP are tarnished by alleged connections to right-wing white racists. But, then again, the ACDP seeks to discredit the claims of nonracialism within gay rights organizations by labeling them white, male, middle class, and professionally elite. Furthermore, each group accuses the other of being foreign-influenced. The "nation" thereby becomes eminently manipulable, deployed by both sides through a selective blending of past and present as a means of inventing a national identity for the future.

Human Rights Are Not Christian:
Conservative Legal Academic Backlash

In South Africa today, public discourse is shaped by the centrality of the language of rights. Even conservative forces such as the ACDP frame much of their position in that discourse. The contours of those rights may be shaped by their interpretation of tradition, majoritarian impulses, and Christian teaching, but nevertheless rights are not eschewed. Right wing white discourse also now resorts to rights talk: minority rights to education, culture, and self-determination.

A somewhat different strand of conservative discourse has come from some quarters of the legal academy. For example, Potgieter (1991) intervened at the beginning of the period of transition with a call for legal "objectivity" and a defense of the South African legal system and judiciary under apartheid. South African common law and the Roman-Dutch legal tradition were "basically sound" and not in need of reform (p. 802). However, in the development of a new constitutional order, he warned that it was imperative that "jurists draw up these documents with scientific care and in an ideologically neutral manner" (p. 803). Relying on the work of Robert Bork, Potgieter argued that "lawyers should rid themselves of ideological prejudice, be it from the political left or right" (p. 803).

Most interestingly, though, he sought to counter claims made by some during this period that human rights were grounded in Christianity. In this regard, he makes a valid point that "attempts to present the political human-rights doctrine as Christian echo earlier endeavours to present apartheid as a Christian system. This approach turns a political ideology into an object of faith" (p. 804). Not that Potgieter espouses secularism; rather, his central thesis is that "Christian justice" is undermined by a "liberal-Western" model of rights:

> The justice created by the liberal-Western model of human rights consists not only in the protection of individuals against arbitrary state

action, but also includes the freedom of individuals to indulge in, for example, pornography, sex shops, free abortion, homosexual "marriages," euthanasia, satanism and occultism et cetera. (p. 805)

Here again the contamination model is employed, but now contamination of the South African nation results from the importation of a Eurocentric conception of human rights. Ultimately, rights discourse is based on a flawed view of the *essential* nature of persons: "It over-emphasises the *alleged* inherent dignity of man and loses sight of his corrupt character" (p. 805, emphasis mine).

In response to the Bill of Rights in the Interim Constitution, Visser and Potgieter (1994) have presented a more expansive critique. The authors emphasize the anti-Christian character of human rights discourse and, in particular, the Bill of Rights. The protection against discrimination on the basis of sexual orientation, which heads the list, is contrasted against the absence of constitutional protection for the "normal" family (p. 494). A variety of other Christian values are discussed: the importance of victims' rights, the "absurdity" of reference to the "human dignity" of prisoners, the importance of crime prevention, low taxes, the right to bear arms, and the injustice of affirmative action.

Out of this rather familiar conservative rhetoric appears an alternative conception of the national identity. Visser and Potgieter (1994, p. 496) point to the difference between "lawful cultural differentiation" and racial discrimination and to the importance of a constitutional right to a cultural identity. Essential group differences are thereby accepted. In this way, the authors seek to reappropriate the colonial discourse of primordial sovereignty, and to strip it of its invidious history, in resistance to the language of universal citizenship. In so doing, they construct an "indigenous" Christian South African constitutional and national identity, shaped by essential ethnicities and conservative Christianity.

They also denounce §35 of the Interim Constitution, which mandates reference to international and comparable foreign case law in constitutional interpretation (Visser and Potgieter 1994, p. 497).[14] This unique provision is read within a model of foreign contamination—of the South African legal system founded on Roman-Dutch law. Section 35 "should not be interpreted to place on the courts an additional obligation to find and apply *alien prin-ciples*" (p. 497, emphasis mine), nor should "comparable [case law] be allowed to interfere with the application of the eminent princi-ples of Roman-Dutch and South African law which have withstood the test of time" (p. 497).

This reasoning is a continuation of past constructions of the South African legal system, which was an important element of the national identity. Historically, South African law was cleansed of its Englishness through "the large cultural labour of resurrecting, re-narrating and representing Roman-Dutch common law" (Chanock 1995, p. 200). That inherently "rational" order could then be con-trasted against a reinvented, subordinate African customary law:

> Marshalling the claims of civilization in Africa involved mobilizing Eu-ropean traditions within a local context, and constantly deploying them against a contested set of African traditions. These were themselves, for the purpose of contrast, re-created in terms of European narratives of Africa. (p. 200)

Visser and Potgieter's (1994) characterization of the legal sys-tem moreover employs many of the same tropes of colonial con-tamination found in homophobic discourse. The Roman-Dutch le-gal system, like heterosexuality, is both natural and yet extremely fragile. Both must be protected from the temptations of the rather glamorous and seductive other, which if succumbed to (even once) will lead to individual and national destruction. The legal system now stands in for the national body, and its boundaries—its meta-phorical borders—must be protected from contamination by the exotic, the foreign, and the seductive.

These rhetorical deployments underscore how the consolida-tion of the indigenous and the foreign is a process of selection and construction, not "natural" or prior to discourse. The legal system serves as an important arena for the consolidation of national iden-tity, but certainly is not all powerful in that process (Chanock 1995, p. 200). In South Africa, where so much tradition has now been discredited, that relationship between the indigenous, the traditional, the innovative and the imported must be blended so as to construct something that can now be labeled "South African." While Visser and Potgieter (1994) provide a politically conservative reading of that relationship, others, in a more progressive fashion, have sought to piece together the foreign and the indigenous to forge a very different national identity.

The uniqueness of the new South African order lies in the way in which it has been created through a process of hybridity (Klug 1996, p. 59). On the one hand, the legal system is strongly influenced by an international order in which legitimacy has been tied to a constitutional culture founded on a discourse of rights (p. 28). The way in which comparative and international law has informed constitution drafting and judicial interpretation underscores this point. On the other hand, the constitutional culture is explicitly grounded in an Afrocentric "tradition," which members of the Constitutional Court have drawn on, for example, in ruling that capital punishment is contrary to the Bill of Rights (*S. v. Makwanyane* 1995).[15] Hybridity is an apt description of such a merging of the international and the local. But "tradition" can never be discovered in a pure, precolonial form, as is apparent in the way in which sexuality has been constructed. Thus, while the constitutional order recognizes the validity of traditional authorities and legal orders, it is widely acknowledged that indigenous law is a product of the colonial encounter, that traditional authorities were manipulated in the service of colonialism and apartheid, and that the universalism of equality rights will not be "trumped" by calls to "traditional" values (see generally Mokgoro 1996). Thus, the uniqueness of the South African national identity may be the way in which the internationalism of rights discourse interacts with the ongoing construction of local traditions, a hybridity that might well inform an understanding of sexual identities and communities in the future.

In this chapter, I have woven together a number of disparate threads to illustrate the potential for the reinvention of South Africa in circumstances where a tradition of essentialist categorical thinking has been discredited. The imagining of nation must avoid the search for essence. The history of South Africa underscores the tragic implications of the ethnic nationalist desire for cultural homogeneity. Rather, the national imaginary might be conceived of as continually in process. Inclusivity becomes the political struggle. The example of constitutional rights claims around sexuality serves as a prism through which to analyze the ways that struggle is fought. Issues of race, gender, sexuality, culture, and nation are all profoundly implicated in the drive for national reconstruction. Ultimately, in order to succeed, reconstruction itself must foundationally shape the meaning of this reimagined nation and all of the identities that constitute it.

4 Queer Nations

Gays and lesbians are full-fledged members of the great Quebec family, and
it is perhaps time to reinvent and enlarge our family. (Fo Niemi, Chair of the
Consultation Committee reporting on Violence and Discrimination Against
Gays and Lesbians, quoted in Quebec Human Rights Commission 1994)

During the 1990s, debates have raged throughout North
America about the desirability of the explicit and specific enumer-
ation of "sexual orientation" as a prohibited basis of discrimination
in human rights laws. In the United States, this has often taken the
form of intense struggles between the Christian Right, lesbian and
gay activists, and the state (see generally Herman 1997). In Canada,
at the federal level of government, the 1996 amendment of the *Canadian Human Rights Act* (which prohibits discrimination by both
public and private actors within the federal government's jurisdictional authority) to include sexual orientation as grounds of nondiscrimination precipitated fierce disagreement and the articulation of vociferous social conservatism in the political arena.

Yet, as North Americans in an array of jurisdictions battle over
the implications and meaning (both practical and symbolic) of laws
that provide remedies against discrimination on the basis of sexual
orientation—debates often framed in terms of whether such measures provide "equal rights" or "special rights"—it is rarely noted
that twenty years ago, in 1977, the Canadian province of Quebec
became the first jurisdiction in North America to specifically outlaw discrimination based on sexual orientation by both public and
private actors, subject to some substantial limitations, in its provincial Charter of Rights and Freedoms. It is also seldom remembered
that this amendment to the Charter was introduced and passed by

This chapter originally appeared as "Queer Nations: Nationalism, Sexuality and the Discourse of Rights in Quebec," *Feminist Legal Studies* V/1 (1997), 3–34, and is here reprinted by permission of Deborah Charles Publications.

the then newly elected nationalist and separatist Parti Québécois (PQ) government.

In this chapter, I consider Quebec as a case study in the relationship between national identities, sexualities, and the discourse of rights by first examining the related background and then contextualizing the discussion with a consideration of the ways in which rights have come to inform national identities today both in Quebec and the "rest of Canada" (ROC). I then look more specifically at how sexuality has proven central to the construction of national identities, often through an oppositional relationship such as between Quebec and the ROC, and conclude by examining how the insights that can be gleaned from an interrogation of national and sexual identification might be employed in conceiving citizenship in the multicultural and multinational state.

Quebec provides an interesting example, one in which, at least at the level of official discourse, nationalism often is articulated through the language both of group and individual rights. National identity appears, in this instance, to leave space for sexual pluralism and lesbian and gay identities. However, Quebec highlights simultaneously the extent to which legal liberalism can be far removed from the complex ways in which national identity is consolidated through its metaphorical deployment in terms of sexual acts and identities and the way in which it may be appropriated within nationalist discourse. Thus, homosexuality serves as both the basis for social movement organization within the national space *and* as a metaphor through which nations constitute themselves and others. The relationship between national and sexual identities proves far from one dimensional.

Rights of/in Nations

In looking back to 1977 and the debates surrounding the amendment of the Quebec Charter to include sexual orientation, it is striking how brief and to the point were the arguments in the National Assembly (the Quebec legislative body). This should not come as a surprise. It often seems that "successful" lesbian and gay law reform strategies involve the speedy enactment of legal change with a minimum of fanfare (see, e.g., Cicchino, Deming, and Nicholson 1995). In this case, the amendment was passed in a midnight session shortly before the Christmas vacation, fulfilling a commitment of the PQ to the lesbian and gay communities. Marc-André Bédard, Minister of Justice, introduced the amendment, explaining the reasons that demanded this legal change in terms of straightforward liberal principles of nondiscrimination against an historically disadvantaged group that had experienced social prejudice: "à mon avis, le rôle de l'Etat n'est pas d'institutionnaliser ces préjugés et de les exacerber en permettant que la discrimination puisse s'exercer contre les minorités dans la société" (*Journal des Débats* 1977, pp. 4883–4884).[1]

He went further, however, and described a relationship between this "progressive" amendment and the changing character of Quebec society. According to Bédard, the amendment symbolized something beyond the letter of the law: "nous avons tous l'immense privilège de vivre et de travailler dans une des sociétés les plus culturellement riches, les plus socialement créatrices, les lus politiquement dynamiques du monde entier. C'est notre conviction" (*Journal des Débats* 1977, p. 4884).[2] But, as Bédard acknowledged, this advanced state was not a characteristic of Quebec society found in its traditions. Rather, the government saw itself engaged in the task of creating a culture of human rights for a new society: "Le Québec des libertés . . . ce n'est pas le Québec d'une liberté acquise depuis des siécles, mais plutôt le Québec qui crée au jour le jour ses libertés" (p. 4884).[3] One of the symbolic effects of the amendment was to repudiate a history of discrimination as part of the process of creating a new, open, rights respecting, and inclusive society:

> I'l n'y a aucun cas comparable en Occident, ni dans le monde, d'une société qui soit passée aussi vite que la société québécoise, d'une façon aussi adulte, avec aussi peu d'aspects négatifs, d'une société fermée, autoritaire, obscurantiste, à une société ouverte, audacieuse et articulée. (p. 4884)[4]

From these passages can be discerned an example of how the amendment of human rights law to include sexual orientation became one of many sites for a new nationalist founding myth—one based on inclusion, openness, and a modernist discourse of progress. This suggests, on one level, that Quebec provides "proof" that nationalist movements, articulating their cause in terms of rights of self-determination, do not necessarily construct lesbians and gays as other to the nation they advocate. Rather, Quebec exemplifies how space can be left for sexual pluralism within the discourse of nationhood. National identity may allow room for identification in an array of important and central ways along other vectors. The PQ government of the time claimed that it envisioned a pluralistic, civic nationalism (as opposed to a narrow and closed ethnic nationalism). A multiplicity of "peoples" (including lesbians and gays), whose rights would be protected through the Quebec Charter, could be incorporated into a new national imaginary. In terms of the way in which sexual orientation was dealt with, Quebec would prove to be (at least) a generation ahead of most of North America.[5]

In this regard, the Quebec Charter has been described as reflecting an important human rights consciousness in Quebec (Sheppard 1997). It remains an unusual document in that it protects individuals against discrimination on a series of enumerated grounds, and it also guarantees numerous "fundamental freedoms" in the form of civic, legal, political, and socioeconomic rights. Furthermore, since its creation in 1990, the Quebec Human Rights Tribunal (charged with the enforcement of the human rights guarantees) has adopted a generous and purposive interpretation of the law. Its approach has been described as symbolizing the possibility of a shared community identity defined in terms of human rights and human variety (Sheppard 1997).[6]

This narrative also underscores the "flip side" of liberal legal rights discourse. That is, the relationship between law and social change is far from straightforward, and the gap between rights, equality, and liberation can be vast. Quebec has a less than illustrious history of human rights protection, a history that many contemporary nationalists vehemently criticize. For example, in the years leading up to the human rights amendment, Montreal police were engaged in a wide-ranging crackdown on gay culture. An October 1977 raid at a Montreal bar provoked Canada's largest street protest (see Lynch 1982), providing a high embarrassment factor for the provincial government. The Montreal police campaign had originated in the months leading up to the Olympic

Games of 1976 (Adam 1995, p. 125). Nineteenth-century federal "bawdy house" laws were invoked, which permitted the arrest of everyone "found in" a place "resorted to for the practice of acts of indecency" (p. 125). A 1976 raid had resulted in the arrest of eighty-nine men and the confiscation of a membership list of seven thousand. The October 1977 raid saw the arrest of 145 men as "found ins" and eight for gross indecency. Such actions had the ironic result (as they so often do) of stimulating the lesbian and gay movement in Quebec, through the creation of the Association pour les Droits des Gai(e)s du Québec (ADGQ) (p. 125). The ADGQ was aligned with the PQ, providing it with credentials within the nationalist movement that, in turn, helps explain the commitment of the PQ to the human rights amendment (p. 125).[7]

The apparent gap between official government policy and police practices, although common in many jurisdictions, has a particular resonance within nationalist discourses in Quebec. Liberal public policy and anti-gay police tactics can be seen as representing two strands of nationalism. The police actions in Montreal exemplified an "old nationalism" that characterized most of the history of a French-speaking Quebec society as inward looking, Catholic inspired, and largely homogeneous. Such a nationalism left no room for a politically informed homosexuality and little space for the articulation of sexuality outside of the confines of marriage. The PQ government, by contrast, was emblematic of what Taylor (1993) has called "new nationalism." It claimed to have little in common with the ideological tenets of old nationalism except the desire to protect the French language and culture, and the recognition of Quebec as the principal homeland of a French-speaking nation.

As Taylor (1993, p. 5) argues, the aim of the new nationalists, beginning in the 1960s, "was not to defend the traditional way of life but to build a modern French society on this continent." The movement was led by a new intelligentsia, which oversaw the development of an urban, modern society led by state participation and, later, a French-speaking entrepreneurial class. The central demand was that French speakers should be able to live and work in their own language, and this would be ensured, when necessary, through the state. The new nationalism is best characterized by economic achievement, social progress, and democratic mores (p. 14). With the election of the PQ government in 1976, separation from Canada became firmly entrenched as the pivot around which nationalist sentiment was oriented.

It is not possible to discuss here the rise of Quebec nationalism and separatist discourse *per se,* nor to analyze why nationalism has come to be articulated chiefly in the form of demands for the independence of Quebec from Canada. As Taylor (1993, p. 42) argues, the question centers on the age-old issue of whether, to survive and thrive, nations must become states—a question that has a particular contemporary currency in Eastern Europe. The argument advanced by separatists in Quebec is, at its most basic, that the preservation of the Quebec nation—a distinct French-speaking society in North America—can only be achieved through independence. Separate statehood becomes the condition for self-rule as well as the necessity for Quebec to take its place in the world. Sovereignty thus is the logical progression for Quebec, whose national identity is principally (but not exclusively) defined in terms of the French language.

Recent constitutional disagreements in Canada have fueled the separatist agenda. Canadian politics in the 1990s has witnessed the failure of governments to achieve constitutional reform in terms of the division of jurisdictional powers between federal and provincial governments, or the constitutional recognition of either substantial aboriginal rights of self-government or Quebec as a "distinct society" (see, e.g., Swinton and Rogerson 1988, Jensen 1993, Bakan and Smith 1995). These arguments have played themselves out in two referenda in Quebec over the sovereignty issue—one in 1980 and the other in 1995—both of which were won by the federalist forces. The result in 1995, however, was extremely close (50.6% to 49.4%), and another referendum can be expected from the PQ government.

Curiously, Quebec's distinctness, as articulated through a nationalist and then a separatist movement, developed precisely as Quebec was becoming *less* culturally unique in many ways (Kymlicka 1995, p. 88). New nationalism developed at the same moment that Quebec experienced "the homogenizing effect of modernity" in the 1960s as it became an urban and professional society (Beer

1995, p. 241). That process of modernization was the *precondition* to new nationalism, which brought with it a new level of self-confidence and saw the tie between nationalism and Catholicism broken. Modernization gave Quebec the resources with which to articulate distinctness in nationalist terms while, simultaneously, it made Quebec more and more like the rest of North America (except for the French language) through the effects of globalization (p. 241). Two seemingly opposing forces—globalization and a localized nationalism—operate together here in a tightly intertwined fashion.

The response of the federal government throughout the 1970s to the new nationalism, under the leadership of Prime Minister Pierre Trudeau, was to attempt to strengthen Canadian national unity through strong federal institutions and a policy of official bilingualism. In the 1980s, the strategy broadened to include the entrenchment of a culture of individual rights. Rights would belong identically to every Canadian citizen, unmediated by smaller place-sensitive communities, through the Charter of Rights and Freedoms, constitutionally entrenched in Canada in 1982. A national identity, it was argued, could be forged through rights discourse, in which the individual as holder of liberal rights would be the basic unit of pan-Canadian citizenship. A national identity would thereby be founded largely on classic liberal precepts, although ultimately the Charter (in a typically Canadian fashion) is something of a compromise of rights among individuals, provinces, collective groups such as First Nations peoples, and multicultural communities with non–place-based identities (see Vipond 1993).

Importantly, the Charter was never accepted by the provincial government of Quebec (the only province not to do so), although it applies by law to all governments in terms of their relationship to individuals. Thus, ironically, one political impact of the Charter has been to further alienate Quebec, which, to a considerable extent, perceives the Charter as an alien document imposed on it. This is not to suggest that a rights culture is *per se* other to the Québécois. After all, the *Quebec* Charter has been a tool for the forging of a new national identity for Quebec around rights.[8] Interestingly, the Quebec Charter is a more wide ranging and powerful tool for progressive social change than the Canadian Charter, providing some of the most progressive rights guarantees in North America (Sheppard 1997).

By contrast, the *structure* of the equality provisions of the *Canadian* Charter have been described as furthering the fragmentation of national identity. The logic of individual and group rights, and interest group politics, are seen as divisive forces in national public life, which may eventually lead to the breakup of the nation state. Here again, a predominant (and probably unrealistic) role is attributed to rights discourse in shaping (and undermining) the nation. The Charter equality provisions are based on a prohibition against discrimination by the state on a series of enumerated grounds (which are left open ended).[9] This structure is significant because it reflects a conception of equality as based on the meaningfulness and centrality of group identity. Furthermore, the equality provisions have been interpreted by the Supreme Court of Canada as designed to ameliorate the historical and social disadvantage suffered by certain groups in Canadian society (see generally Stychin 1995a, chap. 6). The open ended character of the guarantees has meant that the judiciary is empowered to "read in" other grounds, which were not included by the constitutional drafters, based on their "analogous" relationship to those enumerated. For example, the Supreme Court of Canada has ruled, unanimously, that sexual orientation is a protected ground of nondiscrimination because of the social and historical disadvantage suffered by homosexuals in Canadian society (see generally Herman 1994b).[10]

While the identity of the ROC may have gone through a process of fragmentation, a Quebec national identity has not been static either. Increasingly, Quebec has been forced to confront the tension between ethnic and civic nationalism. While old nationalism was inward looking, clerically based, and deeply ethnicist, new nationalism claims to be outward looking, with language central to the construction of identity. These two strands of nationalism continue to be articulated within Quebec, and they represent a cleavage between a homogeneous and a pluralistic collective identity (see Schwartzwald 1990).

Within new nationalist discourse, belonging centers on the speaking of French, particularly in the public sphere. In that way,

Quebec nationalism is compatible with an open, culturally pluralistic society in that the only precondition to full membership in the
group is a working knowledge of the French language. But that is
not to suggest that the ethnic strand of nationalism has ceased to
be relevant. Rather, there is a clear tension between the two forms.
Cairns and Williams (1985, p. 22) have argued that through the
new nationalist language policies and openness to immigration
(necessary to preserve the population base of Quebec), the French-
speaking majority may have greatly expanded its numbers, but at
the expense of a homogeneous ethnic culture. Thus, the creation
of a pluralistic French-speaking society carries with it the side effect that fewer and fewer citizens will share personally in the history of the conquest of the French by the British in North America.
New nationalism, then, cannot be based on a clear conjunction of
language, culture, and history. Instead, a civic, juridical, contrac-
tual nationalism must take its place. In such a nationalism, the metaphor of family (defined as a shared Gallic heritage) must be either
redefined or abandoned. In times of crisis, however, the ethnic
strain comes to be articulated more strongly. On the night of the
1995 referendum defeat for the sovereigntist forces, then PQ pre-
mier Jacques Parizeau publicly blamed immigrants, among others,
for the result. In the face of adversity, then, the *traditional* family
closes ranks, blaming outsiders for the failure to grasp the mantle
of separation.

The policy of the Quebec government of officially recognizing
"cultural communities" inhabits, moreover, an ambiguous political position. On the one hand, the acknowledgment of a range of
cultural communities in government policy suggests an appreciation of the pluralism and diversity of Quebec society. On the
other hand, Shiose and Fontaine (1995) argue that, within official
discourse, cultural communities are constructed as distinct from
the majority. The category *cultural community* becomes a means
through which the other is constructed and is part of a process of
national consolidation around the category *majorité*. All who are
members of cultural communities—no matter what their linguistic background—are not Québécois, and vice versa. Interestingly,
Schwartzwald (1993, p. 265) notes that lesbians and gays at times

have been encouraged to characterize themselves as cultural communities, but their reluctance to do so is hardly surprising.

Queering Quebec

To this point, I have examined how liberal constitutional rights have served as one means for both the construction and, at the same time, the fragmentation of national identities. In this section, my attention shifts to sexual acts and identities, and their relationship to forms of national identification. While the focus turns specifically to sexuality, it remains centered on the construction of the nation's self and others, and on how homosexuality, specifically, is brought into the service of that project.

Importantly, a distinction must be drawn between the legal advancement of lesbians and gays within a particular political community and the ways in which the discourses of nationalism function in relation to sexual identities. In regard to contemporary Quebec, it would be highly problematic to represent the nationalist movement as repressive towards sexual "minorities." On the contrary, the nationalist PQ government and many of its supporters (gay and straight) point to a progressive record in the area and would also claim (rightly) that the nationalist fold welcomes, at least officially, lesbians and gays as full members of the community of Québécois. If anything, it might be argued that the PQ takes for granted the support of the lesbian and gay communities.

It is dangerous to overgeneralize with respect to the relationship between any political movement and lesbians/gays. There is no single lesbian or gay "stance" on Quebec separatism. Lesbians and gays come from all of the linguistic, class, political, and cultural communities of Quebec, and no doubt those identities in large measure inform views on the separatist aspirations of the PQ. It does seem clear, however, that it would be difficult to argue that nationalism, in the form in which it has been given voice by the PQ, is "bad" for lesbians and gays, in either strict legal or social terms. New nationalism in Quebec is no threat to sexual pluralism. Indeed, it is often more "friendly" to it than is the Canadian federation as a whole.

I want to examine, however, the relationship between nationalisms and sexualities in Quebec and the ROC in terms of how discourses constitute nations through the attribution of sexual identities and acts to peoples and places. This theme is well established in the context of the Canadian federal system. It is often said in Canada that the federation is a marriage between French and English, a heterosexual metaphor in which French Canada (centered territorially in Quebec) takes on the female role. This has proven a particularly resilient characterization, one that now frequently extends through the language of divorce, mediation, and possible reconciliation. Its deployment underscores a high degree of gender/national essentialism. Quebec is implicitly (and sometimes explicitly) depicted as emotional, impulsive, and feminized, while the ROC is characterized as rational, moderate, ponderous and, for that matter, "uptight." But the construction of national identities is not limited to a heterosexual frame. The relationship between Quebec and the ROC has long been constructed in homosexual (and homophobic) terms. I hope to demonstrate that this "relationship" is far more complex and contradictory than the marriage metaphor suggests.

It is not my intent to discuss the history of homosexuality in Quebec; such a task is well beyond the scope of this work (see, e.g., Ménard 1985, Higgins and Chamberland 1992). But it is worth considering at this juncture how Quebec's distinctiveness as a society creates a circumstance where constructions of sexuality are influenced by a unique conflagration of factors:

> In discussing French-speaking Quebec's consciousness of, and attitudes towards, homosexuality one must take into account the Latin heritage of tolerance, the puritanical Jansenist influence of the Catholic Church, the important role of homosexual writers such as Proust, Gide and Genèt, as well as the culturally filtered impact of currents from the English-speaking world from Oscar Wilde to Alfred Kinsey. (Higgins and Chamberland 1992, p. 423)

In my view, this melange of influences does create something of a distinct sexual society, at least within the national imagination of the ROC, a point that has been developed most perceptively by Martin (1977, 1994). In his analysis of English-Canadian literary texts dealing with Quebec, Martin argues that Quebec represents the sexually forbidden, exotic other—not unlike the way that the

"Mediterranean" fulfilled this function in the English imagination of the late Romantic period. Quebec allows for the possibility of *jouissance* for the English-Canadian, who can explore the other as a means of escaping the puritanism of the English-Canadian culture and imagination. That otherness has always contained a male homosexual dimension:

> The Canadian colonial imagination, unlike the European, has had no need to travel to exotic places . . . because the exotic and the "southern" were located right next door in Quebec. Its attraction lay precisely in its difference, in its refusal of Anglo-Saxon values. The Montreal of the English-Canadian visitor is thus almost entirely a product of the English-Canadian imagination. (Martin 1994, p. 202)

That iconography deploys the mind/body and universal/specific dualisms. Quebec stands in for the body—for the sensual, the "real," the "authentic," the "earthy"—in a word, for the "natural." That construction exemplifies the colonial discourse of the exotic other in which Quebec performs the role of the colonized (making for interesting parallels to colonial constructions of Africa). Indeed, the Québécois frequently have been described, not only as primitive, closer to nature, less developed, and sexually "natural," but also as physically darker—what Martin (1994, p. 209) calls "the metaphorical brownness of the Québécois body."

The construction of some bodies as closer to nature than others has implications for both the gendering as well as the sexualization of nation. Through the constitution of Québécois women as mothers to the nation, Probyn (1996, p. 79) contends that "women as historical individuals are thrown out of the system of social relations and are deemed to constitute the 'pure materiality' of nature." These constructions thereby further *both* the male homosexualization and the female gendering of nation.

At this point, the connections between national and sexual identity in Quebec can be interpreted through the inside/out binary. As Fuss (1991) has argued, heterosexuality constitutively requires its other in order to construct itself as a meaningful category, and that other must be both coherent and bounded. So too, the ROC *needs* Quebec to constitute itself as a coherent national self. There is a certain political irony in this observation. Although the

current constitutional impasse in Canada stems from the unwill-
ingness of the ROC to constitutionally recognize Quebec as a distinct society, at the same time, without being able to call on that
distinctness, the ROC would lack a sense of itself. Schwartzwald
(1990, p. 18) describes this as the "double bind of calling on Québec's 'distinctness' but being unwilling to acknowledge it within a
new constitutional arrangement . . . [which] explains why many
Québécois feel they are held hostage by English Canada which, un-
sure of its identity, 'needs' Quebec to prove its difference."

In that way, Quebec's relationship to the ROC functions through
the inside/out binary. Quebec is both outside (constructed as other
by the ROC), but also on the inside in that Quebec is necessary for
the survival of the ROC. This is analogous to the double bind in
the constitution of heterosexuality, where homosexuality is both
inside and out. That is, heterosexuality must call on its other in
order to realize a coherent self. Quebec is both inside and out of
the identity of the ROC and, simultaneously, Quebec metaphorically represents both the homosexual male and the female gender
for the ROC's putatively male, heterosexual national identity. Yet,
as Martin (1994, p. 204) argues, the heterosexual ROC enjoys the
taste of the "forbidden fruit" (so to speak), or the proverbial dirty
weekend in Montreal. But despite its penchant for a sampling of
the other, the ROC remains the tourist who emerges with his male
heterosexuality firmly intact on Monday morning and his national
identity strengthened in the process (despite the sexual acts of the
weekend). Martin (1994, p. 203) describes this exploration of "the
other as a means of national renewal and self-liberation without
any intention of becoming the other." In sexual terms, "as Quebec
helps Canada to be more Canadian, so homosexuality helps men to
be more manly" (Martin 1977, p. 29). The ROC in this way has
"used" Quebec sexually so as to constitute itself nationally (and in
a heterosexually totalizing fashion).

The sexualization of the Anglo-French relationship thus is
imagined either as heterosexual or as (male) homosexual. In both
cases, Quebec is female, passive, and penetrated, and the English-
Canadian identity is straight male, albeit with a penchant for "fool-
ing around" (in either direction). Moreover, the constitution of the
ROC demands its self-imagining as dominant and active—as the

universal, coherent, male self. This might explain, in turn, why the relationship constitutively precludes the feminizing of the ROC vis à vis Quebec or the metaphorical use of lesbianism.[11]

This *need* to imagine a masculinized, national self is related to the way in which the national identity of the ROC is subject to a perennial crisis of identity, which is often described in terms of fragmentation, the absence of a founding myth, or lack of a common sense of belonging. I have argued elsewhere that the Canadian national identity (with specific reference to the ROC) is always in some sense self-constituted as the other—the specific and the embodied—because of its relationship to an overarching, abstract, universalized "American" national identity (see Stychin 1995a, chap. 6). The projects of gendering and homosexualizing Quebec by the ROC provide two means of shoring up a beleaguered national/sexual identity. Canada is itself gendered in its relationship to the United States—"the defenceless maiden to the American hulk" (Probyn 1996, p. 80). With respect to Quebec, then, the ROC can attempt to assert its manhood. At the same time, the *sexual* ambiguity of the ROC resides in its relationship to the universal norm represented by the signifier "America." Parker (1993) has described this process of sexual othering, drawing on the work of Canadian filmmaker David Cronenberg. According to Parker, Canada, like homosexuality, experiences boundaries fraught with instability that play themselves out through the sameness/difference, universal/particular binaries. Canadian identity becomes the particular *vis à vis* the United States, and its identity is relatively unstable, inchoate, and in constant danger of fragmentation. As a consequence, it is an identity that must be reconstituted in order to assert its meaningfulness—its difference from the universal.[12]

Thus, there are interesting similarities between Canadian national identity and lesbian and gay sexual and political identities. As Haig (1994, p. 229) astutely observes:

> The parallels between being Canadian and being queer are numerous. . . . Just as gays and lesbians are surrounded by, and barely represented within the larger heterosexual culture, Canadians are awash in a sea of normalizing, hegemonic American culture that rarely depicts them. English Canadians often "pass" as Americans based on hasty assumptions about what is marked as different, just as queers can (and often must) pass as straight. Moreover, both queers and Canadians have

tended to wrest a space for resistance and self-representation by ironically re-reading and re-working dominant cultural texts: camp culture and Canadian traditions of satire and irony can be understood as remarkably similar responses to the experiences of marginalization and lack of voice. Even the rhetoric of "coming out" and being "outed" bear comparisons. In other countries, English Canadians often adopt a strategy of self-affirmation by "coming out" as Canadian, and famous Canadians living and working in the United States are frequently "outed."

While this comparison may strike some as farfetched, the parallels can be seen in comments by United States Senator Jesse Helms on the *Cuban Liberty and Solidarity Act* of 1996 (the "Helms-Burton" law). Pursuant to this legislation, foreign companies that have invested in Cuban assets owned by Americans prior to appropriation by the Cuban government can be sued by American companies and private citizens in U.S. courts. Furthermore, the executives of those companies and their families can be prevented from obtaining U.S. visas. Helms, in cosponsoring the law, turned his wrath on Canada and others in the process, and his anti-Canadian rhetoric mirrored his oft-repeated homophobic language (on Helms and homophobia, see Stychin 1996b). Canadians, like homosexuals, are foolish to believe that their policies/lifestyles will not lead to dire consequences. In the arena of global politics, the peril stems from the naïve appeasement of dictators through political and economic relations (Reuters News Service 1996). In the case of homosexuals, destruction follows from the folly of sinful and dangerous sexual relations. The United States must protect itself (and democracy) against the weakness of its allies (and homosexuals) through tough legal measures to control a menace to the American way of life. Canada is weak, easily corruptible, and succumbs to the seductive temptations of Cuba. Indeed, many Canadians might well hope for a literal seduction on their winter–package-holidays to the island (a privilege not enjoyed by their American neighbors). Only the masculinized United States has the fortitude to prevent the homosexualized and gendered relationship, and to withstand the attempt at seduction.[13]

Not surprisingly, the response from the Canadian government to the Helms-Burton law was to reassert its own national "manhood" through tough talk and retaliatory legislative action. Members of the Canadian government seemed desperate to demonstrate that they were not "wimps"—they were "men"—and could show the Americans that they would not be treated in this way without responding manfully. They thus resisted the inscription of a feminized and/or homosexual identity implicit in the anti-Cuban discourse.

By contrast, Quebec responds to the inscription of a sexual identity upon itself by the ROC differently by *both* appropriating and redeploying homosexuality within nationalist discourse *and*, simultaneously, rejecting a homosexual national subject position. Before developing this thesis further, it should be stressed that Quebec society today defies the stereotype of a parochial, inward looking community that characterized much of its history. The Quebec Charter of Rights and Freedoms exemplifies this progressive human rights context. Moreover, the place of women in Quebec is far removed from their historic role as mothers to the nation (realized both literally and through entry into Catholic religious orders). The last quarter century has seen a dramatic fall in the birth rate, "the most remarkable demographic event to occur in Quebec since the massive emigration of the late nineteenth century" (Langlois et al. 1992, p. 102). Female labor force participation has risen sharply (p. 120), and surveys show that sexual equality has become an important element in the value system of the majority of the population (p. 586). Although women have not yet achieved fair representation in the middle and upper echelons of the public and private sectors, the evidence suggests that the gap is closing (pp. 97–98).[14]

In fact, Quebec is now the most secular society in North America. In the mid-1990s, 64.5 percent of Québécois aged 25–29 were in common law relationships, twice as many as in neighboring Ontario. Between 1971 and 1991, the marriage rate declined by 18 percent in Ontario and by 49 percent in Quebec (Gagnon 1996). Only 21 percent of Roman Catholics in Quebec attend church on a weekly basis (Rawlyk 1995, p. 135). *Practicing* Catholics represented 38 percent of Roman Catholics in 1985, compared to 88 percent twenty years earlier (Langlois et al. 1992, p. 317). Religious orders have experienced a dramatic decline, exacerbated by the transfer of authority over hospitals and schools from church to state during the 1960s (p. 318).[15] This process of secularization makes an examination of nationalist discursive deployments of sexuality more complex than in those societies where old nationalism dominates. When drawn upon by old nationalism, homosexuality is often characterized simply as a betrayal of an individual duty towards the survival of the race, constituted in religious/national terms, based on the assumption that homosexuals are childless (an example being the deployment of homosexuality in apartheid discourse in South Africa).

Interestingly, many have argued that within the popular culture of Quebec there is now considerable space for a homosexual identity (see, e.g., Higgins and Chamberland 1992, Ménard 1985; on lesbians specifically in Quebec popular culture, see Probyn 1996, pp. 97–98). Homosexuality has also been deployed as a metaphor for the place of Quebec in North America, most famously in Michel Tremblay's play *Hosanna* (1974). Within the play, homosexuality is read as the authentic "truth" of the protagonist drag queen Hosanna's being, and the process of coming out represents a coming to terms with this truth. The narrative is frequently read as a metaphor for a "Quebec national collectivity that needed proudly to acknowledge and assert its *specificité* as a necessary prelude to taking its place among the universal community of nations" (Schwartzwald 1993, p. 265).[16]

Tremblay's embracing of homosexuality as a metaphor for the struggle over Quebec's authentic self proved far from unproblematic for many nationalist intellectuals. After all, "Hosanna's rapprochement with his homosexual essence permanently marginalizes him as a sexual minority even as it authenticates him" (Schwartzwald 1992, p. 504). A coming to terms with one's claimed essence does not by itself produce social acceptance, and a celebration of the specificity of Quebec (a coming out) might not mean a place at the table of the community of nations. Instead, the result might be a queer position within North America: "a permanently countercultural society . . . stabilized in its radical difference" (p. 504). While homosexuality might be tolerated in Quebec and even given a particular social role, the argument runs that to adopt it in the service of the nationalist struggle would be both unacceptable and unwise.

Some nationalists have gone further and deployed homosexuality through a variant of the colonial contamination model, which

I have already examined in other national contexts. In this narrative, the independence of Quebec becomes the ultimate step in a maturation process, and homosexuality is characterized in Freudian terms as a form of arrested development (see Schwartzwald 1993, p. 267), which also resembles its deployment in some South African contexts. The failure of the Québécois to seize the moment (twice) in referenda on sovereignty is attributable to the metaphoric homosexualization of society. This facilitates the construction of opposition to independence as feeble and lacking in fortitude. "True" members of the family (who are "grown ups") are sovereigntists, not "immigrants" who voted against sovereignty. Homosexuality (like immigration) becomes one of the stumbling blocks to the modernist logic of nationhood.

In this regard, recent Quebec history has underscored how, particularly in times of crisis, nationalism deploys the ethnic model. But while "immigrant" voters have been constructed as outside the family of Quebec, the lesbian and gay community is given greater space within the national family.[17] In the process, however, lesbians and gays may be constituted as ethnically homogeneous and separatist supporting (francophone, ethnic Québécois) which makes them politically acceptable.[18] They can then be constructed (and construct themselves) as on the "inside" (even if somewhat on the fringes). In the process, those lesbians and gays from the cultural communities may well be erased from the dominant constructions of sexuality.

The openness of the nationalist family to the inclusion of lesbians and gays might be understandable in terms of the culturally specific role of familial discourse and ideology in Quebec. Historically, the family was central to national survival and that role was reinforced through Catholic teaching. In that sense, the family has been "understood and lived as a public institution as well as a private possession" (Probyn 1996, p. 88). References to the Quebec family thus are the product of an ambiguous relationship between public and private. But, with the dramatic decline in influence of the Catholic Church, and the rejection of a matriarchal stereotype for Quebec women, the family as public/national institution has become a site with no essential role or obvious conditions of membership by which lesbians and gays can be excluded (p. 89). In this regard, it is worth noting that lesbian and gay activists in Quebec have been engaged in lobbying the provincial government to fulfill its promise of same-sex spousal benefits and, in substance, a redefinition of the "family" in Quebec law. The outcome of this (family) dispute will demonstrate the extent to which family as a national signifier is open to reworking by Québécois lesbians and gays.

Nationalist homophobic discourse also has had its place, but through the construction of the *federalist* as homosexual (see Schwartzwald 1991). In a reversal of deployments of nationalist sexuality in the ROC, nationalism here is articulated through the colonial contamination model. Those Québécois who support the Canadian federal system are constituted in sexualized terms as passive, effeminate men who, in well-worn homophobic language, are "both violated and craftily seductive. . . . first 'corrupted,' most likely in youth, and who then themselves seek to corrupt" (p. 179).[19] That corruption is the support of federalism and, consequently, the anti-separatist inhabits the position of the *federaste,* a figure that, Schwartzwald (1991, p. 179) argues, "constitutes a significant undercurrent of intellectual discourse about decolonization in Quebec."

In this trope, the federalist represents a seductive and corrupting homosexual whose pederastic eye is turned "against the waifish, innocent Quebec" (Schwartzwald 1991, p. 179). The discourse also conjures up the relationship of priest and altar boy, and its deployment by new nationalists can be read as a rejection of the old nationalism, in which the Catholic Church was central (p. 185). Familial discourse underpins the rhetoric, with Quebec as the family under threat from the *federaste/pederaste* outsider.[20]

Thus, the homosexual is deployed through nationalist discourse, and nationalism is articulated through the prism of sexuality along an array of different trajectories. Sexual identities are called upon to assist in nation building in a complex and sometimes contradictory assortment of ways.

Queer National Cultures

In recent years, much work in political theory (and in the practice of politics) has centered on how citizenship might be conceived in the conditions of pluralism now experienced in Western liberal societies (see, e.g., Young 1990, Taylor 1993). In this section, I focus on one particular attempt at theorizing "multicultural citizenship," which has been developed by Kymlicka (1995). I explore how the relationship between nationalisms and sexualities might enrich a theory of multicultural citizenship, and I continue to deploy the example of Quebec in pursuing this inquiry.

Kymlicka (1995) has sought to carve out a space for minority rights within liberal theory as an important corrective to traditional human rights principles located in the individual. Central to the theory is his constitutive definition of "cultural groups," who are the primary holders of minority rights. Cultural groups are defined as *national* minorities, as opposed to "ethnic" groups and new social movements (p. 19). Kymlicka's focus is on the distinction between individual and collective rights and how a liberal theory must be able to accommodate both (but within the limits of liberal tolerance). There are two kinds of claims that an ethnic or national group might make using the discourse of rights: (1) the claim of a group against its own members, and (2) the claim of a group against the larger society (pp. 34–48). The first is intended to protect the group against the destabilizing impact of internal dissent, the second to protect from the effect of external decisions (presumably by the state). Kymlicka's recipe for mixing liberalism and minority rights is that "liberals can and should endorse certain external protections, where they promote fairness between groups, but should reject internal restrictions which limit the right of group members to question and revise traditional authorities and practices" (p. 37). Thus, the possibility is created, within a liberal framework, for a group-differentiated conception of citizenship.

For Kymlicka, such a theory remains firmly within the liberal universe because its ultimate concern is with the individual, and this is why the notion of cultural groups as the distinguishing feature of national minorities is of crucial importance. *Individual* freedom, Kymlicka argues, is intimately linked to and dependent on culture and, more specifically, on individual membership in cultural groups. But, as a constitutive matter, culture is defined in terms of *societal* cultures—that is, those associated with national groups: "a culture which provides its members with meaningful ways of life across the full range of human activities" (Kymlicka 1995, p. 76). He asserts that only a *national* culture has the staying power to survive globalization and, even then, survival is likely dependent on measures taken by the group to protect itself (which are the defining feature of minority rights). Cultural groups, other than national minorities, will be increasingly marginal (p. 80).

The example that informs Kymlicka's thinking is Québécois culture, and he seeks to theorize the possibility of a group-differentiated liberal citizenship model for Canada. Such a model might be of considerable political usefulness as a means of extricating Canada from its current constitutional difficulties. Kymlicka recognizes that a national identity might not require (or produce) a single set of shared values (Kymlicka 1995, p. 105). The crucial point is that diverse value systems are all restricted to the limits of liberal tolerance. Of course, such a theory is self-consciously created to further (and somewhat revise) liberal hegemony, but, in fairness, it does so openly and honestly. For those national groups that envision a radically different, anti-liberal way of life based on an alternative conception of the good, Kymlicka's approach will be problematic, to say the least.

Kymlicka's theory is closely related, and indebted, to Taylor's (1993, pp. 182–183) conception of multicultural citizenship as based on "deep diversity." According to Kymlicka (1995, p. 190), "members of a polyethnic and multination state must not only respect diversity, but also respect a diversity of approaches to diversity." In this model, national belonging is no longer linked *a priori* to a particular vision of (Canadian) citizenship. Rather, a multiplicity of visions could be accommodated. Some individuals might identify with, and belong to, a country like Canada *through* their identification with a national group; others would belong directly. In this way, citizenship is mediated for some by membership in another collectivity; for others, not. A diversity of approaches to a diverse society is thereby possible. Kymlicka, in developing his theory in explicitly liberal terms, places limits on diversity (namely, the liberal rights of the individual). But within that liberal universe, diversity, as it is articulated through *national* groups, can be accepted.

Multicultural citizenship is undoubtedly an important step in articulating a theory of pluralism and national diversity, although it is somewhat formalistic in its distinction between internal and external limits. Kymlicka's constitutive definition of cultural groups is surprisingly narrow and seems out of step with current cultural theory and practice. To suggest that only national cultures "count," because only they can withstand the homogenizing effects of globalization, is an unrealistically narrow understanding of culture. I suspect, for example, that lesbians and gays (and, for that matter, many others) are skeptical when they read Kymlicka's arguments about culture. For many of us, an important cultural reference point is queer culture, which seems more than capable of surviving (and thriving) in the current cultural conditions.

This point has been developed by Walker (1998), who argues that queer culture is, "even by the most standard definitions, a culture" (p. 507). Walker's concern is that Kymlicka's theory privileges territorially-based cultures over those in diaspora. Furthermore, pushed to its logical limits (by removing the overly narrow definition of a cultural group), collective rights would overload the liberal rights model with innumerable claims. This outcome must force us to rethink the whole notion of multiculturalism and collective rights: "culturalism sets up an aristocracy of difference which attempts to naturalize and depoliticize the struggle over the resources required for differentiation and cultural development" (p. 537).

Walker makes a persuasive argument, particularly in the way in which he recognizes the unduly limited and unrealistic definition of culture Kymlicka offers, and in his discussion of the importance of nonterritorial nationalisms. Kymlicka's nation is also highly culturally specific. But Walker may be underestimating the power of a rallying cry for differentiated citizenship articulated through the language of group rights. Territorial-based nationalisms have a central place in many cultural contexts, including Canada. My interest in this regard is in *how* those nationalisms, and the constructions of national identity in the West (and elsewhere), are *mediated* by other cultural and political identities. Nations are constructed in large part *through* the deployment of other categories: race, religion, language, gender, sexuality, physical ability, etc. Kymlicka radically differentiates this smorgasbord of identities (all of which can give rise to *cultural* groups) from the privileged site of national identity. But national cultures are meaningful, in significant measure, because of the ways in which identity categories, such as homosexuality, are deployed in the construction of the national self and its others. A radical separation between national cultures and other groups hides the ways in which nations are constituted. The role of the homosexual in Quebec and the ROC exemplifies this point.

But what might this discussion suggest for a theory of multiculturalism and citizenship? If we accept the possibility of group based identities and rights—a political reality in Canada throughout its history—then Taylor's (1993) concept of "deep diversity" and Kymlicka's (1995) theory of "multicultural citizenship" are going to be more complicated than we (and they) might first have imagined. That is, it becomes important to consider that national (and other) identities are not formed in a vacuum; they are constructed relationally vis-à-vis other identities. The individual identifies, not only with national cultures, but in other often *no less foundational* ways, such as through a sexual identity. This suggests that Kymlicka is mistaken in the way in which he asserts that national cultural groups are in some sense more primary than others.

It would not be unreasonable, for example, to suggest that an allegiance to nation might be formed *through* sexual identities, interests, and cultures (and vice versa). This possibility was underscored by a newspaper commentary in Quebec written in response to both the sovereignty referendum debates and the contested issue of state benefits for same-sex couples:

> How could queers vote yes [an Anglo might ask] splitting apart Canada . . . just so you could gain legal equality [through the promise of recognition of same-sex couples by the PQ government]? By the same token, Quebec nationalists I know have argued we shouldn't try to sabotage the sovereignty drive, as Quebec still has the best track record on gay rights on the continent. (Hays 1996, p. 13)

In this example, nationalisms are explicitly contingent and filtered through an allegiance to a sexual identity. Similarly, for many Québécois feminists, feminism is filtered through territorial-based nationalism and, at the same time, nationalism is filtered through an identification with feminism (see de Sève 1992, Le Clerc and West 1997). Kymlicka and Taylor seem to envision, by contrast, a one-way process involving a unitary subject, experiencing national identity in a foundational manner, where other identities are experienced *through* that national identification secondarily. Such an approach underestimates the complexities of culture and identity, at both the group and individual levels.

Once multicultural citizenship is recognized in its full diversity, the issue of belonging in the conditions of national fragmentation can then be addressed. That inquiry centers on the force that holds such a nation together (see generally Beiner 1995). This is the same issue faced by new social movements. The question is: How do you maintain group allegiance when diversity creates centrifugal tendencies that seem stronger than the allegiance to the identity inherent in the group identification in the first place? Sometimes the political result is that social movements, like some nations, do fracture and cleave. Social movements and nations fall apart, and people form new collectives that more closely "fit." At other times, movements and nations redefine themselves and accommodate voices that have felt excluded and marginalized. The social movement or nation comes to be redefined.

A theory of how to hold the national community together might look to how a sense of belonging can be maintained when national allegiance does not claim to be totalizing or even primary for the individual (see generally Kaplan 1993).[21] On the one hand, it seems a reasonable observation "that a sense of national identity and belonging does for a very large part of the present population of the world play an important part in individuals' self-understanding" (MacCormick 1996, p. 565). On the other hand, that "fact" suggests that national belonging in the conditions of multiple allegiances demands, as MacCormick argues in the context of European integration, that nationalism be "cut adrift from the absolutism of the sovereign state" (p. 555). My argument is that the reality of national identification can be even further distanced from statism through the appropriation of (civic) nationalism by a plethora of different collectivities holding no obvious claim to territorial "possession." In this model, there is no clear stopping point to multiple national identifications, and less and less likelihood of a totalized, singular nationality.

Deep diversity is a useful and meaningful concept in this regard. Taylor (1993, p. 132) describes it as the product of "a national life founded on diversity, in which the political process takes on a crucial significance, not only as an instrument of self-definition, but as a major component of a national identity which is largely constituted by debate, without definitive closure, between a plurality of legitimate options." The individual might come to identify with a plurality of nations in which state politics has lost its primacy, what Weeks (1995, p. 122) refers to as "multiple belongings" and "a community of communities."

This way of understanding national belongings is dependent on a capacity for national reinvention—a capacity to produce a national identity that is neither essentially fixed nor ethnically based, but rather is alterable, shifting, flexible, and continually in process. Diversity is an experiment in constructing a national life, in which it is recognized *at the outset* that there is no predetermined outcome. While I have argued that national identities parasitically deploy sexuality in constituting themselves, it might be worth thinking about how the experience of those who locate themselves within lesbian, gay, bisexual, and queer cultures might prove useful to the reconception of national identities in the conditions of multiculturalism. Halperin (1995, pp. 101–106), drawing on the work of Foucault, has described the "queer life" in terms of social experimentation and a refashioning of the self. Intuitively, it strikes me that many lesbians, gays, and self-defined queers may see their lives in terms of self-conscious invention (or reinvention), and that this process has been undertaken with little in the way of a road map. In this regard, Blasius (1994, p. 183) has described a lesbian and gay ethos as "a shared way of life through which lesbians and gays invent themselves, recognize each other, and establish a relationship to the culture in which they live." Many of us experience our "exhilarating personal experiment" (Halperin 1995, p. 106) as one in which we are never entirely sure of where our identities will take us; there is no ultimate destination in which identity is finally "fixed."

Lesbian, gay, bisexual, and queer politics and culture can bring to a study of national identities a framework in which identity is self-consciously contingent and in process, characterized by reinvention and an ongoing questioning of borders and membership. A consideration of sexual identities can also bring to the reinvention of nation a sense of *excitement* that comes from "the perpetual inventiveness of a collective sexual politics which stretches towards different ways of being" (Weeks 1995, p. 115). Queer politics in the 1990s, in some of its manifestations, exemplifies this excitement. By contrast, when "mainstream" political theorists such as Kymlicka analyze the options for belonging and citizenship in an age of fragmentation, they often produce angst filled investigations in which the excitement of reinvention is strangely missing. This is one way in which sexual identity politics potentially "produces knowledge that transforms the political world and the way all people understand themselves as living in that world" (Blasius 1994, p. 183).

In analogizing national and sexual identities, I do not wish to romanticize sexual experiments in living. To many, for example, the process of coming out (the paradigm of individual identity reinvention) is painful, involving a loss of faith in previous certainties. And some experiments exact considerable costs from bystanders. But processes of constitution contain within them an excitement generated by the trip. As nations struggle with their sense of self, they could do well to appropriate this excitement of reconstitution, which I would describe as a queering of the nation itself.

5 Eurocentrism

In the 1990s, "Europe" has come to assume a particular significance in the construction of national identity. Within the European Community (the EC, which is now being transformed into a political European Union, the EU), debates rage over the meaning and future of this association of nation states and peoples. This is occurring, not only among academics and politicians but also on the ground, as the EU assumes an increasing role in people's lives. In those countries of the continent of Europe, but not in the EU, membership sometimes signifies an entry into "the West," and all of the economic, political, and social promise that the West has claimed to offer. Meanwhile, in western Europe, attitudes (official and otherwise) toward the continent's "east" and "south" are clearly ambivalent. The European Union aspires to expand its horizons outward, for example, to the former Communist states (the "widening" of the EU). At the same time, many European states are constructed as the EU's other.

The relationship of Europe as an identity to its others will be the focus of this chapter. Europe today is both dependent on, yet also seeks in some sense to transcend the historical construction of, the European nation state and its product, nationalism. This tension proves to be at the heart of the newly emerging political and legal order. The European Union is a product of the history of the Western nation state. Moreover, Europe as a political identity produces its own nationalist discourse through which it differentiates itself from "other" nations (both within and outside the geography of Europe). But it has also been argued that the new European order might serve as a forum for the reimagining of the nation state, if not to transcend at least to reduce the dependence of identity on the construction of the national other. Europe might represent the opportunity for accommodation with cultural, national, and other "difference."

This opposition between the invocation of nationalism, and

challenges to it, is central to the imagining of Europe today. It is intricately connected to the question of what it might mean to be a European citizen. The history of the EC has been characterized by a highly market-oriented conception of citizenship. This is hardly surprising, since the impetus for the European Community was the creation of a free trade area within western Europe. Citizenship, to the extent that it has been a meaningful concept within European law and politics, has focused on the individual as economic actor, as opposed to a more social or political conception of the relationship of the citizen to the polity. Increasingly, however, as the European Union seeks to carve out its own allegiances and to articulate its own identity (whether national, "supranational," or "postnational"), existing alongside those of the nation states, a more political and social conception of citizenship may be developing (the "deepening" of the EU).

This development is connected to questions concerning the future direction of Europe. Some envision the emergence of a federal Europe, where the political institutions of the European Union will assume increased powers at the expense of the member states. Others see the European Union as the opportunity to challenge the centrality and fixity of jurisdictional boundaries in the construction of national space. This vision is related to a reconception of the way in which nationhood and citizenship have been deployed through an exclusionary inside/out binary. Still others see the EU as a means to facilitate national self-interest, and they support integration only to the extent that it is perceived to do so.

Too often, those who envision a European "superstate" and "supranationalism" conveniently forget the legacy of Europe. In extolling the benefits of a European family of nations, the exclusions that have been effected by, and in the name of, nations and nationalisms are ignored. An aim of this chapter is to connect the role played by the other in the construction of national identity in Europe—which was crucially informed by the racializing and gendering of identity—with the ways in which a European identity is deployed today. I will examine the extent to which a "new" European identity replicates the same old constructions of national self and other as opposed to reimagines that relationship.

I also interrogate how struggles by lesbians and gays within Europe exemplify the debates over the role and future of the European

Union. For a number of social movements, Europe has become a site of struggle, in no small measure because it has assumed jurisdiction over many aspects of the lives of those who reside in member states. The European legal order provides a forum where rights discourse is increasingly entrenched, albeit with a limited scope that has been predominantly economic in orientation. For many in European states, where the idea of constitutional rights in the North American sense is absent or "underdeveloped," EU political and legal institutions now provide an alternative arena where an appeal to rights might prove rewarding. European citizenship may be developing through rights that attach to all EU citizens, irrespective of nationality. Thus, once again, I employ lesbian and gay sexualities both to understand how nations and nationalisms are constituted and to look at how struggles around sexuality are challenging (or reinforcing) those constructs.

The Invention of Europe

Much has been written in recent years on the "invention" and "idea" of Europe as an identity (see, e.g., Delanty 1995, Milward 1992, Derrida 1992). The European nation state was the paradigm of the modern Western (and Eurocentric) conception of nation, and that construction in turn served the colonial and imperial project. National identities emerged at a particular historical moment, as did the identity of the "European" (Hroch 1996). Identities *within* Europe were consolidated through an oppositional relationship to other nations (including other Europeans) while, over time, a common European identity also emerged (Pieterse 1991, p. 9; Delanty 1995, p. 6). The latter depended for its coherence on the non-European other (Ward 1996a, p. 89). In this way, Europe was the site both for the construction of the non-European as other and also of others, such as Jews, as non-Europeans (Eley and Suny 1996, p. 28). It was where a modernist logic of nationhood took shape and the arena in which imperialism, colonialism, and empire were fostered (Huyssen 1994). One result of this "ideological labor" has been that nationhood "conspired to eliminate other languages of legitimacy" (Eley and Suny 1996, p. 20).

The current dynamic through which a European identity is articulated can be understood in historical terms as the latest in a series (Ward 1996a, p. 89). The first, a Catholic conception, depended on the construction of the non-European as the barbaric other. This European identity would be refined over time to become "synonymous with modernity" (p. 90). Another, much more recent, instance of European identity formation was undertaken by twentieth-century fascism, "the pretended savior of the European idea" (p. 91; see also Huyssen 1994). Ward suggests that what distinguishes today's conception of Europe is the centrality of law, a point to which I will return.

The historical constitution of European identities was closely tied up with both Christianity and the Enlightenment, through the metaphorical, ideological, and literal creation of borders and boundaries through which national identities were consolidated (Pieterse 1991; see also Blomley 1994). Bounded space facilitates the construction of the other, who can be located literally on the outside. Within the Enlightenment project, that other could be marked as the uncivilized, which in turn justified colonial expansion. European "civilization" thereby represented both a relationship of sameness among European states and a rivalry between them (Pieterse 1991, p. 9), a paradox that continues today.

Race, gender, social class, and sexuality were manipulated to consolidate a European identity, which further served as a justification for colonialism (see McClintock 1995, Balibar 1991). The European nation state has been the product of a "fictive ethnicity," whereby racial "sameness" was invented as a national feature, one that then had to be preserved for the sake of the nation (Balibar 1991, p. 49). In this way, racism in part has been a necessary "supplement of nationalism" (p. 54), but one that is internal to it.

Sexuality and the construction of sexual deviance have been enduring supplements to nationalism. In his important study of male-male sexual relations and the "geography of perversion," Bleys (1996) argues that "the intersecting rhetorics of racialist and sexual discourse were embedded in European civilization, ideology, and scientific innovation at the same time" (p. 11). The historical transition by which sodomy ceased to be understood as a set of acts to which anyone potentially might succumb, and instead became an identity associated with the male homosexual, underscores how sexual deviance became associated with *difference* within and from

Europe (p. 18). Sodomy was described as endemic among indigenous populations in the "new worlds," an "observation" that then justified their suppression through the European civilizing mission (p. 23). But just as the other who was geographically removed from Europe was constructed as deviant, others closer to home, "particularly Muslims, Jews and New Christians" (recent converts from Judaism and Islam), were similarly sexualized (p. 28).

Bleys (1996, p. 81) documents how, over time, at least with respect to male-male sexual relations, "ethnographic reports increasingly emphasized same-sex praxis in relation to cross-gender roles." Sodomy became synonymous with effeminate men, and it was prevalent among uncivilized peoples (both abroad and at home). As a consequence, race could be both sexualized and gendered, as "the very ascription of sexual qualities itself was instrumental in Europe's coming to grips with cultural Otherness" (p. 95). Gender, race, and sexuality coalesced and justified colonialism by virtue of the femininity and sodomy associated with "other" races who were, as a consequence, "naturally" inferior. Through this process there were "generated complicated bodies of discourse around gender inequalities, sexual privilege, class priorities and racial superiority, which in their turn became potently rearticulated into nationalist discourse at home" (Eley and Suny 1996, p. 28).

The dynamic of nationalism in Europe had its own sexual trajectory, which was closely related to the deployment of sexualized nationalism abroad. Mosse (1985) has argued that in the same period that modern nationalism was maturing in Europe in the eighteenth century, an ideal of respectability and a definition of respectable sexuality also developed. European nationalism, respectability (defined in terms of middle class morality), and sexuality were intricately related: "nationalism absorbed and sanctioned middle-class manners and morals and played a crucial part in spreading respectability to all classes of the population" (p. 9). Nationalism provided the means to control sexuality, and it facilitated the normalization of changing social attitudes.

Nationalism also came to assume a particular gender/sex dimension of its own, however, through an aesthetic of the ideal national man and woman (p. 11). The fundamental basis of these deployments was the distinction between normal and abnormal sexuality, whereby national stereotypes were closely tied to a conception of what was considered normal based on fixed, static gender roles as crucial to the survival of the nation (p. 17). Women became the "symbolic bearers of the nation" (McClintock 1995, p. 354). As a consequence, those who "trespassed" beyond the bounds of respectability were considered, not only abnormal, but a threat to the national community (Mosse 1985, pp. 24–25).

Gender stereotypes were central to national consolidation. Nationalism functioned to control women through the ascription of fixed gender roles deemed essential to the flourishing of the European nation (p. 17). White Christian women became the "embodiment of respectability" (p. 97) through the prioritizing of motherhood and the "cult of domesticity" (McClintock 1995, p. 209), which rendered lesbians a specific threat (Mosse 1985, p. 91). Woman became a symbol closely connected to innocence and chastity, and this, in turn, supported the racial basis of nationalism, for "the stereotype of the so-called inferior race filled with lust was a staple of racism, part of the inversion of accepted values" (p. 134).

It is clear, then, that in the process through which nationalism developed historically in Europe—and through which a European identity came to be articulated—racial, gender, and sexual constructions were crucial. If the current attempt to construct a "new" European identity is the latest in a series, then it is worth considering the extent to which discourses of national identity today continue to bear the traces of this legacy. To what extent, it might be asked, is the new Europe really all that novel, in terms of the ways in which race, gender, and sexuality are manipulated? Who are Europe's others, and what is the relationship between self and other in this political and economic union?

Reimagining the Nation State?

It is increasingly apparent that Europe is engaged in a process of articulating a political identity. The European Economic Community (EEC), which began after World War II as a framework to facilitate free trade and other forms of economic cooperation, is now transforming itself into a widening and deepening European *Union*. The goal of an "ever closer Union," and the concept of European citizenship, were officially recognized in the 1992 Treaty on European Union (the "Maastricht Treaty"). The Maastricht Treaty signifies a shift (as well as an ongoing debate) about the meaning of belonging in the EU. For example, some proponents of closer integration cite the importance of deepening the substantive basis of European membership (and citizenship) beyond the market to embrace more wide-ranging political and social concerns. According to this view, a European supranational *political* identity is necessary to make Europe meaningful as a multinational polity: "a European identity that will confer cohesion on a highly diversified but economically and politically united entity" (Guiberneau 1996, p. 114).

But what is the basis for this new European identity, and what is its relationship to the history of European nations and nationalisms? Although it seems intuitive (and appealing) that a multinational union of states might "transcend" discourses of narrow, old nationalism, it has been argued, to the contrary, that "the evolution of the European Community since 1945 has been an integral part of the reassertion of the nation-state as an organizational concept" (Milward 1992, pp. 2–3). The EEC was central to the postwar reconstruction of the European nation state, in that the state was left intact while only limited spheres of sovereignty were turned over to the EEC. The latter thereby helped states adapt to a new era by relieving them of responsibility over particular areas that had come to be more efficiently dealt with at a multinational level. Most importantly, the European nation state was left unchanged *ideologically* as the central locus of citizens' national identity (see Hoffmann 1982).

A key issue, at least among European academics and politicians, is whether the attempt to construct a European political identity will replicate—or alternatively, challenge and undermine—nationalism as it was historically deployed. The centrality of identification with the nation state within much of Europe is what makes the inculcation of a European political identification such a fraught task. For example, the political identity of the "Eurosceptic" in Britain has recently emerged (see Ward 1996a, Herman and Cooper 1997) and is now well entrenched within the British Conservative Party. Eurosceptics argue that increased integration will mean the end of British sovereignty and nationhood, which is assumed to be a self-evident disastrous prospect. But, at the same time, Europeanism sometimes reproduces the same jingoistic tropes that were central to the construction of a European identity in earlier periods. European officials speak of an "essentially European tradition" centered on "freedom, democracy, and autonomy," which is universalized and essentialized as what it *means* to be (and not to be) European (Delanty 1995, p. 2).

Such rhetoric replicates the historical production of European "civilization." Today, as before, a common European civilization relegates some non-Europeans to the category of undesirable and uncivilized others, a point I will elaborate on shortly. This discourse is skillfully employed within the geographical space of Europe. The way in which the former Yugoslavia has been constructed as both dangerously close to, but also profoundly outside of, civilization exemplifies how Europe is a "club" whose prerequisites for membership are more than geography alone. Further, race is used against the nonwhite European, who all too frequently is constructed as the resident "alien" no matter what his or her nationality, residence, or place of birth. Through such deployments, a European identity is further essentialized as white (and, moreover, as northern, Western, and probably Protestant).

Given this ongoing exclusionary discourse of the European, is it realistic to imagine that the political integration now being actively promoted can facilitate a new way of envisioning what belonging to Europe might mean? Many claim that such a reimagination is possible and, increasingly, attention is turning to the idea of citizenship. A "new" European citizenship has been described variously as a "heterogeneity of cultural forms" (Delanty 1995, p. 4), "democratic pluralism" (p. 10), "collectively mediated goals" rather than "totalising visions of identity" (p. 10), and a "post-national citizenship" based on "participation and solidarity" (p. 12). Delanty further proposes a collective European identity based on anti-essential citizenship, "creating the space in which minorities can define themselves rather than having their identity defined for them by the dominant ideology" (p. 162; see also Bankowski and Scott 1996, Backer 1997a).

As a legal matter, the Maastricht Treaty officially introduced the concept of European citizenship. The Treaty speaks of a "European

Union" and then constructs the "citizen of the union," and *nationals* of member states possess the limited rights of EU citizenship. It provides one means through which Europe seeks to transform itself into a political union, where notions of political and social citizenship are grafted onto what began as an economic association between sovereign states, described by one commentator as the creation of a "transnational capitalist society" (Ball 1996).[1]

With the original formation of the EEC came the creation of a new European legal system, albeit one with limited jurisdiction. The norms of that legal system are binding on the courts of the member states, in preference even to national laws. National courts are charged with the responsibility of giving full force and effect to the *rights* that have been created in Community law. Those rights associated with European citizenship traditionally have been grounded in a free market ideology. For example, the centerpiece of European citizenship is the right to mobility, which historically was the right of the economically active citizen to seek employment in any member state of the Community (see d'Oliveira 1994, p. 132).

From the beginning, the EEC recognized the principle of "equal pay for equal work," and "equal treatment" of men and women has become a *grundnorm* of European law (More 1993, p. 45). Rights to sexual equality in the workplace have been central to the "social" dimension of Europe, and to the entrenchment of a discourse of rights around gender issues (see generally Hoskyns 1996). What started as a limited right to equal pay has grown into a more general right to "sex equality," including equal treatment as regards access to employment, training, promotions, working conditions, social security, and pensions (More 1996a, pp. 266–267). Judicial decisions on the employment rights of part-time workers and on pregnancy discrimination might indicate a "progressive" dimension to the law (see More 1993, 1996a).[2] The "equal pay" principle had its origins in concerns regarding fair competition as between member states, in that pay differentials between men and women varied tremendously. It was argued that "equal pay" corrected a distortion of free and fair competition. Only over the course of time did a social as well as an economic justification for sex equality law come to the fore. Even today, within EC law, "issues relating to social policy are viewed as secondary, to be addressed only to the extent that they impact on economic integration" (Ball 1996, p. 309), although economic integration may be broadly defined. With respect to gender, "EC equality law applies to women only in their capacity as 'market' actors," which greatly constrains the scope for European law as a vehicle for *substantive* equality (More 1996a, p. 268).

In terms of this focus on the marketplace, it has been argued that the status of citizenship of the EU might mark a turning point, "a major paradigm shift, from a market-centred integration project towards the formation of a European political space" (Flynn 1996, p. 291). What might be emerging within European political and legal discourse are two competing (or complementary) conceptions of citizenship: the "market citizen" and the emerging "Union citizen" (see generally Everson 1996). The latter concept infuses citizenship with broader, nonmarket elements. Many commentators, especially those of a socially progressive inclination, advocate a broader conception of citizenship through which to expand the narrow economic orientation of European rights that thus far has been predominant (see generally Shaw and More 1996). In the economic model of citizenship, there has been little recognition of a role for the citizen other than as a rationally self-interested, wealth-maximizing actor (see de Lange 1995).

Habermas (1995, p. 265) has characterized the tension around European citizenship as between democracy and capitalism. The issue for the future is whether citizenship can come to mean something *more* than "client" interests, so as to encompass the idea of political rights and obligations in relation to Europe (p. 269). Habermas argues that citizenship must transcend the idea of belonging to a pre-political *ethnos,* a conception of nationhood and citizenship that was constitutively dependent on the exclusion of the other. Instead, Europe might strive to define citizenship in terms of "a common, supranationally shared political culture" anchored in different "national traditions and histories" (p. 264). Each provides a specific "vantage point" (p. 264) on Europe, and each is capable of modifying the rest. Ultimately, "a European constitutional patriotism would have to grow from different interpretations, which the same universalist rights and constitutional principles enjoy by receiving their place in the context of different national histories" (p. 271).

In a similar vein, Weiler (1996, pp. 524–525) has described the Maastricht Treaty as signifying the possibility of "creating a political culture which learns new ways to deal with the Other." In spite of differences between the "peoples of Europe" (a phrase coined in the Treaty), Europe's potential lies in the "coming together on the basis of shared values, a shared understanding of rights and societal duties and a shared national, intellectual culture which transcend organic-national differences" (p. 525).[3] In this Europe, nationality and citizenship would be decoupled, because the EU is made up of individuals who share a citizenship but not a nationality, allowing the individual to "rise above his or her national closet" (Weiler 1995, p. 250; see also Preuss 1996).[4]

Citizens would share a commitment to those values that *transcend* national difference and would identify not only with both their nation state and the European Union, but perhaps in a multiplicity of different ways so that no allegiance could claim an undivided loyalty. This resembles the framework for multinational citizenship that I outlined in chapter four. A reimagined nationalism could prove to be a civilizing force, moderating the excesses wrought in the name of nationalism in the past (see Kristeva 1993). As MacCormick (1996, p. 564) proposes, Europe might facilitate a liberal nationalism in which self-conceptions of belonging might be "always evolving, always diversifying, always contestable." Such a mutable, anti-essential Europe has led to its description as a "postmodern polity" (Ward 1996b), which abandons a totalized and singular political identity and the "foundationalism of sovereignty" (Bankowski and Scott 1996, p. 87; see also Preuss 1995).[5]

This utopian school of citizenship theorists focuses on the potential for rethinking the relationship between the citizen, the nation, and its others to transcend the way exclusions have been effected in the name of nationalism and to reimagine political communities other than through a discourse of sovereignty and jurisdictional autonomy.[6] Whether the current political dynamic of the EU can achieve such noble aims is highly doubtful. Although the Maastricht Treaty raises as a question the identity of the European citizen, it fails to move beyond the nation state as the basis of citizenship. Even Weiler (1994), the proponent of European communitarianism, has recognized that the framework provided by the Treaty likely is inadequate for these goals. As he concludes, "Europe has become an end in itself—no longer a means for a higher human end" (p. 214).

The multiplicity of identities celebrated by Weiler and others can, moreover, prove politically fragmenting (a phenomenon I have also described in the Canadian context). A multinational level of government can facilitate the articulation of common interests by individuals across national boundaries, especially when they perceive their demands (such as the demands of Scotland for self-determination) to be unrecognized and unheeded within the nation state (Shore and Black 1994, p. 291). Although this might suggest that Europe will become nothing more than a "community of local grievances" (p. 291), it also implies that communities, citizens, groups, and regions may find themselves engaged in a process of forging new relationships, movements, and loyalties, thereby undermining the centrality of the nation state as a locus of identification. Thus, transnational interest groups are emerging, "working through common institutions, possibly against the preferences of national governments" (Meehan 1993, p. 185).

Another effect of European integration is to invigorate nationalistic identities within member states. That is, as the primacy of the sovereign state is lessened, other *national* identifications are being articulated with increasing confidence. Under the umbrella of the European Union, nationalist/regional identities are demanding representation, which further weakens the claims to loyalty by member states. The "reawakening of old group ties and loyalties" (Kirsch 1995, p. 67) can result in ethnic nationalism of the most fiercely exclusionary kind. Turner (1994, p. 157) describes this dynamic as one in which the nation state is "squeezed" both by "global pressure and local/regional/ethnic challenges" (see also Darian-Smith 1995a, Kearney 1997).

While the local challenge stems in part from regional loyalties, one of the global pressures on the nation state comes from the discourse of rights and, especially, rights that are characterized as universal human rights (see Turner 1994). This development is a product of the globalization of political issues, and it is particularly apparent within discourses surrounding European law and politics. The idea of common rights shared by citizens, and protected through European law, is one of the means through which a "common bond of political loyalty" can overcome the limitations of economic citizenship (Preuss 1996, p. 549) and provide a means to moderate or potentially transform nationalism.

European rights discourse, though, has traditionally operated within very narrow confines. The European Court of Justice (the judicial arm of the European Union) has stated that Community law may confer legal rights on citizens and can be enforced against member states in national courts (see Meehan 1993). This "individual remedial structure" has meant that the recognition and development of rights discourse is a product of individual and group pressure (Shaw 1996a, pp. 245–246). The content of those rights—free movement of labor within the Union, rights to social security for citizens across the Union, and sex equality rights—has been largely justified economically. More critical European scholars, in contrast to the utopian school, argue that the content of rights within EC law is based largely on a conception of the rational, self-interested, wealth-maximizing legal person (see, e.g., Ward 1996b, Everson 1996, Ball 1996). Rights, after all, are a *means* by which to enforce the positive obligation on member states of the EU. The consequence of legally entrenched and binding European norms, therefore, is that "an economic right must in the existing legal order be enforced over any domestic though substantively ethical right" (Ward 1994, p. 327) because of the European Court's "pervasive socio-economic vision and its determination to effect rights derived solely from an immanently economic teleology" (p. 326). A broader conception of citizenship and rights, according to some critics, has yet to be adequately articulated.

The "universalising tendency of economic rights" (Bankowski and Scott 1996, p. 91), however, can serve to deepen citizenship beyond a narrowly market-oriented conception of Europe. While economic rights are geared towards the efficient running of a transnational, capitalist order, one necessary ingredient of efficiency is sometimes seen to be a minimum floor of social rights for individuals across the EU (e.g., state and employee benefits and educational opportunities). While rights claims may be couched in the language of the rational free market, their recognition, it could be argued, might help moderate that market (see Bankowski and Scott 1996). Thus, while there is clearly an "instrumental relationship between the Community's social policy objectives and liberal economic goals," those social policy objectives have taken on a life of their own, justified by the need for equality between states to ensure an efficient capitalist system (Ball 1996, p. 314).

The European Court of Justice, for example, has been prepared to develop the beginnings of a social rights discourse that challenges a market ideology and a conception of citizenship defined solely in terms of free market values. The Acquired Rights Directive (a piece of European legislation) has been interpreted broadly to protect the rights of employees in the event of a "transfer of undertakings," including the "contracting out" of services by companies (see More 1996b). As a consequence, employees have a right to be employed on the same terms and conditions after contracting out, a ruling that employers and some national governments argue undermines the principle of employer "flexibility" in the free market. In this way, it has been recognized that "social and other noneconomic factors must be taken into account in determining how best to attain the economic objectives of the Community" (Ball 1996, p. 361).[7]

The Community Charter of Fundamental Social Rights of Workers (the "Social Charter") might also be construed as an attempt to provide a uniform level of workers' rights throughout the EU. Once again, the justification for guaranteed social rights is to ensure a common EU floor for basic terms of employment, thereby preventing "social dumping"—business exploiting "varying standards of social protection by moving to countries with the lowest requirements in these matters and therefore the lowest costs" (Boch 1993, p. 9). The entrenchment of social rights can serve to moderate the effects of the marketplace and supplement the historically predominant ideology of the EC.[8]

The European Convention on Human Rights provides an alternative arena for mobilization around rights, but one that is on the periphery of EC law. The Convention, though, *has* been incorporated into domestic law by most EU countries, and even those that have not "generally abide by the provisions as interpreted by the European Court of Human Rights in Strasbourg" (Bellamy 1995, p. 153). Membership in the Council of Europe, which is responsible for the Convention, is a prerequisite for joining the EU, and "new members of the Council must agree to ratify the Convention" (Sanders 1996, p. 81). Because this system for the protection of civil and political rights exists largely outside the scope of European law proper, it might be considered the civil and political other to the central role of economic rights in the EU; I will return to some of its legal implications shortly.

An optimist might argue that the emerging language of rights in Europe, at least in the social sphere, creates *space* for the articulation of values other than those of the market (see generally de Búrca 1996). Rights, to the extent that they come to transcend purely economic interests, could enhance the "moral standing" of Europe and help "capture the idea of the individual as part of a broader political community involving reciprocal rights and duties" (p. 42). In that way, rights discourse may prove to be a tool for further integration within the European Union, with its focus on commonality, universality, and a shared cultural tradition. But, at the same time, the deployment of rights in social struggle might equally be seen to have very little to do with the assertion of a European identity *per se* and could be a source of political fragmentation.

Even if the language of rights facilitates the uniting of groups and individuals across national boundaries, the basis on which rights are recognized within the EU remains ambiguous. At a strict legal level, the source of rights is not always apparent within the judgments of the European Court of Justice. At times, the European Convention on Human Rights has been cited. In addition, the Court has grounded citizenship rights within the constitutional traditions of the member states, preferring "to invoke these general principles as an interpretative criteria rather than to identify a precise list of human rights attached to the individuals within the scope of EC law" (Closa 1994, p. 112). European rights discourse, as a unifying force, thus is "invented" through an appeal to common traditions, which, in the process, are socially (or, more accurately, judicially) constructed.[9]

Rights can also prove a *divisive* force when individual member states do not claim allegiance to the common constitutional "tradition" being articulated and legally entrenched. Furthermore, rights can be a site of conflict "when community rights are seen to impinge on what is considered to be primarily a matter of state competence" (de Búrca 1996, p. 48). In those situations, the perception is that the European superstate is obviously and erroneously inventing consensus and uniformity through rights discourse, where no such tradition is shared.

Rights may serve as a force for facilitating coalitions between social groups within nation states and *across* nation states. Groups and individuals may find that concrete benefits can be achieved through activism around rights, especially in the face of a lack of national consensus within a member state. However, de Búrca (1996) notes that rights are not the sole preserve of the historically or socially disadvantaged within the EU, a point that is hardly surprising given the centrality of economics in the historical development of Europe. Rights discourse thus can serve as an empowering tool for those who otherwise would be "excluded from the political processes" as well as for those who are advantaged by them (p. 53).

Reracing the National Imaginary

The potential for empowerment through rights discourse is fundamentally dependent upon *who* can deploy rights within the European legal and political order. On this point, the critique of Europe centers on the fact that rights flow largely from the status of being a Community national. In that sense, "the Treaty [on European Union] has failed to make the leap from the protection of fundamental Community rights to concern for human rights proper" (P. M. Twomey 1994, p. 123). Instead, rights talk provides an easy justification for discrimination as between member state nationals and those of third-party countries, even those who are long-time *residents* of the EU.

This relates back to the foundational issue of how Europe creates and relates to its others. In a continuation of old nationalist discourse, the creation of the other today turns largely on race and ethnicity. Even within the geographic space of Europe, some nations and peoples are other—Europe's periphery—namely, those states that are not (currently) members of the European Union. Furthermore, some *members* of the EU are nevertheless perceived to be on the edges. For example, the member states of southern Europe are frequently constructed as on the fringes because they supposedly are barely able to live up to the economic conditions of membership set by the north. The southern members are also characterized (in the north) as having lax border controls.

As I have already suggested, an increasing importance is placed on the need to *create* an identification by citizens with the machinery of European government, which, it is hoped, will lead to European "loyalty." One mechanism by which this has been attempted is the construction of a common legal heritage, shared by all EU members, which is the basis for the individual rights of Europeans (Hervey 1996, p. 98). But this focus on "universal" rights and equality between citizens only superficially masks the particularism and socioeconomic inequalities of Europe. After all, rights apply only to *nationals* of member states, thereby excluding those millions of people who are long-time residents of the EU, but who lack European nationality (and who may be unable to qualify for it under the rules propagated by member states, who remain the "gatekeepers" of European citizenship).[10]

This exclusionary logic is part of a broader ideological framework, wherein a shared European culture and history is constructed in the hope of inculcating a common European identity (and a concomitant loyalty to EU institutions). This development has been referred to as the "contemporary cultural fundamentalism" of Europe (Stolcke 1995, p. 4), in which "formal political equality presupposes cultural identity and hence cultural sameness is the essential prerequisite for access to citizenship rights" (p. 8). Culture becomes defined as those values and supranational traditions that have been passed down to "us" by "our" (white, Christian) European ancestors. The construction of a European culture is thought necessary to enhance the status of the institutions of contemporary European governance: "there is a growing sense that Europeans need to develop a feeling of shared culture and identity of purpose in order to provide the ideological support for European economic and political union that will enable it to succeed" (p. 2; see also English 1997).

Legal and political developments support this thesis. The achievement of an "internal market" in Europe in 1992 included a framework for the demise of internal borders. Simultaneously, it provides for the strengthening of a common European border to the outside, combined with uniform visa rules and the targeting of non-EU nationals for "restrictive internal policing measures," through coordinated policies on asylum seekers and the movement of non-nationals between countries (Paliwala 1995, p. 78). While the borders within the EU are coming down, the Union will be secured through an (imagined) impermeable border to the outside world. European integration in this way serves to reproduce an opposition between the "good" (authentic) European (citizen) and the "criminal/illegal other" (the nonwhite "immigrant") (Bhavnani 1993, p. 34). Black and Third World peoples continue to be constructed as undesirable, because they do not share in the pan-European cultural heritage of civilization, and, therefore, in the European tradition upon which rights are founded.

Consequently, a common European identity is constructed by overlaying a "shared" tradition on the cultural and historical diversity between and within nation states. But, in so doing, an underlying racism is invoked: "one way of achieving commonality in the idea of 'European' is to stress *otherness* or the alien nature of those from outside, the non-Europeans" (Hervey 1996, p. 98). This is apparent in EU publications that refer to the promotion of European culture. As Hervey notes, while they contain no definition of culture, documents emphasize commonality between member states in terms of values and heritage, through which minorities are excluded *per se*. What Berlant (1991b, p. 20) has described as the "national symbolic"—that is, "how the imagery of nation enters the lives of people"—continues to be racially coded (see also Fitzpatrick 1997).

It is clear that the European national symbolic remains racially constituted. This is hardly surprising. As Mosse (1985) has argued, European nationalism has historically deployed race, gender, and sexuality so as to invent itself through the idea of respectability. The partitioning of Europe after World War II served to physically divide space into the respectable, enlightened West and its other. But what of other exclusionary bases upon which European nationalism historically constituted itself? To what extent does the national symbolic continue to be informed along these trajectories? I now want to consider how a "new" European identity incorporates, rejects, or assimilates what has been constructed, throughout much of the history of European civilization, as transgressing European respectability, namely the homosexual.

Euro-sexual Identities?

I have already touched on the close historical links between race, gender, sexuality, and European nationalism in which the racial other defied respectable gender and sex roles. The homosexual was often constructed in racial terms or, at a minimum, as a threat to the nation state. And European nationalism was articulated to respectable sexuality. In the 1990s, the process of racial othering as a means of consolidating a European national identity continues. In the arena of sexuality, how do lesbians and gays negotiate a space and place within Europe today, in light of their long histories outside the norms of respectability on which a European national identity was founded? If race continues to be a central pivot around which the European other is constituted, do lesbians and gays, by analogy, continue to be located outside the national symbolic? How do they fare in the new Europe? Finally, to what extent might the emerging discourse of European rights be deployed so as to construct an inclusive sexual citizenship?

In considering how lesbians and gays negotiate a place within Europe, it might be asked whether any "room" is left in the bundle of rights for those interests and concerns that flow specifically from lesbian and gay identities. In other words, is the discourse of citizenship and rights a useful concept, as it is currently understood, with which to make claims on behalf of lesbians and gays in member states of the EU? Alternatively, can lesbian and gay rights claims be deployed so as to challenge and widen the existing paradigms of citizenship and rights?

Throughout this chapter, I have underscored the "double edged" character of citizenship—both its inclusionary and exclusionary aspects—as it has developed in the European context. In considering how lesbians and gays respond to that dynamic, it must be kept in mind that how any particular lesbian woman or gay man views her or his role and place within the EU is no doubt highly dependent on a range of other identities, and on the role of identity politics in her or his national community.

European institutions have long addressed issues of sex equality (whether adequately or not is another matter). The legal basis of this drive towards equality is the Equal Treatment Directive, a piece of European legislation that has effect in all member states and that directs governments to implement equal treatment for men and women workers. Within Europe, there has also been some space in recent years for feminist groups to apply political pressure on the Community for progressive social change (see Andermahr 1992, Hoskyns 1996). Whether these groups represent the specific interests and needs of lesbians is debatable. However, the ability of feminists to organize across national boundaries has meant that lesbians have had a vehicle for (at least limited) participation in the European arena (see Kaplan 1997). As I will discuss shortly, European activism around sexuality often reflects a gay male agenda, making feminist coalitions a more appealing alternative for many lesbians.

Racial identification *profoundly* shapes the experiences of European lesbians and gays, given the centrality of the racial construction of Europe today. Given the importance of an economic conception of citizenship, employment status has also been a prerequisite to the enjoyment of rights. Citizenship rights have been the preserve of the economically active, a group constructed within European law as wage earners or self-employed persons in terms of participation in the marketplace.[11] For those whose lives do not fit that model, few rights have been available. And rights depend almost entirely on *being* a citizen of the Union which, in turn, depends on citizenship of a member state. The EU does not dictate to member states the conditions of national citizenship, and the choice of immigration rules within member states are not currently subject to review. Thus, a plethora of different lesbian and gay legal and political experiences exist within Europe, and they are the product of a combination of ranging variables.

The historical and cultural specificity of sexual identities must also be considered. Within Europe (however defined), the existence and role of lesbian and gay identities, and the relationship between sexual acts and sexual identities, varies greatly. The experience of being a middle-class white, gay, professional man living in central London is a world apart from being a working class woman who lives with another woman in rural Greece, or of being a married man who has sex with men in Spain. European societies also exhibit wide variations in the ways in which sexism and racism are articulated, which overlap and connect to homophobia and heterosexism in different ways throughout the continent. All of these factors make generalizations about gay and lesbian life in Europe extremely precarious (see generally Rieder 1992). Europe thus raises the central question of whether collective identities can ever be universalized. That is, in struggles around sexual orientation, to what extent is an Anglo-American model of identity politics being transplanted unthinkingly across the European political arena? Not only does the relationship between acts and identities vary widely across Europe, but for some nation states like France, identity politics sits uneasily with republican notions of citizenship (Marshall 1997).

The stark differences in life experiences of those who identify as lesbian or gay in Europe (and those who have same-sex sexual relations but do not identify as lesbian or gay) tends to get buried or erased in discussions of sexual citizenship. In part, this erasure may stem from the growing centrality of rights discourse both in academic commentary and in social movement mobilization.[12] Lesbian and gay activism, as I will argue, increasingly focuses on rights claims as Europeans and, consequently, a unitary sexual identity is articulated, with demands that it be *included* within the framework of citizenship.

The appeal of rights activism emerges in part from the different degrees of success that have been experienced by lesbians and gays within their *national* political arenas. For example, activists from the Netherlands come to the European political and legal system having achieved considerable advances in social and legal reform domestically (see Waaldijk 1993). They turn to Europe, then, with a relatively high level of confidence, and from a national culture strongly committed to European integration. By contrast, other activists come from national cultures where the political and legal structures have proven unreceptive to their claims—such as the United Kingdom, which was under Conservative Party rule from 1979 to 1997 (see generally Cooper and Herman 1995). In the U.K., where rights discourse is comparatively underdeveloped domestically (for better or worse), Europe provides a new arena for social and legal struggle. In this venue, the language of rights is seen to have more potential, and activists perceive that EU political actors are more supportive of and receptive to their claims for inclusion in a European polity. British activists are increasingly turning to Europe. In so doing, European institutions are seen as "liberators in the face of existing social and legal discrimination" (Bamforth 1995, p. 115). The strategy deployed by lesbian and gay activists in relation to the institutions of Europe might best be described as one that erases differences in an attempt to construct a common European lesbian/gay identity. In this regard, activism replicates some of the ways in which European integration is pursued through the consolidation of an invented, common European tradition.

This is particularly apparent in a major study undertaken by the European Human Rights Foundation at the request of the European Commission, a central and powerful organ of European government (Waaldijk and Clapham 1993). Published in 1993, it was "the first ever study of the situation of lesbians and gay men in the EC" (Ashman 1993, p. 4). The introduction begins with the sweeping claim that:

> in the huge diversity of peoples who make up the human race, there are a number of universal constants which have always been part of the human condition. One is that people who are different inspire fear which often leads to prejudice; another is that a proportion of the human race is homosexual. (p. 3)

This statement sets the tone for the remainder of the book, which focuses on the claimed universality and essential "sameness" of homosexuality, rather than, for example, how the homosexual role has been important historically to the project of European nationalism. Nor is there any attempt to connect the homosexual within discourses of European nationalism to imperialism and colonialism—the legacy of Europe. This universalizing of homosexuality as a transhistorical and cross-cultural essence might itself be regarded as a form of European neocolonialism. That is, the 1990s western European (or, perhaps, Anglo-American) gay male becomes a universal and universalized subject position.[13] Leaving aside the ways in which activism here replicates wider deployments of nationalism, the question remains whether the strategy of constructing a single, universal European gay subject has been "successful" as a political strategy.

In fact, the resort to legal and political institutions of the EU for social and political advancement has had some limited success in eradicating national legislation that criminalized same-sex sexual activity between men in private. This deployment of rights as a means of "trumping" state law was effected through the application of the right to privacy in the European Convention on Human Rights (see generally Wintemute 1995). The strategy proved particularly successful in the Republic of Ireland. A challenge to legislation that criminalized same-sex sexual acts between men failed before the Irish courts (*Norris v. Attorney General* 1984; see also Flynn 1995). It was then taken successfully to the European Court of Human Rights (see Rose 1994, pp. 39–40). However, as a legal matter, the Convention is unenforceable domestically in Ireland. Nonetheless, the decision of the European Court of Human Rights was an important political victory for Irish lesbians and gays, in part as a means of mobilizing and energizing a movement (see generally Rose 1994). Furthermore, in combination with a rapidly changing political and social climate, the victory facilitated a wide ranging reform of laws (and perhaps social attitudes) in the Republic of Ireland (see Ryan 1996, Flynn 1997).[14] This shift is closely bound up with a reimagining of Irish national identity, and Ireland's relationship to Europe (see Kearney 1997). As Flynn (1997, p. 495) has argued, historically, a "vision of Irish-ness, centring on a Gaelic, Catholic culture" focused specifically on the family and rural life "as sources of 'authentic' Irish experience" (not unlike Quebec). Homosexuality was incommensurable with that national identity, standing as a symbol of modernity in a society wedded to tradition (Walshe 1997).[15]

In Ireland today, by contrast, efforts at legal and social reform are connected to attempts to redefine the national identity "Irish" so that lesbians, gays, and other "others" can be accommodated within a reimagined Irish "family" located within Europe (Flynn 1997, p. 507). Familial discourse remains important, but the family *may* have become more welcoming and inclusive. In this regard, Flynn (1997, p. 506) argues that "a remaking of 'Irish-ness' was a central condition for the successful law reform strategy."

The dynamics of this refashioning of national identity might be characterized as *both* forward and backward looking. Interestingly, one discursive deployment now is a mythologized, "authentic" Irish/Celtic identity grounded in a distant, precolonial past (resembling some constructions of "tradition" in South Africa). This identity is sexually constituted as permissive, passionate, and uncorrupted by the sexual repression of British colonial rule. As a consequence, "homophobia can be regarded as part of the colonial inheritance" (Rose 1994, p. 8), a colonial contamination from which the Irish people are just recovering their authentic spirit of tolerance of sexual diversity (and of sex in general).[16] This articulation is a reversal of earlier nationalist deployments of homosexuality in the late nineteenth century, in which homosexual scandals among colonial administrators were used to foster Irish nationalist resistance (p. 6). In this way, "mainstream revolutionary discourse projected a particular image of the Irish male as antithetical to the feminised versions of Irishness projected by colonial propaganda" (Hanafin 1997; see also Walshe 1996). This again exemplifies the colonial contamination model, but as a mirror image of the current dynamic. Finally, the appearance of postcolonial nationalist struggle in the space of Europe might be read as a "queering" both of Europe and of a postcolonial identity (Walshe 1997).

As well as looking backward, lesbian and gay activists deploy forward-looking rhetorical strategies in calling for social and legal change. In combination with other progressive social movements and individuals in Ireland, particularly those active on the reform of abortion laws, lesbians and gays have argued for the transformation of an insular society into an outward looking, cosmopolitan state in a new European order (Rose 1994, p. 43).[17] The *Norris* case, with its turn to Europe and the consequent rebuke of Ireland from Europe, is one step in that process. Irish progressive social actors in general have a strongly pro-European integrationist leaning, focused on the reimagination of Ireland through the turn towards Europe and the bypassing of England (Walshe 1997). By contrast, some social conservatives have adopted an anti-European stance, including opposition to the Maastricht Treaty. In this reading of Europe, the *Norris* case, abortion rights, and greater European integration are linked, and *Norris* becomes "another example of Europe imposing its ethical values on Ireland" (Rose 1994, p. 47).

The Irish example highlights an interesting dynamic of nationalism, sexuality, and the emergence of a European identity. However, it is worth noting that European human rights law played a largely *symbolic* role in the struggle.[18] Domestic law criminalizing male same-sex activity in private provided a relatively "easy" case to argue before a court of human rights, and any other result would have been surprising (although it was only a majority decision).[19]

Beyond the issue of the criminalization of same-sex sexual activity, the European Court of Human Rights has not proven a particularly worthwhile forum for lesbian and gay legal rights struggles (see generally Wintemute 1995).[20] However, in 1997 the United Kingdom government decided not to contest a case challenging Britain's unequal age of consent for gay sex after the European Commission of Human Rights ruled that the inequality violated Article 8 (respect for private life) and Article 14 (discrimination) of the European Convention on Human Rights (*Sutherland v. United Kingdom* 1997). This may well lead to a change in the law. In general, though, the focus is shifting away from the Court of Human Rights towards the institutions of the EU proper. In geographic terms, this is a shift from Strasbourg to Brussels and Luxembourg, from human rights to the (primarily socioeconomic) law of the European Union.

In turning to the institutions of the EU, lesbian and gay activism has experienced most of its successes before the European Parliament, an elected body of members regarded as the least powerful branch of European government. In 1984, the European Parliament passed a resolution on sexual discrimination in the workplace that called for an end to discrimination against homosexuals both within member states and at European Community level (Ashman 1993, p. 4). In May 1995, it further resolved that the Treaty of the European Union should forbid discrimination on the basis of sexual orientation in member states, and it "also extended certain employment benefits to the same-sex partners of its employees" (Sanders 1996, p. 84). But the European Parliament had no power to implement resolutions in any kind of substantive way. Rather, it called upon the European Commission (which does possess substantial powers) to draft a detailed recommendation to member states for "equal treatment" of citizens regardless of their sexual orientation (Bamforth 1995, p. 114).

By focusing reform efforts at the institutions of the EU, the tension between an economic free market oriented Europe, and a conception of European citizenship rights which deepen that vision, is underscored. For example, the English law reform pressure group "Stonewall" has explicitly pitched its arguments to Europe in terms of economic rights of citizenship for lesbians and gays (Tatchell 1992, p. 20). The most fundamental and powerful rights in European law are the Internal Market Provisions, which guarantee the free movement of labor, services, goods, and capital and forbid discrimination by member states on the movement of these factors of production.

Stonewall's argument deploys a model of the wealth maximizing citizen. The claim is that the widely varying levels of discrimination and legal protection for lesbians and gays in the various member states undermine the commitment of Europe to the "harmonization of regulations" and "constitutes a barrier to the free movement of people" (Tatchell 1992, p. 20). Similarly, the pressure group Lesbian and Gay Employment Rights (LAGER) has argued that discrimination against lesbians and gays in the workplace is "a waste of human resources" and "a restriction on free competition," which "denies employers the opportunity to take on the best person for the job" (p. 21). These arguments replicate the original justifications for "equal pay" provisions in EC law, namely, the perfectibility of the market and the classic liberal separation of public and private spheres.

In this way, discrimination against lesbians and gays is "translated" into a distortion of the market and as economically inefficient, so as to fit the dominant discourse of European rights. Lesbian and gay political activism, to a large extent, seems not to envision its role, at least in this example, as challenging the pre-vailing paradigm of rights. Instead, rights claims are made within the dominant, market based, rational choice model. At the same time, as I have already argued, some within Europe are actively seeking to expand that paradigm to encompass a political vision of citizenship that is grounded in something other than the market-place. But lesbian and gay activism has not particularly served in that project to date.

In reply, it might be argued that struggles around rights, in or-der to have some chance at gaining victories, must articulate claims within the language game currently being played. Thus, it has been asserted that:

> by placing the argument for the need to prevent discrimination against lesbians and gay men within the sphere of economic fairness and equal-ity (i.e. those conditions that are necessary to compete successfully in the labor marketplace), there is no need to engage in the type of norma-tive or moral considerations that lesbians and gay men, as a minority often not viewed well or understood by the majority, are likely to lose. (Ball 1996, p. 385)

This justification underscores the dilemma of the deployment of rights discourse, which is especially pronounced in an arena where rights have had such an individuated, economically conser-vative, market driven orientation. In response to Ball, it can be ar-gued that rights claims in large measure are important sites of struggle *because* they provide an arena to make "normative" or "moral" arguments that can serve an educational and, ultimately, transformative function (see Herman 1994b). That, in part, is what provides rights with their radical edge as a strategy of social change—their ability to alter society. In adopting the strategy out-lined by Ball, by contrast, the instrumental function played by rights discourse within EC law, rather than being challenged or broadened, instead is replicated and further reified.

As a consequence, the substantive rights claims made within the European arena often deploy the logic of the market. Activism has centered, for example, on the rights of EU workers to be joined by their spouses and dependents in a country of residence (where the lesbian or gay "spouse" is not a national of the European Union) (see Tanca 1993). To date, this issue has not elicited a result at European Community level, although gains have been made in some member states (such as the Netherlands). The underlying argument is that a "truly" free and efficient labor market depends on workers' ability to bring their immediate families with them to their country of residence. Otherwise, the worker might not relocate to where his or her factor of production will be rewarded through the highest wages and opportunities. The effect of the failure to recognize some "families" in law becomes economic inefficiency. Rather than drawing into question the prevailing paradigm of insiders and outsiders of Europe, such a strategy merely redefines some outsiders as on the inside, based on the degree to which their relationships with European citizens replicate a traditional heterosexual, Eurocentric model of marriage.[21] While this issue might serve as a site of contestation over the meaning of "family," such a conflict has yet to emerge within public discourse.

Great stress has also been placed on the expansion of European sex discrimination law, which covers employment, training, and working conditions, to include discrimination on the basis of sexual orientation. The question has arisen whether European law that prohibits discrimination in the workplace on the basis of "sex" implicitly includes discrimination against gays and lesbians. A positive result has not been forthcoming in law, but in adopting this strategy, the differing dynamics of discrimination based on gender and sexual orientation (and their relationship) can easily be erased (see generally Currah 1996).[22] A case has been decided by the European Court of Justice (ECJ) in which a lesbian railway employee claimed that her employer's failure to extend to her female partner benefits automatically available to unmarried female partners of male employees amounts to sex discrimination in pay (*Grant v. South-West Trains Ltd.* 1998; see also Armstrong 1998). The Court refused to accept that sexual orientation discrimination *is* sex discrimination. A victory would have forced employers to "pay out" (or to terminate all such benefits). Such strategies can be subject to critique for the way in which they further a model of citizenship based on the replication of heterosexual marriage. That institution, after all, was historically central to the construction of middle-class respectability within discourses of European nationalism, which, in turn, served to constitute the homosexual as the deviant other, and to preserve rigid and fixed gender roles.[23]

More generally, it has been argued that the agenda for activism is largely shaped by gay male issues, a phenomenon that is hardly unique to Europe (Andermahr 1992). The different priorities of some lesbians (for example, donor insemination and child custody rights) are ignored—a product, in large measure, of the relationship between social movement activism and available paradigms on offer for the articulation of rights claims. The prevailing rights framework has also been subject to critique for its underlying gendered view of citizenship. Flynn (1996, p. 291) has argued that, historically, European law has been a masculinist construct because of the way it conceives the citizen as an economic unit of production (the rational, wealth maximizing, male wage earner). Gay activism, in its deployment of rights strategies, may serve to reproduce that gendered dynamic.

While European rights claims may be framed within the logic of the market (in large measure so as to ensure a more receptive hearing), that may not negate the role of rights in social change. The *visibility* of lesbians and gays facilitated by employment (and other) discrimination claims and the *justice* of those individual cases, presented in the public sphere, may well be important steps. The caveat I (like many others) would add is that those engaged in rights struggles must be sufficiently self-reflexive so as to recognize that "success" in narrow instrumental terms ought not to overwhelm the agenda. In this regard, the lawyerization of activism, when it comes to center on rights struggles, is a phenomenon that is ever present.

What will be interesting for the future is the extent to which a discourse of rights and citizenship expands its horizons beyond the economic to embrace a political and social dimension. For lesbian and gay legal activism, such a wider focus, and an awareness of both the potential *and* limits of rights discourse in Europe, may be essential to ensuring that any transformative potential is realized.

In this chapter, I have attempted to connect the ways in which Europe and European nationalism were historically invented through the constitution of various others to current deployments of European identity. Within the European Union today, rights discourse has come to serve as a bond of commonality through the language of universality and citizenship. But the construction of citizenship replicates many of the historical exclusions wrought in the name of European nationalisms. The economic grounding of rights is itself exclusionary, albeit moderated by the emerging discourse of social rights. Moreover, policies that seek to create a "Fortress Europe" through literally impermeable borders between Europe and its others further reproduces historical exclusions.

Rights struggles around lesbian and gay sexualities may have a growing role within Europe, but they frequently reify a logic of European citizenship that has centered on the economically active. Whether rights discourse might serve as a forum for transforming the place of lesbians and gays within the national symbolic of Europe remains to be seen. At the same time, the constraining character of rights, especially within the context of European law and politics, suggests that rights as a site of political struggle has its limits. A circumscribed role for rights within the activist agenda may be called for.

In the end, rights discourse in the EU is but one side of the challenge of integration and citizenship. The other is the need for democratic institutions to which citizens feel allegiance. Rectifying the deficit in both rights and democracy is key to reconceiving citizenship and national identity in this emerging order. That is part of the challenge to be faced by a Europe that continues to widen its membership and deepen its identity.

6 Reimagining Australia

In this final case study, I focus on a national culture in which, for the past several years, the relationship between national identity, sexuality, and rights has been a central focus of public discourse. Australia is a society in which national identity is perhaps the least "naturalized" of any that I have considered so far. Nation in Australia is most explicitly and widely recognized as a social construction—one that is in process—and capable of reimagination for the next century. It is a social order in which the public, for a number of years, has been saturated with the question of what an Australian national identity might signify. This has taken the form of debates over the creation of a republic (as opposed to Australia's current status as a constitutional monarchy with Queen Elizabeth as head of state); occasional attempts to create an entrenched, comprehensive constitutional bill of rights (which does not currently exist at either the federal or state levels of government); Aboriginal justice through recognition of historic land rights (an ongoing issue that has achieved both success and setbacks in the judicial and legislative process); and the meaning of multiculturalism in a society historically dominated by white "Anglo-Celtic" peoples but that now must come to terms with the importance of its relationship with "Asia."

All of these issues are bound up with the reimagination of the place and role of Australia in the current global order. As a "settler society" of the British Empire, Australia's geographical isolation was tempered by its links to the United Kingdom, symbolized by the role of the British monarch as head of state. Subsequently, in the post–World War II era, its ties (and dependency) shifted to the United States, and Australia, unlike most Western allies, participated actively in the Vietnam War. That event served as a catalyst for the articulation of an oppositional, countercultural vision of Australia through a series of vibrant movements. Social movement politics has played an important and ongoing role in the imagination of an Australian identity.

In the 1990s, national identity has come to be associated with the imagination of an independent, international role for Australia—the carving out of a place on the international stage, with a particular focus on the Asia-Pacific region. Such a role marks a departure from Australia's history as a British colony, and then as subsumed in the American sphere of influence. Yet, at the same time, American culture permeates most national cultures today, although to varying degrees and in different ways. As Australia seeks to define a place on the international stage, it has also been forced to consider how it will meet and respond to international "standards" such as those of "human rights." This has been particularly apparent in Australia's recognition of Aboriginal rights and, more recently, the rights of lesbians and gays. Some argue that for Australia to be credible internationally, it must accept and implement international agreements and judgments. Australia has long entered into a range of treaty obligations and has sought to abide by treaty terms domestically. The increased role of treaties, in areas such as human rights, exemplifies for some an uncritical acceptance of international judgments that necessarily undermines both the national sovereignty of Australia and its federal distribution of powers (because it is the federal level of government which enters into *all* treaty obligations). This more isolationist position is articulated to the language of sovereignty and states' rights, in opposition to the internationalist stance.

The so-called "bill of rights debate" in Australia, which has been sporadic for many years, sometimes has been fueled by a sense that the nation is being left behind other national cultures in its lack of entrenched and enforceable individual rights. Such rights, some claim, could prove both a means of nation building and a symbol of maturity as a nation state. Further, international human rights discourse has an increasing place and role in both the enactment of legislation and judicial decisionmaking, as a standard that can be applied domestically. In these various ways, the national legal culture increasingly defines itself through the international legal order, albeit with vociferous dissenting voices. In this chapter, my argument is that rights discourse is playing an increasing role in the reimagination of national identity in Australia through the intersection of the international, national, and local legal orders.

It has been in the specific context of struggles around sexuality—state laws criminalizing male same-sex activity—that these connections most recently have come to the fore. As the criminal law falls within the legislative competence of the individual states pursuant to the Australian Constitution, attempts to repeal these laws through national and international legal and political claims confronted the competing discourse of states' rights. After all, federalism has also been an essential historical component of the Australian national identity. Increasingly, claims grounded in the rights of states to enforce local norms and values are being forced to give way in this and other disputes by virtue of the enactment of national legislation aimed at protecting rights that have been recognized at the international level and accepted nationally through treaties.

I explore this range of issues as follows. I begin with an historical consideration of the various constructions of national identity in Australia. The role of rights discourse, as well as federalism, prove central. Following on from this, but still related to it, is how rights discourse has informed lesbian and gay struggles in the past quarter century. Social movement activism around sexuality has had a particular dynamic in Australia, with some interesting results. Finally, I will look more closely at the *Toonen* case and controversy—which concerned laws regulating same-sex sexual acts in the state of Tasmania—as a recent example of how issues of national identity, rights, and sexual identity have come together, placing Australia center-stage in a developing international human rights jurisprudence. It is in the *Toonen* case that these conceptions of national identity come to be articulated most clearly.

The Reinvention of Australia

The claim that the Australian national identity is a social construction, and one that has been subject to frequent reimagination throughout its history, is well established (see, e.g., Eddy 1991, Price 1991, Kapferer 1996). In his landmark study, *Inventing Australia,* White (1981) attempted to tell that story, and he found that an Australian national identity was a particularly malleable construct, subject to considerable change over time. While early nineteenth-century Australians may have been tainted with the history of the convict system (which existed from 1788 to 1868), "convictism" came to be displaced in the course of the nineteenth century. During that period, Australia was associated with opportunity, social mobility, and an "idealised Arcadian society, a rural Utopia" (p. 33). In addition, Australian national identity, to a significant degree, was constituted derivatively as a "new America" or as "another England" (p. 50).

Discussions of national identity in Australia, however, as in so many other cultures, cannot be separated from historical ideas of racial purity. Traditionally, the preservation of the Australian "character" was understood as dependent upon the maintenance of the purity of the white race, which was achieved, first, through the literal and metaphorical "erasure" of the Aboriginal people. The basis of Australian colonization in international law was the doctrine of *terra nullius* (an empty land), devoid of civilization (see Povinelli 1994). The other means of maintaining racial purity was manifested in the legislative action of the first Commonwealth of Australia Parliament in 1901 (the Commonwealth was created that year through the joining together of the various colonies as a self-governing, federal, but still colonial dominion of the United Kingdom).[1] Parliament passed the *Immigration Restriction Act,* which established the "White Australia" immigration policy that would remain in force until the 1960s (Castles, Kalantzis, Cope, and Morrissey 1988, p. 19). These discourses of race, as I have argued throughout this book, cannot be separated from the gendered construction of white (in this case, Anglo-Celtic) women as reproducers of the national race.

The twentieth century has seen a frequent focus in Australia on national identity, articulated to a discourse of increasing maturity, sophistication, and independence (White 1981, p. 151). In the post–World War II period, Australia was constructed as an outpost of "freedom" and "democracy" in the context of the cold war in the Asia-Pacific region (p. 158). Furthermore, from the 1950s, the United States became the standard by which Australians, like many in the world, measured the success of their way of life. For

Australians, that lifestyle revolved around consumerism, suburban sprawl, and, for white immigrants from a non-Anglo background, assimilation into an imagined Australian way of life and identity (Castles, Kalantzis, Cope, and Morrissey 1988, p. 12).

That consensus broke down in the late 1960s. Participation in the Vietnam War inspired strong and vociferous anti-war social movement activism, followed by a series of movements demanding progressive social change led by feminist, lesbian and gay, anti-nuclear, environmental, and anti-racist activists (Altman 1988). At the same time, claims for Aboriginal justice were made, often through demands for the reparation of land rights (Inglis 1991, p. 30). The consensus was further shaken by the breakdown of the "White Australia" immigration policy in the mid-1960s (Castles, Kalantzis, Cope, and Morrissey 1988, p. 51).[2] The change in policy was provoked in part by the perceived need for closer (economic) ties with Asia, and it opened the way for a greater orientation of Australia towards Southeast Asia through immigration (p. 53). It has provoked a very significant white backlash in Australia, which nostalgically yearns for the postwar consensus on an Australian way of life. The backlash has been most recently manifested in the election to Parliament of Pauline Hanson, the self-proclaimed leader of the "One Nation Party," on an explicitly anti-Asian immigration and anti-Aboriginal rights platform. Some opinion polls have indicated that One Nation has the support of up to 10% of the electorate (Megalogenis 1997), illustrating the current strength of racist backlash.

Increased immigration, from a vast diversity of national cultures, led to the abandonment of a policy of assimilation in favor of "multiculturalism" (see generally Beckett 1995, Inglis 1991, Smolicz 1995). A term first used by the immigration minister in 1973, multiculturalism has emerged as a "comprehensive ideology of what Australia was supposed to be and to become" (Castles, Kalantzis, Cope, and Morrissey 1988, p. 4). It has been defined as the attempt "to uphold and develop an overarching framework of Australian values in which the right of individuals from minority backgrounds to retain their ethnic identity was assured" (Smolicz 1995, p. 6). Multiculturalism sought to provide a flexible framework of shared values through which a diversity of cultures could flourish (or, less charitably, would be normalized and disciplined). At the same time, it has conveniently served as an ideology through which the historic connection between Britain and Australia could be severed (Gunew 1990, p. 104). An Australian national identity grounded in internal pluralism (and equality) was seen as a means of replacing a British colonial identity and, at the same time, as resistant to the gravitational pull of the American cultural sphere. More critically, the *ideology* of multiculturalism has been described as exemplifying how, in the conditions of economic globalization, "as the nation-state loses many of its former functions and powers, becoming more and more an empty shell, it suffers a crisis of legitimacy. It needs powerful ideologies to shore up its crumbling walls" (Castles, Kalantzis, Cope, and Morrissey 1988, p. 141). Multiculturalism becomes one of the few "grand narratives" readily available to the nation state. Multiculturalism can also obscure the specificity of Aboriginal claims through the construction of aboriginality as simply another ethnic variant, and it has tended to focus on a celebration of postwar *white* immigration, masking structural inequalities between groups (Gunew 1990, p. 104).

The policy in recent years has exemplified an Australian willingness to deploy the state to achieve social policy goals, and this is associated specifically with the Australian Labor Party. Multiculturalism under Commonwealth Labor governments of the 1980s and 1990s had a social democratic focus, which included the recognition of a duty to ensure equal access to government services for members of all cultural groups, the recognition of multiculturalism as an important element of all government policies, and a requirement of consultation with groups in the development and implementation of policy (Castles, Kalantzis, Cope, and Morrissey 1988, p. 73).[3] The preparedness to deploy the state to achieve a multicultural society exemplifies a more general feature of Australia, namely, a more interventionist role for the state compared to some other Western countries (Sawer 1991, p. 269). The welfare state has long been entrenched in the Australian national identity, and Australia avoided many of the debilitating attacks on it that occurred in the United States and United Kingdom during the 1980s (p. 276), only to have them emerge in the mid-1990s with a political turn to the right.

The policy of multiculturalism also underscores a historical transition in the way in which national identity is conceived, from a customary to a conventional account (Yeatman 1994). In the customary narrative, a shared common culture defined by British origins is emphasized, and those who do not share personally in that story are expected to assimilate as best they can. The conventional account, by contrast, focuses on national institutions as a unifying bond, and on shared Australian values such as equal opportunity and participation. In terms of national identity, a conventional account looks to "processes of self-fabrication" (p. 100), and this orientation assumed an increasing prominence through the 1980s and 1990s (similar in this regard to the construction of a Canadian national identity). This period is noted for the increasing centralism of the polity, arguably at the expense of the values of federalism.

Australia today might be described as manifesting a tension between customary and conventional accounts of nationhood. Backlash against nonwhite immigration, Aboriginal justice claims, feminism, and gay rights appears to be on the increase. Race, gender, and sexuality remain central to how the "symbolic boundaries" of the nation are imagined by many Australians (Phillips 1996). Australian right wing discourse seeks "a return to the traditional values and beliefs which have historically characterized Australia" (p. 117). The defeat of the Labor Party in the national election of 1996 is inseparable from imaginings of nation, particularly given its implementation of many of the policies associated with a conventional account of national identity and its support for those groups that have been historically imagined as outside the national symbolic. The election of the right of center Liberal-National Coalition government—on a platform of nostalgia, support for "ordinary" Australians, and "traditional" values—represents the reascendence of the customary account of nationhood.

By contrast, under·Labor administrations during the 1980s and up to 1996, the women's movement in Australia, for example, had more of an impact on the state than in most other Western countries (Sawer 1991). While women had the right to vote from 1902, it was not until the 1980s that feminism was successful in acting through and within the state and bureaucracy to achieve social change. The policy of monitoring the outcomes of all government programs for their impact on women exemplifies this commitment (p. 262). A close relationship between the state and social movements is also apparent around HIV issues. From the outset of the epidemic, there has been a close working relationship between AIDS activist groups and the state, giving rise to a radically different experience of government response from that of many Western nations. An activist state through which social movements have had an effect on policy has been an important facet of the Australian national experience, which has clearly come to shape identity—although, as with all features of national identity, it is still open to redefinition in the face of a reaction against that activism (Altman 1988).

The focus on the (re)definition of national identity became something of a national obsession in 1988, the bicentennial of white arrival in Australia (see generally Bennett, Buckridge, Carter, and Mercer 1992). This is roughly the same period in which the effects of globalization in the financial markets were felt, marked most in the public mind by the floating of the Australian dollar on the currency markets in the mid-1980s. For the Labor government then in power, marking 1988 was a delicate task. The "celebration" of the conquest of the Aboriginal peoples—in a society officially committed to Aboriginal redress, gender equality, and multiculturalism—highlighted the tension between different accounts of nationhood. Three issues assumed a prominence that continues to this day: multiculturalism, aboriginality, and republicanism (Phillips 1996, p. 118). The government's approach was to attempt an imagination of a new kind of national community in "an attempt to manufacture a consensual position," focusing on "journeys" as a universal Australian experience of migration (Cochrane and Goodman 1992, p. 178). Despite this imaginative effort, 1988 primarily underscored the demands for Aboriginal reparation and the difficulty of constructing a coherent national identity based on a policy of multiculturalism, with its focus on "difference."

One answer to that conundrum, which came to assume a particular prominence, has been the drive spearheaded by former Prime Minister Paul Keating in the 1990s to make Australia a republic by the turn of the century. On June 7, 1995, Keating announced in Parliament his desire for an Australian head of state by the turn of the century, replacing Queen Elizabeth, to mark the centenary of Australian federation (Bulbeck 1996, p. 43). Thus, the next "celebration" would have a genuine unifying, national meaning: the end of the British link and the symbolic maturity of the nation, a century after it began. The republic question remains one of the key sites of struggle over an Australian national identity, and a popularly elected constitutional convention will determine in 1998 the form of a referendum on the issue. Parliament has ratified that agenda.

The republican movement, however, manifests its own gendered dynamic. While republicanism is frequently described as the "natural" endpoint of a process of maturation, it is also embedded within a discourse of masculinity (Irving 1996). Republicans "assert their independence by masculinising their country" (Bulbeck 1996, p. 45) and, symbolically, the desire for a republic represents a "revolt against the femaleness of Britannia" (p. 46). This discourse of "muscular independence" (Irving 1996, p. 91) may explain in part why the republican movement in Australia is identified predominantly with white men with a "lack of articulation between feminism and republicanism" (p. 95; see also Howe 1995). Antirepublican discourse is also heavily gendered. The queen is frequently portrayed as the dutiful monarch—the ideal "woman"—untouched by the dirt of party politics and, consequently, the perfect head of state in a parliamentary system (Irving 1996, p. 91).

One reason many observers now consider a republic to be inevitable is the way in which the republican movement constructs its goal as a simple constitutional change. In this way, while a republic is constructed as symbolically important for national identity, it is equally described as substantively minor. Of more constitutional significance would be the linking of republicanism to the entrenchment of a constitutional bill of rights, along the Canadian, South African, and American lines. The bill of rights debate has had a role in the imagination of an Australian national identity, but the likelihood of its realization in the foreseeable future is remote due to a lack of political and popular will. The role of rights in the Australian national identity has been subject to considerable contemplation (see, e.g., Galligan, Knopff, and Uhr 1990; Alston 1994b). Collins (1985) has described Australia as a "Benthamite" society in which legalism, utilitarianism, and positivism have been ideologically central. In such a culture, it is not surprising that the discourse of rights historically was limited to the rights of states. The "inherited constraints of utilitarian liberalism" have meant that there was little scope for a model of individual rights that transcended the geographically based communities in which the individual was member (p. 161).

At the same time, "equality" is a value that now centrally informs Australian culture, linked to an activist state and creating "a collectivist political economy with important social justice purposes" within the constraints of a federal model of government (Galligan 1994, p. 62). A discourse of equality, as I have shown in other national contexts, articulates readily to individual rights. The emergence of this discourse of rights, in turn, cannot be separated from another historical development in Australian constitutionalism, namely, increased centralization and the strengthening of the Commonwealth government at the expense of the states (see Eddy 1991, p. 27). This, too, has been a partisan political issue. Since the 1970s, the Labor Party has advocated some form of bill of rights and, on various occasions when in power, has tried to introduce one that is binding on both federal and state governments. All of those attempts ended in failure. In this context, rights are perceived by advocates as a tool for the forging of national identity. By contrast, opponents claim that rights function as a means to furthering the centralization of authority in the Commonwealth government and eroding the power of the states. A decentralized federal system, it is argued, is the best protector of the individual. States rights and enumerated, entrenched individual rights thereby are constructed oppositionally:

> The structure of Australian human rights law has been shaped by both the politics of federalism and a dedication to legalism as the appropriate mode of legal reasoning. These two forces have operated in the same direction to create a culture wary of the discourse of rights. (Charlesworth 1994, p. 21)

Historically, skepticism about legally entrenched rights was linked to faith in responsible government (the accountability of the executive to the legislative branch in a parliamentary system) as the best protector of the individual. Further, a federal system operates as a check on power by dividing jurisdiction. Thus, the Australian "founding fathers," while certainly aware of the U.S. approach to rights, replicated only the federal aspects of the American Constitution, leaving both levels of government sovereign within their respective jurisdictions (Charlesworth 1994, p. 22). However, with the increasing centralization of the Australian polity, advocates of a bill of rights argue that the executive power of the Commonwealth government can best be checked through the creation of common rights of citizenship, given the declining role of federalism as an effective brake on the executive. Constitutional rights become both a means for greater nationalization of political life and, simultaneously, "a counterbalance to greater centralisation" (Galligan 1994, p. 68). Opponents of a bill of rights also frame their arguments in the language of rights—states' rights in a decentralized system of power—in which federalism "promotes rights-oriented citizenship" (Galligan, Knopff, and Uhr 1990, p. 56).[4] Opposition to entrenched individual rights is linked to support for strong states as well as to opposition to creeping centralization and the increased executive power of the federal government. But many advocates of a bill of rights are skeptical of claims that federalism is the best defense for the individual. Traditionally, state governments have often been noted for a particular brand of conservative politics that was deleterious to the rights of minorities and others (p. 66)—an example of which can be found in the *Toonen* case, which I will consider shortly. A further aspect of the national culture is the centrality of an ideology of legalism. In this regard, opponents of a bill of rights fear that "constitutional rights could both politicise the judiciary and legalise public policy" (Charlesworth 1994, p. 26), which would undermine the rigid boundaries between the legislative powers of Commonwealth and states.

The failure of Labor governments to entrench rights constitutionally does not mean that a discourse of individual rights is without currency in Australia. In the 1990s, rights have played a substantial role within public discourse. One reason this has occurred is a particular conjunction of the local, the national, and the international, whereby rights claims—grounded in the international legal sphere—have come to possess increased weight domestically.

Furthermore, the assertion of an Australian national identity has been realized in part through a more prominent and independent role on the international stage. One example of this outward looking mentality has been Australia's entry into numerous international legal conventions, dealing with everything from labor law to the environment (see generally *Sydney Law Review* 1995).

As a matter of law, in this regard, it is within the exclusive jurisdiction of the Commonwealth government to enter treaties concerning *any* legislative field (see generally Saunders 1995). This led to the question of the federal government's ability to implement, through legislation, those treaties that deal with subject matters falling within the legislative competence of the states. For example, the *Racial Discrimination Act* was enacted by the federal government in 1975, and the jurisdictional basis upon which the government relied was the fact that it had previously entered the International Convention on the Elimination of All Forms of Racial Discrimination. The legislation closely followed the Convention, and its validity was upheld by the High Court (the supreme court of Australia) under the external affairs power (Galligan, Knopff, and Uhr 1990, p. 58).

More famously, in the *Tasmanian Dam Case* (1985), the issue centered on the federal government's ability to act pursuant to international environmental agreements to halt a dam project undertaken by the state government of Tasmania (see generally Rothwell and Boer 1995). The High Court answered affirmatively, finding the existence of a *bona fide* treaty sufficient to ground federal action. It is widely recognized that "the scope for Commonwealth invasion of traditional state jurisdictional areas sanctioned by the Dam decision was enormous" (Galligan, Knopff, and Uhr 1990, p. 59), and the decision fueled attempts to introduce a constitutional bill of rights on the basis of the federal government's entry into the International Covenant on Civil and Political Rights. Although a comprehensive rights document lacked the needed political and popular backing, several rights protection acts have been enacted nationally by "piggybacking" on international obligations (including, besides race discrimination, sex and disability discrimination acts and more general human rights and equal opportunities legislation) (see Mathew 1995).

Internationalism has thus become a force for the nationalization of rights discourse and the basis for federal legislative action in areas traditionally outside of its jurisdiction. It has provided a justification for the centralization of legislative power to protect the individual, and has led to a readiness by Labor governments to enter international agreements knowing that their powers to implement are unimpeded constitutionally. These developments have been controversial, and the disagreements over the proper scope of the external affairs power "are virtually identical to the entrenched differences regarding human rights protection in Australia" (Tenbensel 1996, p. 11). International agreements are associated with an activist state, in addition to concerns about the centralization of power.

At the national level, these points have been taken up by the Liberal-National Coalition, which now governs federally. Thus, the relationship of rights, federalism, and centralization is a partisan political issue, as is international activism more generally. At the same time, political rather than legal constraints have ensured that there are some limits to the federal government's powers of treaty implementation. A policy of "cooperative federalism" in the 1990s led to a Standing Committee of senior officials to ensure cooperation between levels of government (Tenbensel 1996, p. 14). Labor governments "continued to seek the views of the States before ratifying international human rights agreements," although they made clear that unreasonable delays would not be tolerated (Charlesworth 1994, p. 43). The Liberal-National government, by contrast, has adopted new procedures that involve greater cooperation with state governments.

The debates over international treaty implementation and the desirability (or not) of a bill of rights are closely connected in terms of how they translate into partisan politics: "in the human rights debates, conservatives are content with the state of play and see no reason for substantial changes, [while] the situation is reversed in relation to the treaties debate" (Tenbensel 1996, p. 15). The two discourses are linked in the way in which an Australian national identity is increasingly conceived in more internationalist terms. For example, the absence of a bill of rights suggests, to some rights advocates, that "Australia has remained outside of the international mainstream," which is assumed to be a negative effect (p. 9). At the same time, international treaties in a range of areas are being entered into, providing Australia with international standing and, simultaneously, forcing it to measure up to international standards (from which it can then judge others).

For supporters of individual rights discourse, federalism is a constraint on the development of uniform citizenship defined by internationally recognized rights (Charlesworth 1994, p. 44). The rights of geographically based communities and those of the citizen—the latter of which are constructed as universal through the discourse of international human rights—are read, not only as in tension, but ultimately as irreconcilable. The federal government becomes the guardian of international standards, as a result of which the nation gains a stronger sense of (anti-isolationist) national identity and greater credibility internationally. Rights thereby are integral to the internationalization of Australia, which facilitates the construction of national identity (along with multiculturalism and republicanism). In the process, "geographically guaranteed autonomy" would come to be replaced by "individual autonomy" through rights, which would serve to protect against increasingly centralized political power (Sawer 1976, p. 152).

A more critical appraisal could be made of the attempt to constitute national identity through the implementation of international standards. While the floating of the currency was cited by the government of the day as a sign of national maturity, it also exemplified the way in which "the powers of the nation state are cut back to make way for an 'efficient' order of production and trade" in the conditions of globalization (Cochrane and Goodman 1992, p. 175). As a result, other tropes of nationhood—such as republicanism, rights, and multiculturalism—must be invoked to sustain national identity in the face of "a new and disciplining openness to the world" (Goodman 1992, p. 193).[5] In other words, while international agreements may secure a place on the international stage, the effects of economic globalization profoundly undermine governance by the nation state in more fundamental ways through telecommunications, capital flows, financial markets, free trade, etc.

Whether or not the "internationalisation of culture" (Cochrane and Goodman 1992, p. 176) represents an attempt to shore up the nation state in the face of the upheavals of economic globalization, Australian legal culture has not been immune from this process. Rather, discourses of international law, and particularly human rights, can be seen "seeping into" the domestic legal system at several sites, particularly in some judgments of the High Court of Australia.[6] For example, the High Court has been prepared to "find" certain limited fundamental rights protected within the Australian Constitution, despite the absence of a bill of rights, with the argument being that certain rights are "implied" in the Constitution.[7]

A primary source for the "discovery" of rights is international law. This reflects something of a departure from the traditional skepticism of rights. Today, the judiciary increasingly describes domestic law as "informed" by international and comparative rights jurisprudence. This is particularly apparent in the High Court's landmark judgment in *Mabo v. Queensland* (1992), where the Court squarely faced another central trajectory of Australian national identity: the historical treatment of Aboriginal people and the claims for reparation now framed in the language of land rights. Six of seven members of the Court were in agreement that "the common law of this country recognizes a form of native title which, in the cases where it has not been extinguished, reflects the entitlement of the indigenous inhabitants, in accordance with their laws or customs, to their traditional lands" (p. 15). According to Justice Brennan, "the common law does not necessarily conform with international law, but international law is a legitimate and important influence on the development of the common law, especially when international law declares the existence of universal human rights" (p. 42). Furthermore, "no case can command unquestioning adherence if the rule it expresses seriously offends the values of justice and human rights (especially equality before the law) which are aspirations of the contemporary Australian legal system" (p. 30). While international law historically was deployed to construct Australia as uninhabited prior to conquest, the situation now becomes reversed: "his argument thus establishes a link between the international law doctrine and corresponding common law fiction of uninhabited land, and then rejects the latter partly on the basis of the International Court's rejection of the former" (Patton 1996, p. 58).[8]

The decision in *Mabo,* along with other recent developments, suggests an ongoing process of national reimagination that challenges the notion of Australia as a customary community through the language of international human rights. It symbolizes a shift from the colonial conditions of a settler society to the postcolonial world, where the role of the state as guardian of a clearly delineated customary community with recognizable conditions of membership has become increasingly unsustainable (Povinelli 1994, p. 136).

While *Mabo* represents how the international order informs national legal culture, reaction to the judgment underscores how economic globalization disciplines that legal order. Among the international business community, the reaction to *Mabo* was apprehensive, with concerns that it threatened "socioeconomic progressivity," foreign investment, and the ability of Australia to maintain a "modern" economy (Povinelli 1994, p. 144). Criticism was also grounded in the language of states' rights, with a fear that the High Court (appointed by the federal executive branch) had gone too far. This perception has been further exacerbated by the High Court's subsequent decision in *Wik Peoples v. Queensland* (1996), in which a majority held that the granting of a pastoral lease in land by government to a non-Aboriginal does not necessarily extinguish all aspects of Aboriginal title to the property in issue. The negative reaction to this decision by business, government, and the public is unprecedented.

With this background in mind, I now turn to how rights claims around sexual acts and identities fit within this emerging conjunction of rights and national identity. In recent Australian history, these claims have proven a central site of contestation over internationalism, federalism, multiculturalism, individual rights, and "special" interests, reproducing the tension between customary and conventional accounts of community. Thus, homosexuality has become one of the registers through which competing notions of national identity are played out.

Rewriting the Sexual/National Narrative

As I have already suggested, prior to the late 1960s, Australian national identity was understood largely as a way of life centered on the suburban nuclear family. Sexual identity, gender roles, and the white immigration policy were closely bound up with this conception. In that context, it is hardly surprising that in the post–World War II era, when an Australian way of life based on democracy and consumerism was at its ideological zenith, homosexuality was constructed as "the greatest menace facing Australia," leading to intense police surveillance, harassment, and draconian law reform (Wotherspoon 1991, p. 58). Indeed, it *was* a threat to a national order founded on traditional gender roles and social conformity. The reaction also illustrated the international impact of McCarthyism, which was also felt in Britain and elsewhere.

That way of life came to be challenged more broadly by feminism, antiracist struggles, and the gay and lesbian movement in Australia. The latter began with the formation in 1970 of the Campaign Against Moral Persecution (CAMP) (Altman 1987, p. 77).[9] For gay (especially male) activism, law has been one of the central discourses in which an engagement with the state has occurred. A drive for the decriminalization of same-sex (generally male) sexual activity occurred over a long period across all of the states and territories: South Australia (1972), Australian Capital Territory (1976), Victoria (1980), Northern Territory (1983), New South Wales (1984), Western Australia (1989), and Queensland (1990) (Bull, Pinto, and Wilson 1992, p. 178). The fact that the state of Tasmania did not decriminalize male same-sex sexual activity until 1997 led to a major international law dispute, which I will examine shortly. Further, equal opportunity legislation has been widely amended to cover discrimination with respect to sexual activity or sexual preference (except in Western Australia and Tasmania) (Human Rights and Equal Opportunities Commission 1997, p. 6). The Commonwealth government has declared that sexual preference is a ground of discrimination for the purposes of the International Labor Organization's Discrimination (Employment and Occupation) Convention 1958 (p. 4), and it has created a statutory mechanism by which claims of employment discrimination can be considered by the Human Rights and Equal Opportunity Commission, although no enforceable remedies can be granted—another example of the federal use of the external affairs power (p. 6).

But such changes have not been wrought without resistance.

Widespread police harassment was a regular feature of gay life throughout the 1970s and 1980s and occurs in many parts of Australia to this day. Most famously, in July 1978, police attacked an activist rally in Sydney, leading to riots and arrests (Wotherspoon 1991, p. 59). Ironically, that event is the direct precursor to today's Mardi Gras festival in Sydney, which has assumed international standing as a celebration of lesbian and gay life (p. 60). The 1980s and 1990s have also seen the continuation of violence directed at lesbians and gays by the public at large (Kallen 1996, p. 212), and homophobic violence is an important site of lesbian and gay activism.[10]

Because Australia is a federal jurisdiction, activists have been forced to mobilize at both state and federal levels, and progress has come at different speeds across the country. Current areas of controversy include custody and parenting issues, superannuation benefits for lesbian and gay partners, social security and health care benefits, the legalization of same-sex relationships, equalizing the age of consent laws in some states, and access to donor insemination for lesbians, among others. The dominant discourse in which these claims have been framed is equality rights, and progress on many of these issues speaks to the resonance of that discourse in Australian society today.[11]

It is significant that a national culture so centrally informed by migration, journeys, and (increasingly) multiculturalism created a space for successful activist struggles around gay and lesbian immigration. This is a uniquely Australian example of activism undertaken by the Gay and Lesbian Immigration Task Force, which involved a close working relationship with a member of the federal cabinet, and is an issue that has a particular resonance in Australian society (see generally Chetcuti 1992, Hart 1992).[12] By negotiating with officials, activists managed to achieve a change in the interpretation of the immigration law as a matter of public policy and, subsequently, secured an alteration to the immigration regulations to allow the partner of a lesbian or gay Australian to immigrate on the basis of that relationship. The regulations now include a category of close and enduring relationships of "emotional interdependency" with an Australian national. When enacted, the provision created "hardly a bang or a whimper of public disapproval" (Chetcuti 1992, p. 179).

Others have noted that there is something specifically Australian about this outcome. Hart (1992), for example, suggests that it stems from a national identity as a "land of migrants" with an appreciation of the "tyranny of distance" (p. 121). Kallen (1996, p. 221) makes a similar point, arguing that the successful activist strategy "relates in large part to the geographical isolation of Australia from other, EuroWestern societies. What this means for the small gay and lesbian minority is that the supply of same-sex partners is very limited." Echoes can be heard in this description of the "White Australia" policy and the history of bringing young brides to Australia for the white, male settlers. The fact that the Task Force, when the policy originally turned on the exercise of ministerial discretion, ensured claimants had "lookalike heterosexual relationships" makes the analogy more compelling (Hart 1992, p. 131).

The policy's history has other resonances as well. If Australian national identity is characterized by the turn from the Anglo-American orbit to Asia, then it is not surprising that many of the relationships processed under the regulations involve the immigration of Southeast Asian men as partners of Australian nationals. Hart (1992) has documented these cases, and his findings underscore the colonial construction of race and sexuality. These relationships often replicate the "Asian marriages" of Western men and young, dependent Southeast Asian women and appear to reproduce the gendered Western/developing nation dyad. However, like relationships between nations, these emotional and sexual relationships can reveal a more complex dynamic. The immigration/relationship scenario constitutively creates a situation of dependence and power imbalance. In the end, Hart concludes that:

> the European colonization of Australia and the relationships in the Colony of gender and race have made attitudes to sexuality deeply ambiguous. Perhaps this provides a key to understanding why Australia, so notoriously male homophobic and contemporaneously homosocial *quietly* developed the arrangement for same-sex migration and then measured relationships against the traditional family form of a primary and dependent migrant pair. (p. 132)

The example also highlights a relationship between national identity and social movement activism by lesbians and gays. The way in which national identity is conceived in this case created the circumstances in which activism could achieve its goals. It was also initiated by a newly elected Labor government that was attempting to reimagine what "Australia" (and citizenship) signified.[13]

If, in the immigration example, national identity left space for activism to realize its objectives, the next section examines a case that has garnered enormous publicity both in Australia and worldwide in recent years where activists have had a much rockier road: the *Toonen* controversy.

When Legal Orders Collide

As I have argued, in recent years the relationship between federalism and rights in Australia has become controversial. The federal power to enter international treaties, and then to implement them, in an era of increasing importance for such agreements, has facilitated the centralization of power. By impacting upon state jurisdiction through the international sphere, the federal government has come to mediate directly between the local and the international. This process is exemplified by Australia's ratification of the International Covenant of Civil and Political Rights (ICCPR). Drafted by the United Nations Commission on Human Rights, this wide ranging document, which became operative in 1976, covers a variety of fundamental rights (life, liberty, freedom of conscience, speech, and privacy, among others) and political rights, including the right to equality before the law. As an international treaty, it binds those countries that have ratified it. One mechanism by which state compliance with the covenant can be ensured is the First Optional Protocol. When a country signs up to the Protocol, it recognizes the jurisdiction of the UN Human Rights Committee (HRC), made up of eighteen "experts" nominated by member countries of the ICCPR to hear "communications" from individuals within the state who allege that they are victims of a violation of an ICCPR right. Signatories are not required to ratify the Protocol, so compliance in fact is voluntary.

The Australian government ratified the ICCPR in 1980, and at that time included a reservation to the effect that it was a federal state and implementation would be a matter for the government jurisdictionally responsible in the particular case (Opeskin and Rothwell 1995, p. 47).[14] Subsequently, Australia signed up to the First Optional Protocol on September 25, 1991, after "protracted debate," and it came into force on December 25, 1991 (p. 48).

The communication procedure of the Protocol applies only to individuals who can demonstrate that they are "victims" of a violation (and therefore have the requisite standing before the HRC) and that they have exhausted all domestic remedies of redress before proceeding internationally (Morgan 1994a, p. 741). The opinions of the HRC are not directly legally enforceable. Rather, the role of the HRC is to publish its "views" regarding those communications that come before it. Because Australia has not directly incorporated the rights protected in the ICCPR in domestic law at either state or federal level, and because there is no entrenched bill of rights, signing up to the First Optional Protocol is a significant step "in enhancing human rights protection in Australia because it opened the possibility of individuals communicating directly with the UN Human Rights Committee with respect to alleged violations of the ICCPR" (Opeskin and Rothwell 1995, p. 49). There may well be increased scrutiny of Australia's laws internationally because there is no domestic, explicit rights framework within which individuals can first bring their claims (Alston 1994a, p. 5). That fact already has led to arguments that legal sovereignty has been turned over to unaccountable "foreigners" through the First Optional Protocol.

It took no time for the Protocol's potential for promoting legal and social change to become apparent. On December 25, 1991 (the day the Protocol came into effect), a communication was lodged with the HRC in the name of Nick Toonen, with the organizational backing of the Tasmanian Gay and Lesbian Rights Group (TGLRG). It alleged that laws in the state of Tasmania criminalizing some sexual activities "violate Australia's obligations under the ICCPR to respect the author's privacy and equality rights" (despite the fact that the laws had not been enforced since 1984) (Morgan 1994a, p. 742).[15]

The communication did not occur in a political vacuum. It was the product of several years of political mobilization in the domestic arena. A 1991 attempt by the then state Labor government to decriminalize same-sex sexual acts failed to pass the upper house of the Tasmanian legislature. A subsequent change of government effectively foreclosed the possibility of successful lobbying at state level. Thus, accession to the First Optional Protocol opened a new avenue of activism, using the language and institutions of international human rights, which potentially could force the Commonwealth government to take action pursuant to its external affairs power under the Constitution and its legal obligation under the Protocol. This is precisely what happened.[16]

In the communication, the arguments made by Toonen turned on privacy and equality rights. The privacy arguments were based on article 17 of the ICCPR, read in conjunction with article 2(1).[17] The equality arguments were grounded in article 26.[18] The communication argued that these rights were violated in various ways. As for privacy, the primary argument was that the laws permit "the police to enter a household on the suspicion that two consenting adult homosexual men may be committing a criminal offence" (reproduced in Aldous 1995, p. 8). Such an action is an arbitrary violation of the right. Further, the communication alleged that the laws violated Toonen's right to equal protection and freedom from discrimination, in so far as the "Tasmanian Criminal Code does not outlaw any form of homosexual activity between consenting homosexual women in private and only some forms of consenting heterosexual activity between adult men and women in private" (p. 8).[19] Men thus are the primary focus of concern. An attempt was then made to link the laws' existence with acts of discrimination more broadly, including private violence inflicted on gays. The argument was that the laws contributed to Toonen's low self-image, alienation, vilification, denial of HIV/AIDS prevention information, stigma, police harassment, and loss of employment (Morgan 1993, p. 281). The submissions mentioned that "Australia is a pluralistic and multi-cultural society whose citizens have different and at times conflicting moral codes" and, in view of this fact, that the criminal laws should avoid moral judgments (Joseph 1994, p. 397). The submissions thus argued that the threat of enforcement violated the author's right, as well as that the continued presence of the laws impacted on public and private actors by fueling "discrimination and harassment of, and violence against, the homosexual community of Tasmania" (*Toonen* 1994).

The communication to the HRC faced two hurdles: admissibility and the merits of the case. The admissibility issue demanded Toonen establish that he was a "victim" of the alleged breach, despite the fact that he was never prosecuted under the law. The HRC, in this regard, was satisfied that "the author had made reasonable efforts to demonstrate that the threat of enforcement and the pervasive impact of the continued existence of these provisions on administrative practices and public opinion had affected him and continued to affect him" (*Toonen* 1994). He also had to establish that domestic remedies were exhausted, not a serious obstacle given the absence of a remedy in domestic law for the violation of an international human right. The admissibility issue was not argued by the "state party" (the Commonwealth government) despite a request to do so by Tasmania, the first indication in this case that the Australian government would not act simply as a conduit for the state directly concerned (Morgan 1994a, p. 743).

As for the merits of the dispute, here again the state party was the Commonwealth government, rather than the Tasmanian state, and the government did not actively contest Toonen's submissions (Morgan 1994a, p. 744). Instead, it conceded that consensual sexual activity in private falls within the scope of article 17 and requested guidance from the HRC on whether it was also a breach of equality rights. While Australia made clear its view that "domestic social mores may be relevant to the reasonableness of an interference with privacy," in the Australian context "there is now a general Australian acceptance that no individual should be disadvantaged on the basis of his or her sexual orientation" (*Toonen* 1994). In the case of the Tasmanian laws, furthermore, "their impact is to distinguish an identifiable class of individuals and to prohibit certain of their acts. Such laws thus are clearly understood by the community as being directed at male homosexuals as a group" (*Toonen* 1994). The government rejected Tasmania's arguments that the laws were justifiable on public health and moral grounds.

The HRC's eventual result was hardly surprising. The Commonwealth submissions largely accepted Toonen's complaint, although the Tasmanian government's submissions were sent to the HRC. But the Tasmanian government had no independent standing to make its case, highlighting the inability of international bodies to recognize the legislative realities of a federal system. The

Commonwealth attorney general at the time, Michael Lavarch, responsible for the government's handling of the issue, in retrospect described the process to me as one in which:

> internationally you have to speak with one voice, and sort out within your political system how you arrive at that position. The Tasmanian government's views were taken into account in crafting the material that went to the Committee but it's the prerogative of the Commonwealth as to how the case . . . is operated. (Lavarch 1997)

The HRC's process and qualifications would prove a central area of attack for critics of the decision domestically, a point to which I will return.

The HRC accepted Toonen's arguments on privacy grounds. It recognized that consensual sexual activity in private is included within article 17 and that "Mr. Toonen is actually and currently affected by the continued existence of the Tasmanian laws," even if unenforced (*Toonen* 1994). The HRC's focus here was on the *potential* for criminal prosecution, which interfered with the privacy right. On whether such an interference was arbitrary, the HRC rejected Tasmania's two claimed justifications: HIV prevention and morality. As for the latter, the HRC pointed to the fact that the provisions were not enforced actively as relevant to whether the law is essential for the protection of morality (*Toonen* 1994). This argument is somewhat disingenuous, given that much of the author's argument was grounded in the alleged wider, social consequences of the law: "if, as the Committee accepted, the existence of the sections has a 'pervasive impact' on 'administrative practices and public opinion,' then the fact that they are not enforced would not necessarily mean that they are 'not deemed essential for the protection of morals in Tasmania'" (A. Twomey 1994, p. 11). Given the HRC's finding that the law constituted an arbitrary interference with the right in article 17, it did not deal with the question of whether sexual orientation constitutes an "other status" for the purposes of equality rights law. But, in an offhand and potentially significant comment, the HRC baldly stated that "the reference to 'sex' in articles 2, paragraph 1, and 26 is to be taken as including sexual orientation" (*Toonen* 1994).[20]

The decision in *Toonen* perfectly underscores the tension between federalism and the discourse of international human rights.

Although the law in issue was within the constitutional jurisdiction of the Tasmanian government, which was ready to defend it before the HRC, it was the Commonwealth government that has sole standing internationally, and the Commonwealth government was not prepared either to defend the law or to simply pass along Tasmania's arguments without making its own views known. An Australian national consensus on the decriminalization issue was presented (with Tasmania as the holdout) to further the claim that the law could not be justified on a moral basis. Moreover, Toonen argued that Australia's international interventions in favor of the recognition of sexual orientation in international human rights law, including its call "for the proscription, at the international level, of discrimination on the grounds of sexual preference," were relevant (*Toonen* 1994). In response, it might be argued that such a national culture of acceptance is irrelevant to the Tasmanian law. The criminal law is within the jurisdiction of the states, presumably, because it was deemed more appropriate that the criminal law reflect the values of localism, rather than a national consensus.

To argue that Tasmania is culturally "different" from Australia as a whole would be a variant on the "cultural relativism" argument that seems to be implicit in the opinion. As the TGLRG's legal advisor noted prior to the HRC's opinion, the aim was "to convince the Committee that the laws cannot be justified as 'reasonable' in light of prevalent community attitudes" (Morgan 1993, p. 288), hence the focus on Australian values as a whole and Australia's position in the international arena. TGLRG recognized strategically that:

> it will be impossible for the Human Rights Committee to find any international consensus in favour of decriminalisation and in favour of increased protection for gay men and lesbians. If anything, the international consensus points in the opposite direction. . . . Much will depend upon the willingness of the Committee to adopt a "cultural relativity" attitude to the rights contained in the Covenant [and judge] in light of prevailing Australian attitudes. (p. 289)

The deployment of a discourse of cultural relativism, though, is extremely problematic. While it "works" in this case, because of an illiberal law that can be interpreted as a reactionary holdover in a liberal, Western nation state (and therefore a violation of a right), the scope of rights in relation to sexual orientation might become inversely correlated to the acceptance of a lesbian or gay identity in the national culture. Following this logic, there would be no internationally recognized privacy rights to same-sex sexual activity where "cultural attitudes are indisputably hostile to homosexuals" (Joseph 1994, p. 405).

The cultural relativism approach draws on the reasoning of the European Court of Human Rights, particularly its judgment in *Dudgeon v. U.K.* (1981) that criminalization of homosexual acts in Northern Ireland was contrary to the European Convention.[21] Despite finding against the state, the Court in *Dudgeon* recognized that "where there are disparate cultural communities residing within the same State, it may well be that different requirements, both moral and social, will face the governing authorities" (p. 166). Although the HRC does not pursue this line of argument in *Toonen*, the communication attempts to answer any argument based on the cultural "peculiarity" of Tasmania. Toonen claimed that support for decriminalization was widespread in Tasmania, and included a list of associations and groups that endorsed the principle (*Toonen* 1994). In this way, the cultural context can be portrayed as that of a state government unwilling to respond either to claims grounded in the language of rights or to popular will. Indeed, the 1991 legislative attempt at decriminalization stalled because of an upper house of Parliament that did not respond to the actions of a "responsible government" (Tenbensel 1996, p. 19). Thus, an argument grounded in the cultural relativism of Tasmania was difficult to mount on the facts of the case. Theoretically, though, it underscores the tension between federalism and rights as they are enunciated in the international arena.

The HRC concluded that Toonen was entitled to a remedy and "in the opinion of the Committee, an effective remedy would be the repeal" of the laws (*Toonen* 1994). Having signed up to the First Optional Protocol, it was *Australia* that was obliged to provide a remedy for a *state* law that infringed a right.[22] The wider implications, in terms of the federal system, are clear:

> Most alleged violations of the ICCPR are likely to be the result of actions taken by, or laws existing in, the various Australian States and Territories. Yet it is the Commonwealth government which has the re-

sponsibility of submitting Australia's position in relation to communications, and the Commonwealth government which will have the responsibility of acting in response to the views the Committee takes. (Morgan 1993, p. 289)

Those states found in violation of the ICCPR are given a three-month period to respond to the HRC's findings (Opeskin and Rothwell 1995, p. 51). In this case, that time involved discussions between the Commonwealth and Tasmanian governments. The Commonwealth indicated that legislation would be brought forward in compliance with its international obligations, although action by the Tasmanian government was to be preferred (p. 52). On April 6, 1994, the Tasmanian government announced that it would not change its position (or its laws) (Joseph 1994, p. 403). In the words of the Tasmanian attorney general, "this was a decision by a faceless group of people telling the Tasmanian Parliament how it should legislate for its citizens. It doesn't hold any water for us" (p. 402). The tension between federalism and rights had reached its logical culmination.

Nationalizing Privacy

This dispute might have appeared to provide an ideal opportunity for (generally) conservative opponents of federal intervention to make political capital, deploying the language of national sovereignty, responsible government, states' rights, localism, democracy, and perhaps even the merits of the law. As the then attorney general described the situation, some state governments "make an artform of bashing Canberra [the seat of the Commonwealth government] for political consumption. In that sense, the issue didn't really matter. . . . It wasn't a human rights issue, but a bit of political game playing" for advocates of states' rights (Lavarch 1997). In the period following the HRC opinion, those discourses were taken up by conservative states, federal opposition politicians, citizens groups, and the Tasmanian state (see generally Tenbensel 1996). Most strongly, the Tasmanian government combined arguments grounded in states' rights and national sovereignty, asserting that:

"a democratically elected Parliament should not have its decisions vetoed by a remote UN body" and expressed concern about the "ability

of an Australian government to govern without international bodies in-
truding into areas of domestic law that are properly the jurisdiction of
either the State or the Commonwealth." (p. 17)

Given that opposition to federal intervention could be articulated to so many related concerns—national sovereignty, states'
rights, responsible government and due process (in terms of HRC
procedures), in addition to the substance of the law—the federal government had no easy task in negotiating what might have
become a political minefield. After a four-month period, during
which consultative attempts with Tasmania failed, the government
introduced the *Human Rights (Sexual Conduct) Act 1994.* The political shrewdness of the legislation is demonstrated by the fact that
the federal opposition chose not to oppose the bill, although some
members of Parliament defied that decision (Tenbensel 1996, p. 16).
This division within the opposition benches proved "a very nice
side benefit" for the government (Lavarch 1997), although some
opposition members sought to deploy it against the attorney general, claiming that he was playing politics with rights. The same
argument would be made by TGLRG. The Act is a minimalist one
that sought to meet, at least in a formal sense, Australia's obligations under the First Optional Protocol.[23] At the same time, it cau-
tiously avoided inflaming states' rights discourse because it did not
directly override the Tasmanian law. This was a deliberate strategy
on the part of the attorney general, who "took a political judgment"
on the issue. As he described in our conversation, "having to secure passage through the Senate where we didn't have control, and
to win the political argument and to paint the opposition of Tasmania and to an extent the federal Coalition and to outmanoeuver
them . . . it was smarter in my view to go down the privacy path"
(Lavarch 1997). As a consequence, there seems no doubt as to the
constitutionality of the law in federalism terms, especially given
how closely it mirrors the HRC opinion, and in light of previous
jurisprudence on the breadth of the external affairs power of the
Commonwealth government. By creating a universally applicable
but limited *right,* few would be willing to contest the bill on its
merits. In walking this fine line, a high level of political consensus
was realized, and the law came into effect on December 19, 1994.

The strict legal impact of the federal legislation on the Tasmanian law was widely assumed to be as follows:

> Applying general constitutional principles, the relevant sections in
> the *Criminal Code* are invalid to the extent of the inconsistency with the
> Commonwealth Act. Invalidity in this context does not mean that the
> offending sections of the Tasmanian Code cease to exist; rather they are
> simply rendered *inoperative* to the extent of the inconsistency. Thus, the
> sections dealing with "unnatural sexual intercourse" and "acts of gross
> indecency" would still apply to sexual conduct between males which
> (i) occurs without consent; or (ii) involves parties under the age of
> 18 years; or (iii) does not occur in private. (Bronitt 1995a, p. 225)[24]

The law was widely viewed as a shrewd political move by the Labor government, in large measure because it was couched in the general language of a right to sexual privacy for *all* Australian adults no matter what sexual orientation. This made the right-of-center opposition's position more difficult, given its commitments to the liberal principle of individual freedom from the state and privacy rights in particular. The government also avoided a political confrontation with the mainland states (for those states abandoned their opposition to federal government intervention when the bill was introduced) in a period immediately preceding a general election (which Labor ultimately would lose anyway).

The government did, however, face a vociferous and wide ranging debate in Parliament when it introduced the legislation, despite the opposition's decision not to officially oppose it. The attorney general sought to frame the issue so as to avoid the claim that national sovereignty was undermined by the Act. Instead, he argued that the Act was central to the national identity of Australians: "these principles are central now to our national identity and international reputation. . . . These basic rights are universal and cannot be limited by national or state boundaries. They are the birthright of every human being and of all Australians" [House of Representatives 1994 (October 12), p. 1775]. Rather than undermining sovereignty, the legislation demonstrated the maturity of the Australian nation state: "it displays our confidence in our capacity to meet the same standards which Australia contends internationally should be met by all nations" (p. 1777). Federalism concerns were met by the assertion that "only individuals and not governments enjoy rights. Governments exist to protect rights, not to enjoy them at the expense of the individual" (p. 1777).

This theme of the compatibility of internationalism with sovereignty was taken up by other supporters of the legislation. One government member waxed eloquently on the connections between the national identity and the legislation: "we are now a much more inclusive society, willing to take its place in the world . . . not so much frightened by distance and isolation but willing to break down the barriers to Australia's place in the international community" [House of Representatives 1994 (October 12), p. 1831, Mr. Latham]; "with advances in communications, transport and trade Australia must accept its role in the international community. . . . The whole thrust of our national policy is to integrate Australia's economy and social fabric with the international community. . . . Those values are reflected in the International Covenant on Civil and Political Rights" (p. 1833). Loyalty to Australia, another member argued, "will not be superseded by our growing recognition that we are members of an international community" (p. 1797, Ms. Worth).[25]

The way in which the legislation was drafted forced the Liberal-National Coalition to describe the Act as underlining a tension between two principles: privacy and "the right to the proper sharing of powers between the Commonwealth and the states" [House of Representatives 1994 (October 12), p. 1780, Mr. Ruddock]. Faced with that choice, they officially chose not to oppose the legislation. However, many members of Parliament criticized it on a variety of grounds. The national sovereignty argument was one of them. Supporters' claims that the Act reflected Australia's maturity as a nation were met by arguments that the process amounted to a transfer of sovereignty to a United Nations committee. Thus, opponents argued that it was ironic for the Labor government to have abolished appeals from Australian courts to the Judicial Committee of the Privy Council in the United Kingdom in 1975, but now be prepared to transfer sovereignty to the UN [House of Representatives 1994 (October 13), p. 1960, Mr. Truss].[26] Furthermore, the Labor government's espousal of republicanism led to similar arguments: "I find it absurd that a government which professes horror at the place of the

Australian Crown in the Australian Constitution should now be placing us under the influence of the United Nations Human Rights Committee" (p. 1982, Mr. Abbott). This argument was combined with vociferous criticism of the credentials of the HRC:

> Let us have a look at this particular UN Committee. It has 18 people on it from different parts of the world. Five of these 18 countries have laws against homosexuality similar to those of Tasmania. Not only that, four of those countries have not even signed the first optional protocol. Its members deign to comment about the rights of people in other parts of the world when in their own countries they have done nothing about it at all. [House of Representatives 1994 (October 12), p. 1841, Mr. Miles]

These interventions were closely bound up with claims about an Australian national identity, and specifically, the democratic and accountable character of Australian institutions in which due process was always respected. By contrast, the HRC was painted as a body that met in secret, where evidence was not subject to cross-examination, rules of procedural fairness and natural justice were ignored, and members were little more than "faceless diplomats" [House of Representatives 1994 (October 13), p. 1931, Mr. Scott] and "unelected Third World delegates" whose beliefs "are in line with contemporary left wing ideology" (p. 1971, Mr. McArthur).[27] The explicit (and racially based) contrast here is to the rights-respecting and procedurally-fair Australian institutions. The claim that power is being turned over to the HRC is interpreted as a direct threat not only to national sovereignty, but to the traditional protections offered the individual under the Australian constitutional framework (see Galligan 1994, p. 66). This position is grounded in the notion of responsible government as foundational to the protection of rights. Resort to the HRC undermines that principle: "Australia's parliaments and courts are ultimately accountable to the Australian people. These institutions also have a knowledge of Australia's law, history and other institutional arrangements that an international agency could never hope to acquire" [House of Representatives 1994 (October 12), p. 1849, Mr. Rocher].

This argument, however, despite some intuitive appeal, was difficult to sustain. Parliamentary supremacy was not abandoned, for ultimately it is up to the Commonwealth Parliament to determine how it will respond to the views of the HRC, and whether it should respond at all. In that respect one senator asked the astute question, "Can the government pick and choose which decisions or findings to accept, and what will be the reaction of individuals if the government chooses or tries to choose not to accept a decision?" [Senate 1994 (December 8), p. 4336, Senator Kemp]. Thus, arguments grounded in national sovereignty have some currency to the extent that they are formulated in terms of how political realities may make it difficult for the government to ignore a decision of the HRC in the future. But critics of the government seemed unable to move beyond a narrow conception of legal sovereignty, where their position was weak, to the impact of internationalization on *political* sovereignty more broadly.

On the other hand, government members sought to broaden the debate, placing this case in the context of an increasingly globalized political reality. Economic agreements, the attorney general claimed, also required the implementation of international obligations domestically, and had a far greater impact on the Australian nation [House of Representatives 1994 (October 19), p. 2283, Mr. Lavarch]. As Burmester (1995, p. 129) argues:

> The impact on Australian freedom to formulate economic policy is already much more significant as a result of international agreements like the General Agreement on Tariffs and Trade (GATT) and the Organisation for Economic Co-operation and Development (OECD) than any limitations applicable in other areas of government policy.

As a consequence, the discourse of sovereignty seems increasingly archaic. Only one opposition member was prepared to consider sovereignty more widely, and he expressed a broad-based isolationism:

> It seems now that Australians do not really run Australia. In the field of trade, GATT controls all of our trade decisions. . . . In the field of the economy, the international money changers seem to have taken over. They told us to deregulate the banks. . . . in the area of social mores, international conventions are once again telling us how we should run our country. [House of Representatives 1994 (October 13), p. 1973, Mr. Katter] [28]

But this brand of isolationism lacked the political currency to achieve any sort of predominance. Rather, arguments grounded in national sovereignty were marginalized.

In contrast, federalism concerns were more central to the claims of opposition members, with the primary argument being that the Commonwealth's ability to enter into and implement treaties was damaging the jurisdictional boundaries of federalism. This position had a primary role in the debates and was articulated to a critique of the alleged desire of the Labor government for a more centralized state. The external affairs power, through which treaties can be implemented federally, was "undermining the system of checks and balances that the original division of powers between the states and Commonwealth was supposed to guarantee" [House of Representatives 1994 (October 12), p. 1846, Mr. Rocher]. Abolition of the states was described as the ultimate goal of the government, which would be realized incrementally through the implementation of international agreements (p. 1846, Mr. Rocher). The constitutional basis of Australia was jeopardized by the federal government's approach to treaty implementation.

This defense of states' rights was framed, first, in a discourse of responsible government. Critics argued that the essence of a federal system was that an elected legislature is entitled to make laws within "the natural province of state administrations" [House of Representatives 1994 (October 13), p. 1931, Mr. Scott]. The forces of internationalization, according to this view, cannot be allowed to undermine the division of powers. Second, the values of a federal system were stressed and the argument made that individual rights were best protected through responsible government attuned to local conditions and social mores: "the fact is that our liberties and democratic system are best protected when the commitment to our federal system is strong" [House of Representatives 1994 (October 12), p. 1848, Mr. Rocher]; "centralised, interfering, impersonal governments which go beyond their constitutional authority will never provide individual liberties" [House of Representatives 1994 (October 13), p. 1969, Mr. McArthur]. This argument ignores what the *Toonen* dispute evidences, namely, that "those who are members of minorities or relatively powerless groups in our society cannot hope to have full input into the legislative process" (Mathew 1995, p. 187).[29]

The meaningfulness of states as geographically based communities possessing rights was cited by some speakers as a central feature of national identity, one that was being eroded by a Labor government more responsive to "minority pressure groups" than the legitimate aspirations of states to develop the criminal law so as to respond to local values [House of Representatives 1994 (October 12), p. 1850, Mr. Rocher].[30] In this way, a defense of Tasmania's right to legislate was transformed into the defense of a minority group—Tasmanians—whose rights were being trampled on by a government committed to protecting (other) minorities: "this government is now using the external affairs power based on a UN treaty to override and destroy the law based upon the values of the Tasmanian people, which they have every right to hold and every right to enact laws based upon" [Senate 1994 (December 8), p. 4327, Senator Minchin]. Similarly, another speaker analogized the policy of multiculturalism to a defense of states' rights: "we celebrate and we promote the diversity of multiculturalism . . . yet we would have our states a pale reflection of each other. The states, dating back from between 110 and 206 years, have also had rich diversities and these also need to be respected and celebrated" [House of Representatives 1994 (October 13), p. 1985, Mr. Neville]. One member likened Tasmania's right to legislate to the "self-determination" of a people (p. 1989, Mr. Filing). In this way, the defense of states' rights becomes more complex, encompassing a reverence for responsible government, with claims about the responsiveness of local government to individual rights, the meaningfulness of states as signifying diverse rights holding communities, and the importance of maintaining the constitutional structure devised by the "founding fathers."

The defense of states' rights never realized its full potential, however, in part because the federal legislation was not an explicit attack on Tasmania. Instead, because it was framed as a general right to sexual privacy, it was argued that universal human rights transcended the distribution of powers: "we are dealing here with a fundamental human right in an area in which all Australians should be equal before the law, no matter where they live" [Senate 1994

(December 8), p. 4311, Senator Spindler]. The tenuousness of a discourse of states' rights, in the context of a "human" rights issue, meant that there was limited support for the idea of human rights as being relative between states.[31] Rather, the more widely accepted view in Parliament was that rights are uniform across the nation (and, in that sense, rights are an emerging, developing, and unfolding component of the national identity). The attorney general could point to the fact that the external affairs power is also central to the original constitutional structure, and the Act was no departure from the founding compact [House of Representatives 1994 (October 19), p. 2282].

The factual background to the HRC opinion made claims about responsible government at state level difficult to sustain. The then Labor government of Tasmania did attempt to repeal the sex laws in 1991, only to be halted by the upper house of the Tasmanian Parliament. Thus, it was the *failure* of responsible government, due to the antidemocratic element of that Parliament, that prevented the vindication of rights through the democratic process (see Tenbensel 1996, p. 19).[32] Arguments against federal intervention, grounded in the accountability of democratically elected state legislatures, faced a political history that undermined their very claims. That history problematized the argument that those legislatures provide the best possible protection for individual rights. The case demonstrated instead how the intervention of outsiders was necessary to promote legal change (p. 20) and provided evidence for supporters of a bill of rights as to why a national "mediating" rights discourse was desirable between the international and the local (see Alston 1994a, p. 11). All of these arguments helped undermine mainland opposition to the HRC opinion.

Given the focus on national sovereignty and states' rights, there was relatively little space in the debates for a consideration of the merits of the Tasmanian legislation. The discussion that did occur focused primarily on the educational and symbolic value of law. Members on all sides agreed that this was primarily what was at stake in the debate, and differences centered on the appropriateness of a state government deploying the law to this symbolic effect. Opponents of federal legislation argued that the Tasmanian laws "illustrate the values and concepts that are important for a society" [House of Representatives 1994 (October 12), p. 1840, Mr. Miles]. Senator Watson from Tasmania went further in elaborating on how demands for federal intervention were the thin end of the (gay rights) wedge:

> Law has educative, as well as preventive roles which set out the standards of acceptable behaviour within a community. In Tasmania, there is a considerable body of community concern that, because their sexual behaviour is illegal, militant homosexuals are hampered in the achievement of their far wider social, legal and educational agenda. [Senate 1994 (December 8), p. 4326, Senator Watson]

For TGLRG and for some supporters of federal intervention, this was precisely the reasoning that forms the basis of their arguments. As Minister of Justice Kerr explained, "laws do have an educative effect. They tell homosexual men in Tasmania that they are criminals. They tell the Tasmanian community that homosexuals are second-class citizens" [House of Representatives 1994 (October 19), p. 2276, Mr. Kerr]. One senator representing the Green Party went further, taking up TGLRG's argument that sodomy laws "lend support to people who continue to discriminate against, physically assault and vilify lesbians and gay men . . . until we reform our laws, we cannot absolve ourselves of responsibility for this sort of violence" [Senate 1994 (December 8), p. 4330, Senator Chamarette]. Members on both sides thereby agreed on law's powerful symbolic and educational role, and they basically concurred on the type of message that these laws send out. The disagreement turned on the *right* of a state community to deploy that particular message versus the prerogative of the federal government to curtail it on the basis of an individual *right*. In this regard, an analogy was drawn by one senator to the federal government's racial hatred bill, "which introduces criminal sanctions on the quite explicit basis of their educative effect" (p. 4328, Senator Minchin). Yet this senator opposed federal intervention because it was within a legislature's power to deploy law in this way: "the Tasmanian parliament, based on its sovereignty and the wishes of the Tasmanian people . . . chooses to have laws based on the educative effects in relation to sexual practices" (pp. 4328–4329). This reasoning begs the question of what *type* of education is reasonable for the state to propagate, which was the pivotal point of division.

Finally, in framing the legislation in the language of a general right of sexual privacy—equally applicable to all Australians—there was very little space for a discussion of homosexuality and the material effects of sex laws on individuals. Supporters of federal intervention cited the deleterious impact of the laws on HIV prevention programs [see, e.g., House of Representatives 1994 (October 13), p. 1951, Mr. Griffin], while opponents referred to the low rate of HIV in Tasmania (p. 1959, Mr. Truss) (a statistic that supporters dismissed on the basis that individuals were less likely to be tested there because of the laws). As for sexuality, both sides for the most part avoided any discussion. Opponents in general sought to distance themselves from the substance of the legislation, focusing instead on states' rights and national sovereignty. Government members could support the legislation as applicable to the (heterosexual) marital bedroom as equally as anywhere else. Those few supporters who did mention homosexuality deployed a discourse of biology. For them, the injustice of Tasmania's laws turned on "genetic" origins—how "homosexuality is not a lifestyle choice but an orientation which for many is impossible to change" [Senate 1994 (December 8), p. 4322, Senator Woodley]—and, far more interestingly, how "the bottom line is that genetically, biologically, we are all bisexual. I will not go into the fascinating embryonic details of the matter" [House of Representatives 1994 (October 13), p. 1943, Ms. Henzell]. As a political strategy, the government's approach was to avoid the construction of the legislation as a "special" right for gays, so it is hardly surprising that little room was left in the debate for an explicit consideration of sexual identity, beyond many supporters' claims that they were not condoning homosexuality in their support of the bill. In that sense, the government's strategy achieved its political aim, but it undermined the effectiveness of the parliamentary debate as an opportunity for any consideration of law reform to be a site of *positive* social transformation.

Not surprisingly, TGLRG was unimpressed with the Act. As its legal advisor described, the federal legislation was "practically and ideologically flawed" and "fails to comply with Australia's international obligations to protect human rights" (Morgan 1994b, p. 409), in part because it provides "no remedy for the violation of rights" (p. 411). That is, TGLRG sought a more proactive reaction from the federal government, namely, a law stating that homosexual sex would not be subject to criminal penalty by the states. In this way, it would have been *explicit* that the Tasmanian laws were inoperative, thereby not requiring a court ruling on whether Tasmania's laws were an arbitrary interference with a right to sexual privacy. For TGLRG, the weakness in the Act was that while it would provide a defense to a criminal charge, *unless* someone was criminally charged (an unlikely occurrence) the Tasmanian laws would remain on the books unchallengeable. This is important because TGLRG's central argument was that the "mere existence" of such laws "amounts to a continuing breach of human (gay and lesbian) rights" (p. 412).

In that sense, the federal law did not meet TGLRG's central claims, which seemed to be accepted by the HRC:

> The issue is not whether gay men are prosecuted for having sex in their bedrooms. The issue is the clearly inferior status these laws place on gay and lesbian Tasmanians. The Tasmanian Government and individuals within Tasmania regularly cite that "homosexuals" are "criminals" to justify discriminatory practices. (Morgan 1994b, p. 412)

Numerous examples of this "indirect" effect of criminalization have been documented. They include police harassment, intimidation, the banning of a TGLRG stall from a market in the Tasmanian capital Hobart on the basis that it was "promoting an illegal lifestyle," the refusal to enact antidiscrimination laws, the refusal of permission to screen a number of films at festivals, and a ban on any reference to homosexuality in Tasmanian schools except for the distribution of a pamphlet by an anti-gay group encouraging students to "develop fulfilling heterosexual lives" (Croome 1995, p. 283).

This list of public policy examples suggests several things. First, it raises the question of the impact the simple invalidation of sex laws will have on Tasmania. As TGLRG campaign coordinator Croome (1995, p. 284) recognized, "a High Court invalidation of Tasmania's anti-gay laws will not eliminate homophobia, but it will force conservative regimes to find other less convenient camouflages for their hatreds." Whether alternative justifications would be forthcoming is open to speculation, but TGLRG's view was that the existence of the law largely foreclosed both positive representations of lesbians and gays in the public sphere and the possibility of progressive social change. Second, the list of homophobic policy decisions suggests that arguments grounded in the "cultural relativism" of Tasmania might actually have some validity. TGLRG's arguments *do* make Tasmania appear a radically different society from the rest of Australia, one in which tolerance, pluralism, multiculturalism, and a liberal "consensus" seem not to exist. Pushed to its limits, the argument might suggest that this is a case where there is no single national standard on the acceptability of certain sexual acts. Rather, as one member of Parliament claimed, these laws "reflect the social mores and traditions of that state" [House of Representatives 1994 (October 13), p. 1986, Mr. Neville]. More generally, this line of argument underscores a difficulty that may be faced in making gay rights arguments in international human rights discourse. While the documentation of an anti-gay animus in the state may be necessary to fully elaborate the impugned impact of the laws, in the process the claimant paints a picture of a culture in which the tolerance of homosexuality is culturally foreign. As a consequence, the cultural relativist argument can be invoked by the state party to make the claim that no internationally recognized right exists in the specific national culture. What made the *Toonen* case unique was that the state party was not prepared to challenge the arguments put forward in this (or any other) respect.

Another problem highlighted by TGLRG is the reification of the public/private distinction in the *Human Rights (Sexual Conduct) Act 1994*. As its legal advisor Morgan (1994b, p. 413) explained:

> The words emphasised clearly give clause 4 a geographical focus. Sexual conduct *in a private place* is protected. This mischaracterises the right to privacy set out in Article 17. Article 17 protects private choice rather than private place, and the UN Committee's jurisprudence makes this clear . . . the geographical focus of clause 4, its emphasis on gay and lesbian rights only in a "private place," could be analogised to a statement that our rights will only be protected if we "stay in our closets." . . . This reading is reinforced by the fact that neither the Bill nor the explanatory memoranda ever mention the words "gay" or "lesbian." [33]

While the discourse of privacy—which was deployed by TGLRG in its arguments before the HRC—was taken up in the federal law, it was now within the context of private places, rather than private choices. From TGLRG's perspective, that private space was too constricted.

Globalization, Localism, and the Politics of Rights and Identities

Given TGLRG's argument that the law had an impact on Tasmanian gays and lesbians beyond the potential of criminal prosecution, their negative response to the federal bill was predictable. But TGLRG's legal advisor was also well aware of the limitations of rights discourse (see Morgan 1994a). As Morgan has argued, international human rights law "masks" the connections between state institutions and abuses of rights by "private" actors, and the rhetoric of privacy often allows courts and tribunals to "maintain and reinforce their stories about the *dangerousness* of homosex" even when recognizing the existence of rights (p. 753). Morgan posits that the usefulness of rights discourse is in its ability to act as a "site of cultural intervention" (p. 741), by bringing sexuality into the public sphere and out of the private: "it is not the outcome of law reform that is of sole (or even primary) importance. The importance of law reform lies in its power as a site at which lesbians and gays can intervene in popular cultural discourses and dispute institutional discourses about homosex" (p. 756; see also Walker 1994). In that sense, this rights strategy was reasonably successful, given how the Tasmanian government was isolated in its defense of the merits of the law and ultimately repealed the law in the face of a High Court challenge.[34] However, the parliamentary debates left *relatively* little room for a discussion of lesbian and gay sexualities in affirming terms, although there were certainly some instances of that. But, then again, defenders of states' rights generally avoided arguing the merits of the Tasmanian law (and often came out against the substance of the law). In addition, the HRC opinion, as it was interpreted by some Australians, may have acted as a "type of legitimation vehicle" for gays and lesbians (Morgan 1994a, p. 750).

But TGLRG's disappointment with the federal government's response to the HRC opinion, which Morgan (1994b, p. 413) argued "hardly amounts to taking gay and lesbian rights seriously," suggests another conception of rights, one in which they are recognized as something *more* than a tool for cultural intervention.[35] It could be argued that TGLRG held a legalistic conception of rights, to the extent that it advocated the separation of law and politics— that lesbian and gay rights should be protected through law unsullied by the "vagaries of the political process" (Charlesworth 1994, p. 47). Rights, in this interpretation, must somehow be "beyond politics" to be taken "seriously." But, conversely, the reason TGLRG fought so hard for a more direct federal override of the Tasmanian law was that it was a goal which it thought was realizable within the cut and thrust of the political process (Morgan 1997).

Australian rights discourse has been described by Charlesworth (1994, p. 48) as grounded in a faith in law which is shared by "pro-rights" and "anti-rights" actors alike. For rights supporters, individual rights should be above and beyond the political process and the inevitable compromises that are the outcome of political struggle. For their opponents, law and politics are assumed to be separate, and the concern is that constitutional rights will lead to "a politicised judiciary" (p. 48). Law (and the High Court specifically) will be sullied by the politics of rights. This position was taken up by many opponents of federal intervention in the parliamentary debates, where opposition to the Act was frequently bound up with a critique of a constitutional bill of rights. The Act, as described by one member, "is all part of a gradual process by which issues are transferred one by one to fall within the jurisdiction of the courts and not the people through their elected representatives" [House of Representatives 1994 (October 13), p. 1969, Mr. McArthur]. According to a senator from Tasmania, "bills of rights undermine the principles of parliamentary democracy . . . [and] judges inevitably become legislators beyond the control of the democratic will. This not only threatens the principle of democracy, but also the position of the judiciary, which would, over time, become politicised" [Senate 1994 (December 8), p. 4360, Senator Harradine]. A separation of law and politics is both assumed to exist traditionally and seen as necessary for the integrity of the judiciary. Similarly, TGLRG, while it expounds a broad, cultural, and critically informed interpretation of rights, desired an outcome that represented the triumph of law (in the form of rights recognized under international law) over state politics. However, it sought to achieve this through the federal *political* process.

In my view, the events surrounding the *Toonen* case underline the degree to which rights and the HRC were taken "seriously." Individual rights "trumped" states' rights, in a dispute that centered on the *politics* of federalism and rights. This might suggest that the historical skepticism about rights discourse in Australia is being eroded to some degree.[36] More likely, it demonstrates that sex laws of this type are now unlikely to be supported on their merits by the mainstream, and, in that case, any "grand theories" about rights and identities would be unwise. Not all issues disputed before the HRC may give rise to the same respect for rights (and the UN Committee), which would raise interesting questions about the value of *Toonen* as a precedent for federal action in the future.

The *Toonen* case does not so much represent a shift away from the legalistic and positivistic foundations of the Australian political and legal identity, but instead underscores their ongoing importance. The reaction to the HRC report was, in many respects, highly legalistic, as the federal government argued that it was under a political and legal obligation to implement an opinion delivered by an international legal body with jurisdiction (while also arguing that this was a decision made by a sovereign Parliament). The then attorney general described the position of the government to me as follows: "the reality is that the findings can't simply be ignored with great ease because it is an express finding about a very specific Australian law" (Lavarch 1997). The government sought to meet what it perceived to be its political and legal obligations while avoiding a backlash over states' rights and by keeping much of its lesbian and gay constituency on the government's side.

These events underscore how rights discourse involves legal and political tradeoffs, and the discourse of international human rights magnifies those choices on a larger stage. In this case, international bodies, the Commonwealth government, the states, and national courts are engaged in a relationship that might be described as dialogical, where the resolutions emerge over time and where they appear more politicized than naturalized. The repeal of the sex laws in Tasmania in 1997 is a step in that process. It was entirely appropriate that TGLRG launched a legal action seeking a declaration from the High Court of Australia on the status of the Tasmanian laws in the face of the *Human Rights (Sexual Conduct) Act 1994* prior to their repeal, to determine whether "Tasmania's anti-gay laws are an arbitrary interference with the right to sexual privacy" and therefore inoperative (Croome 1995, p. 283).[37] Yet, by being forced to enter the domestic legal arena, the group needed to allocate resources to a fight that it wished the federal government had resolved definitively. Had the laws not been repealed, it would have been interesting to see the extent to which a broad rights-based discourse informed the High Court's judgment or, alternatively, whether a more narrow, legalistic approach prevailed. Of more interest now will be the extent to which the Act is invoked as a defense to criminal charges in other spheres of sexual activity, and the willingness of the judiciary to apply it beyond the Tasmanian sex crimes context. That was one of the major criticisms of the legislation when it was debated in Parliament—namely, its potential as a thin end of a bill of rights wedge, which would inevitably involve the judiciary in "political" decisions and social engineering. As the then attorney general has acknowledged, "it is really the first time that a broad based statutory right has been enacted by the Commonwealth Parliament that would be similar to the sort of rights you would see in a bill of rights" (Lavarch 1997). Moreover, the Act may be representative of how any future legislative rights protection will be achieved: "if we're ever going to get a bill of rights in this country, then maybe we're going to do it bit by bit"—an "Australian solution" to the rights debate (Lavarch 1997).[38] Consequently, judicial reaction to the law will be important in shaping public opinion. A wide reading (striking down prostitution laws, for example) would "lend weight to people saying you can't trust the judges" (Lavarch 1997).

This was a central issue for opponents of federal legislation. One of their primary concerns was that the Act exemplified "the government's intention to introduce a de facto bill of rights through the use of international covenants and the foreign affairs power" [House of Representatives 1994 (October 13), p. 1962, Mr. Truss], and they focused on the claimed lack of correlation between rights documents and individual liberty: "the operation of this country has given us the greatest freedoms on earth without codifying rights" [House of Representatives 1994 (October 19), p. 2272, Mr. Charles]. Codification becomes synonymous with limitation. Furthermore, opponents seized upon the generality and brevity of the legislation, combined with a skepticism about the predictability of judicial interpretation. The phrase "arbitrary interference with privacy" was interpreted by some as sufficiently vague to render inoperative laws dealing with abortion, incest, prostitution, pornography, and female circumcision (see, e.g., pp. 1993–1994, Mr. Tuckey). The argument was made that the courts must be kept away from "political" decisions, as they will act in an unconstrained and unpredictable manner because they are unelected, unaccountable, and irresponsible (the specter of a *Roe v. Wade*-style judgment, for example, was mentioned specifically several times).[39] Interestingly, the fact that Parliament could always legislate to clarify the law in the face of such a court ruling (since the Act is not an entrenched constitutional right and Parliament remains sovereign) was never raised.

To the extent that the Act gets invoked in different contexts, it may underscore how rights discourse provides a new vocabulary in a political and legal culture that historically was characterized by a legalism averse to rights, in which judges were assumed to somehow operate "beyond" politics (Charlesworth 1994, p. 50). Mathew (1995, p. 178), for example, argues that "the use of international human rights norms has done much to bring the language of rights into Australian legal discourse." In Australian national culture, responsible government, within a federal division of powers, was assumed to offer protection of the rights of the individual. *Toonen,* to some degree, undermined that belief, and in so doing, it exemplified how rights discourse:

> offers an alternative language to that of the mainstream culture and challenges the mythology of the neutrality of the law, making clear the political choices in any constitutional catalogue of rights. In this sense, rights discourse can disturb and reshape existing patterns of Australian legal thought. (Charlesworth 1994, p. 50)

But the malleability of rights means that, in a politically conservative period, progressive public policy achievements of the past can be recharacterized as "special rights" to be rolled back in the name of the "majority."

Although the rights critics had a number of supporters among opponents to the sexual privacy legislation, others in Parliament criticized the government for its narrowness and selectivity in implementing rights. These members took the opposite position from the rights critics, suggesting that a more comprehensive approach would be preferable, "if the government were serious about protecting Australians' right to privacy" [House of Representatives 1994 (October 12), p. 1788, Mr. Williams]. Some referred to other internationally recognized rights, such as the interpretation of freedom of association as including the right not to belong to a trade union [see, e.g., House of Representatives 1994 (October 13), p. 1983, Mr. Abbott]. They challenged the government to enact *that* right in domestic legislation. Still others, from the opposite end of the political spectrum, criticized the government for not using the HRC opinion as an opportunity to introduce national sexual orientation antidiscrimination legislation, which has been advocated by the Australian Human Rights and Equal Opportunities Commission [see, e.g., Senate 1994 (December 8), p. 4313, Senator Spindler]. Such parliamentary maneuvers further underscore the inevitably political character of rights discourse.

The HRC opinion, and the subsequent actions of governments, serve to undermine the legalistic, positivistic belief in the separation of law, politics, and rights. At the same time, other categories that have been traditionally "bounded" are problematized. For example, the opinion illustrates the complex character of legal sovereignty today, and the porousness of the so-called watertight compartments of jurisdiction (both at the state and national levels). For some time, it has been clear in Australia that state powers are not classically sovereign given the scope of the Commonwealth external affairs power. Furthermore, because of the role of international bodies generally, the contingency of national sovereignty is becoming apparent (see Burmester 1995). In an era of increasing economic globalization, that trend will undoubtedly be exacerbated in the future (see generally *Sydney Law Review* 1995).

In that sense, the argument the opposition fell back on—that the federal government should take steps to ensure that international treaties do not undermine the division of powers between federal and state legislatures—rang hollow (see generally Opeskin and Rothwell 1995). Although Burmester (1995, p. 129) suggests that economic agreements are regarded as having a less pernicious impact on sovereignty than "perceived international intrusions into land management or human rights," in this case of the alleged internationalization of human rights, sovereignty arguments generally fell flat. For a geographically remote nation state with a small population, it may well be that isolation is singularly lacking in viability and popular appeal.

The High Court of Australia, in cases such as *Mabo* (1992), has relied explicitly on international legal standards in the interpretation and development of the common law. Some opponents of the Act expressed anxiety at the possibility that it would lead to the further internationalization of the common law because courts might well turn to international law materials as an interpretive aid. This "is cause for concern, because these sources are, philosophically, from outside the legal system which applies in this country" [Senate Legal and Constitutional Legislation Committee 1994 (dissenting report)]. The *national* common law (the external origins of which are not acknowledged) becomes in danger of infiltration (and corruption) from international influences.[40]

A more accurate reading of the use of international legal standards by the High Court would be as sources from which to articulate "'enlightened' expressions of community values" that are widely accepted in Australia (Mathew 1995, p. 200). Judicial value judgments can then be legitimated by the Court in the language of universalism and law, a point that refutes the claim that rights discourse necessarily exposes the politics of law. This is the most persuasive interpretation of *Toonen,* underscoring the extent to which the attribution of a faith in legalism is rightly ascribed to the Australian national identity. While the sources of law may shift from the domestic to the international arena, the judiciary can still construct itself as apolitically "finding" legal standards that can be "neutrally" applied. In such an environment, as Alston (1994a, p. 11) suggests, calls for state sovereignty might be more effectively delivered by linking them to the advocacy of a domestic rights document to mediate those international standards. However, that is unlikely given the political conjunction of states' rights, national sovereignty, and responsible government among opponents of *Toonen.*

The *Toonen* case underlines the unexpected and unpredictable results of that overused term, globalization. The explanation for the Tasmanian laws—an anomalous legal situation in Australia—is, as Australians will readily explain, the cultural "peculiarity" of Tasmania, an island state removed from an island continent. A distrust both of federal institutions and the interference of outsiders were conjoined in this instance with hostility directed to a perceived link between gay rights and environmentalism: "antipathy towards homosexuality was often interlinked with an antipathy towards a loosely identified green movement" (Morris 1995, p. 81). Remember, the external affairs power previously, and most famously, had been used to halt a Tasmanian state dam project on the basis of environmental concerns. Environmentalists and gays to some extent were similarly constructed as outsiders, "who had been brought into Tasmania to destabilise existing values" (p. 82).

The cultural uniqueness of Tasmania rests both in its geography and history. The island geography "allows the imagination to toy with the idea of creating or maintaining a social structure untarnished by outside influences" (Morris 1995, p. 115), and this imagination of identity has come to be translated into the language of states' rights. Historically, the island first was imagined as a "dumping ground" in the era of convictism and, curiously, the prevalence of "homosexuality appears to be one of the main reasons for the cessation of transportation" (p. 115). Subsequently, Tasmania was cleansed through state coercion and religion to create a "delicate social fabric" where a premium was placed on cultural homogeneity and a disciplined social order (p. 117; see also Altman 1995 for a fictionalized account). It is hardly surprising, therefore, that TGLRG deliberately chose a complainant who was Tasmanian born and bred as a means to counter the construction of a gay identity as so firmly other to a Tasmanian identity. Tasmania is a society where divisions in political opinion are particularly sharp and entrenched, a state where multiculturalism has not had the impact it has had in the rest of Australia, and a place where population is declining. This is a small society that rarely appears on the global stage, except, most recently, in the tragic circumstances of the massacre of thirty-five people in 1996 by Martin Bryant, a product of that social order.

The *Toonen* developments show that even Tasmania, however, is not isolated from the impact of an increasingly globalized rights discourse. TGLRG achieved much in placing a local law on the international stage. In May 1997, in the face of a pending challenge to its sex laws, the Tasmanian government (now in a minority position in the legislature), finally chose to repeal them in the face of TGLRG's legal challenge (Montgomery and Hughes 1997). The

Tasmanian attorney general argued that the laws had "become a negative for Tasmania" (Montgomery 1997, p. 1). The extent to which this law reform campaign results in social change is already being felt by way of a more receptive government attitude to HIV education and services (Morgan 1997). For TGLRG, the frustration is that progress could have been advanced by three years with a more explicit federal law. What has been witnessed, however, is a particular intersection of the international, the national, and the local through the language of rights, invoked by all sides in the dispute and unlikely to be reproduced in any other national context.

Australian national culture is self-consciously in the process of reinvention. This has been demonstrated in recent years by an emphasis on multiculturalism as a defining cultural feature, a fervent discourse of republicanism, and the possibility of an entrenched bill of rights (realized most likely in a "piecemeal" way) so as to create national standards of citizenship. Australia is also a society seeking, in a tentative way, to make reparation for the conquest and deterritorialization of Aboriginal peoples. However, an increasingly conservative climate may well mean the end of these attempts. Sexuality, too, plays a role in constructions of national identity. Struggles around lesbian and gay rights have functioned to frame national debate in the language of rights (a change from previous conceptions of national identity) and to locate the nation within an international community, where obligations will be implemented in domestic law (for an American view of this process, see Grant 1994, p. 5).

National identity in Australia (as elsewhere) is increasingly defined and constituted within a globalized context, in which the very boundaries of nationhood may seem under threat. Perhaps, however, Australia is a society in which threats to sovereignty discourse will be less successfully (and hysterically) invoked than has been the case in other parts of the world (an example being "Euroscepticism" in the United Kingdom). It may also be a national culture in which lesbians and gays will be able to appropriate a discursive space because of an increasingly effective conjunction of rights and internationalism within national politics.

National cultures are always subject to reconstitution and redefinition, and recent trends may well be subject to reversal. The election of the Coalition government in 1996 signals, for many, an end to the era I have described in this chapter. This government was elected in part on its claim to speak for ordinary Australians, rather than the "special interest" groups that have had an important role in reshaping what it means to be Australian. The future may see the revitalization of a customary account of nationhood, which relies on a traditional narrative of an Australian "people" and way of life. This is also a time in which there is an increasing backlash against immigration and, by extension, against the notion of a meaningful multicultural citizenship. Furthermore, it sees a vociferous critique of the High Court's recognition of Aboriginal rights, and questions being raised (especially by state governments) about the legitimacy of the High Court's invocation of rights discourse more generally, along with concerns about its "politicization." As 1997 drew to a close, the Commonwealth government introduced a new native title bill designed to protect the rights of ranchers, farmers, and miners who had leased government land, by limiting Aboriginal rights to make land claims. It is worth noting that Prime Minister Howard pointedly refused to endorse the 1997 Sydney Mardi Gras Lesbian and Gay Festival in February. During this same period, there was widespread controversy over a tribunal finding that the denial of alternative insemination to a lesbian woman was a violation of her right to sexual equality under law (Pollard 1997, p. 1). Events such as these suggest that progressive social change is always a tenuous process, with setbacks (and successes) always looming with changes in the political winds. As Australia enters its second century of nationhood at the beginning of the millennium (and hosts the Olympic Games as a suitable symbolic marker to these historic moments), the question of what it is celebrating—of what Australia understands itself as in the process of becoming— remains firmly on the national table.

7 Concluding Remarks

Although the national cultures that I have considered are diverse, there are a number of unifying threads that have emerged with implications for both politics and theory.

Tradition, Modernity, and the Nation

It has become apparent that same-sex acts and identities have frequently been deployed in the construction of national cultures. The homosexual is a particularly malleable subject position that has often been brought into the service of nations, especially in times of perceived crisis. We have seen in these studies how homosexuality has been associated with Communism, fascism, bourgeois capitalism, colonialism, the West and north, the east and south, environmentalism, Europe, and North America. In the project of nation building, homosexuality is a ready discursive tool that can be conflated with any enemy of the state, in the process becoming the enemy within.

This use of homosexuality has been exemplified by the colonial contamination model. In this guise, same-sex acts and identities are seen through the lens of colonialism, and homosexuality becomes a symbol of modernity, contrasted to a "traditional" way of life based on heterosexual marriage and strict gender roles that existed before the perversion of the colonial encounter. But the appeal to tradition is not limited to the postcolonial state. In the West, homosexuality is constructed as undermining traditional values and is associated with the urban, which, in turn, is assumed to be in decay and social decline. Nostalgia for a mythical past, which predates the emergence of a gay or lesbian identity, is invoked. The controversy over the Boston St. Patrick's Day Parade, for example, in many ways was grounded in an appeal to history, tradition, and nostalgia for a "simpler" time.

This longing for the past cannot be separated from the forces of globalization. While economic transnationalism has been embraced by some as a liberating force—usually those who are well off, educated, and mobile—for most people the future is filled with economic and social insecurity.[1] As a consequence, nations and citizens look to sexuality for certainty in a changing world. An appeal to the heterosexual nuclear family becomes an anchor to grab in an increasingly confusing "new" world order. Economic globalization is met with a defense of localism, and a traditional way of life, in which "outsiders" have no right to dictate the terms of how communities define and constitute themselves and others. For example, localism provides one explanation for citizen-initiated ballot measures designed to repeal "gay rights" laws in the United States (see generally Herman 1997, pp. 137–169). It also explains the strength of opposition to the repeal of sex laws in Tasmania.

The increasingly globalized political climate can, however, create opportunities for lesbian and gay activism. The deployment of the discourse of international human rights in Australia, and gains being made through the European Union, exemplify this side of transnationalism. In these moments, activists tend to deploy the language of universality, rights, and modernity to answer the calls of tradition and localism. Law proves central to these social struggles, and the language of universality can resonate in the legal arena.

Legal discourse, as we have seen, can be unpredictable. On the one hand, law is receptive to the discourse of rights and citizenship expressed in universal terms. On the other, it is apparent that legal systems are a means for the construction of national identities, and claims to rights are sometimes interpreted as illegitimate; grounded in foreign ideas and outside influences; and a contaminant of an indigenous, traditional, "pure" national legal order. Conservative legal opinion in Australia and South Africa, and Euroscepticism in Britain, exemplify this discourse. Gay rights claims become constructed as other to the national legal identity.

Rights claims articulated to identity-based groups are sometimes read as a force for the fragmentation of national identity. Terms such as "special rights" and divided loyalties are employed, not only by conservative political actors, but advocates of class politics, to undermine these claims. This phenomenon has been particularly apparent in Canada, where rights are sometimes constructed as eroding the national identity by overloading the system with interest group claims. South Africa provides an interesting contrast in that rights, defined through social groups, seem central to the reconstitution of national identity. The constitutional structure now blends "tradition" and internationalism. The extent to which that experiment is successful will unfold in the years to come.

While the power of rights discourse lies in its claims to universality, I come away from this project with the belief that a somewhat different deployment of rights may be preferable, at least in some instances. In South Africa, gay identities have the potential to combine appeals to universality and modernity, with selectively appropriated "traditions" and local knowledges and practices. Given the way in which the South African Constitution blends both of these elements, such a "hybrid" understanding of identity strikes me as appealing and worth considering in other cultural contexts. It also provides a means to break out of the conundrum of the universality versus cultural relativism binary, which I described in chapter six, because the universality of rights can be *linked* to the specificity of culture.

Such a deployment of culture, which I sought to engage in my discussion of South Africa, speaks a cautionary tale of which Western activists and theorists should be aware. For some time, activists have sought to put lesbian and gay rights on the international and transnational political agenda. As capitalist societies in the West increasingly recognize the rights of lesbians, gays, and bisexuals, I expect that those Western actors—activists, non-governmental organizations, and governments—will turn their attention outward to the "east" and the "south" in an attempt to bring "enlightened" perspectives to bear on those cultures that fail to protect the rights of sexual "minorities." There is a danger here of colonization by an Anglo-American model of identity and the appropriation of local struggles (a dilemma feminist politics has long grappled with). In addition, I worry that the specificity (and rich historical diversity) in the relationship of same-sex acts and identities, as well as in how the "sexual" is constituted, will be erased as cultural relativism is answered through claims of universality.

Sanders (1996, p. 74), an advisor to the International Lesbian and Gay Association, exemplifies this point in his strategy for advancing lesbian and gay rights on the international stage:

> According to some accounts, gay male activity was common and accepted in classical Greece and Rome. Christianity was apparently tolerant until the 13th century. The Kama Sutra has a full chapter on same-sex love and lesbian and gay homoerotic carvings feature on the famous Indian religious temples of Kanarak and Khajuraho. In addition, male homosexual activity was accepted by some of the Muslim rulers in India. A gay male classic from 17th century Japan has recently been translated. At many points in Chinese history "homosexuality acted as an integral part of society, complete with same-sex marriages for both men and women."

This is not a parody but a serious academic attempt to answer relativism on the terrain of culture. A claim to universality is maintained, but only through effacing all cultural difference across place and time, in an attempt to "prove" that "homosexuality" is not only universal, but also essentially the same everywhere throughout history. Like cultural relativists, this universalist argument understands culture as static and capable of being tested in terms of authenticity. I have argued, by contrast, that a more contextual, historically grounded approach is to be preferred, one that acknowledges the history of the colonial encounter and the way in which sexuality was deployed in the construction of "tradition." Answering charges that a "gay" identity is other to some cultures demands an interrogation of the way in which homosexuality has served the project of nationalism and continues to do so.

Towards a New National Narration

Throughout this book, I have analyzed how national cultures deploy sexuality as a means to interrogate the construction of national and sexual identities more broadly. I have not called for the abandonment of national identification. Such a call is both unrealistic, given the historical and ongoing importance of national identity, and ignores the powerful ways in which the language of nation has been used to resist occupation, colonialism, and the oppression of minority groups. Instead, I have argued for a more anti-essential conception of identities, turning away from "ethnic" models toward a recognition of the multiplicity of ways in which people relate to all identity categories. Identity might be regarded as an ongoing process, rather than one fixed by any final essence.

This framework has implications not only for national identities, but sexual (and other) identities as well. It demands that sexual identity politics be understood, not as ethnically based, but as a coalition of diverse interests (see Phelan 1994, pp. 131–159). The nation state might be equally understood in coalitional terms, and this is one way in which sexual politics can contribute to the reimagining of nationhood. Experiments in multiculturalism as a constitutive feature of national identity in Canada and Australia underscore the potential and pitfalls of an anti-essential understanding of national identity. This raises the issue whether identities—national, sexual, or otherwise—can survive if they are conceived in these fluid terms. It is a theoretically unanswerable question. National identities today are in flux, and some nation states (especially those that are coalition based) are fracturing, but no one ever claimed that coalitions were easy to manage or that realignment is necessarily a bad thing.

Sexual identity politics can contribute in other ways to the re-imagining of national cultures. Claims to inclusion within the national imaginary by lesbians and gays have the potential to challenge and undermine the masculinizing and heterosexualizing of national identity. This is a worthwhile project, not least because, as I have argued through several case studies, this imagining of nation has impacted negatively on the ways in which nations relate to each other as well as to citizens and noncitizens. For example, I remain convinced that the struggle for the inclusion of "out" gays and lesbians in the United States military, and the fight for same-sex marriage rights, *could* be discursively deployed to reimagine these central national institutions, and by extension, the ways in which the nation state has been gendered and sexualized. Although I am very skeptical as to whether activism is interested in such a project, these struggles may contain within them the *potential* to destabilize the construction of nation.[2]

This is one reason the St. Patrick's Day Parade issue is significant. Bringing sexual identities out in the public space of the parade—especially given the way that public space has been nationalized—challenged the ways in which the public/private distinction has been deployed around sexuality. The construction of public and private not only has served to keep lesbians and gays in their closets, but it also has been historically deployed to construct women's duties as citizens exclusively within the private sphere of the home (a passive form of citizenship). Problematizing public and private space is an important strategy for challenging the gendering and sexualizing of nation.

This brings me to the issue of citizenship, a term I have invoked in several contexts throughout the book. Rights claims around sexuality, grounded in the language of citizenship, are of importance both in redefining the national imaginary, and in making political gains. In the United States, for example, the majority of the Supreme Court in *Evans v. Romer* (1996), in striking down Colorado's anti-gay rights citizens' initiative (which would have amended the state Constitution to prevent any gay rights laws in the future) held that inclusion within civil rights laws is something every group of citizens should be able to fight for within the political process: "a state cannot so deem a class of persons a stranger to its laws" (p. 1629, per Justice Kennedy). The discourse of national rights and citizenship thus "trumped" competing claims grounded in local democracy (see also Backer 1997b).

Part of the power of an appeal to citizenship for gays and lesbians, as well as for other disenfranchised groups, lies in the potential to disturb "common sense" assumptions about who belongs to the nation state. I have often thought, in frustration, that a suitable response to the seemingly endless attacks on public funding for any gay- or lesbian-related cultural project is an appeal to citizenship and, specifically, on the rights of gays and lesbians as taxpayers to get a return on their investment in the nation. But such an argument underscores the limitations, as well as the strengths, of citizenship discourse. As I have argued in the context of the European Union, citizenship has been constitutively built on exclusions. My intuitive reliance upon claims as a taxpayer highlights how the invocation of citizenship can result in gains for some, but at the expense of others through their exclusion from that discourse. Are indigent people not entitled to the same rights? What about refugees and illegal immigrants?

Thus, care must be taken in the way in which citizenship is

deployed by gays and lesbians in the deployment of rights claims. Arguments about inclusivity in the national imaginary must not be built on new boundaries of exclusion, but instead on challenges to the inside/out dichotomy. I see the dangers here as twofold. First, in attempting to achieve legal victories, lesbians and gays seeking rights may embrace the ideal of "respectability," a construction that then perpetuates a division between "good gays" and (disreputable) "bad queers" (see Robson 1994, pp. 985–991). The latter are then excluded from the discourse of citizenship. Second, to the extent that lesbians and gays do become included in the category "citizen" within the Western nation state, there may be an increased tendency to reproduce the construction of the "south" and "east" as the nonrights respecting, uncivilized other. The colonial discourse of the civilizing West comes to be replicated as the recognition of formal legal rights signifies progress, modernity, and Western "civilization."

Part of the value of citizenship discourse is in the way in which it can be deployed to reimagine the nation as a space for the performance of a range of different projects, in which there is no single authentic way of relating to the nation. This demands an understanding of national identities as capable of reinvention, shifting, in process, and having borders and membership that are subject to ebb and flow. In the end, rights discourse might contribute to that project, and I am convinced that sexual identity politics in the future will become increasingly globalized and articulated to rights discourse. How we *use* rights—to what end and through what means—is the question with which I have tried to grapple.

The relationship of national cultures, sexual identity politics, and rights discourse is dynamic. As I write this in Britain in the autumn of 1997, I am aware that the domestic political climate has experienced a significant (albeit certainly not revolutionary) change in the last several weeks. The election of a Labor government has signaled the end of nearly two decades of right wing Conservative Party rule, in which the nation was frequently invoked in a variety of exclusionary terms (see, e.g., Cooper and Herman 1995; Stychin 1995a, chap. 2). Labor is committed to the incorporation of the European Convention on Human Rights into domestic law; has overseen referenda, the results of which will lead to the significant "devolution" of governmental powers to new elected assemblies in Scotland and Wales; claims to stand for a more "positive" engagement with the European Union; and has announced that foreign policy will be informed by "human rights." In these times, the national identity *feels* less fixed and rigid than it did only a short while ago. By contrast, Australians sense that an era of liberal inclusivity and national reimagining has come to an end with the election of the Liberal-National Coalition, which embraces traditional values, is averse to "special interest" groups and Aboriginal land rights, and advocates neoconservative economic policy. Things have come full circle.

In the late 1990s, the nation state sometimes seems to be caught between the local and the global. For example, the breakup of Canada seems increasingly likely, with perhaps a redefinition of the historically sexualized relationship that I argued has existed between Quebec and the rest of Canada. At the same time, steps are being taken in Europe to expand the European Union eastward to create both a more "inclusive" Europe and, simultaneously, a newly drawn Iron Curtain based on economic viability, Western-style democratic institutions, and perceived respect for the rights of individuals and groups. The other thus continues to be constituted within Europe, and no doubt that construction will remain gendered, raced, and sexualized. The imagining of nation continues.

Notes

Chapter One

1. Anderson's thesis has been subject to critique from a variety of angles; see, e.g., Balakrishnan 1996, p. 208, arguing that "the cultural affinities shaped by print-capitalism do not in themselves seem sufficiently resonant to generate the colossal sacrifices that modern peoples are at times willing to make for their nation"; Chatterjee 1996, who notes the specificity of anticolonial nationalism in Asia and Africa; Eisenstein 1996, p. 52, arguing that Anderson "does not recognize that nationalism is an instance of phallocratic construction. . . . Nor does he recognize racism as part of the historical articulation of the nation." For my purposes, it is Anderson's insight that national communities are "imagined" which is of prime importance.

2. I will return to the impact of membership in the European Union on national identity in chapter five.

3. The role of legal discourse in the constitution of national identities is itself an interesting issue and one I return to throughout this book.

4. I consider this point in greater detail in chapter four.

5. One of McClintock's particular areas of interest is South Africa, and I will focus specifically on gendered and sexualized constructions of national identity in South Africa in chapter three.

6. I develop this argument in more detail in chapter five.

7. As Halley 1996, p. 95, cautions, "reading native culture from a western perspective may occlude everything that is distinctive about it; mining native culture as a source for legal reform can be a gesture of neo-colonial appropriation"; see also Harris 1996.

8. On national/sexual "panic attacks," see Edelman 1994, Harper 1994.

9. Sinfield 1996, p. 281, interestingly refers to this phenomenon of the enemy within as "a kind of reverse diaspora."

10. For Berlant 1991a, p. 113, it is "the power to suppress" the white, male body that signifies this cultural authority. This point bears interesting connections to Yingling's 1994 analysis of HIV and national identity. In particular, the disfiguring effects of some HIV related diseases—particularly Kaposi's sarcoma—are graphically embodied, thereby erasing any cultural authority previously possessed by the bearer. I consider these themes in the specific context of the United States in chapter two.

11. On lesbian feminist theory and politics, see, e.g., Phelan 1989: "the core of lesbian feminism is the position that sexism and heterosexism are 'hopelessly intertwined,' that the oppression of women and of lesbians is 'the prototype for all other oppressions, since the oppression of women and of lesbians crosses boundaries of race, class, and age'" (p. 47, footnotes omitted).

12. For example, in some ways "queerness" might be read as quite assimilationist in its slogan "we're here, we're queer, get used to it," and in the way in which it arguably seeks in some moments to depoliticize sexuality. There are also many forms of anti-assimilationist lesbian and gay politics that are not "queer," such as socialist-inspired activism.

13. Interestingly, McClintock 1995 has provided substantial evidence that historically nationalism and imperialism were transmitted through commodity fetishism.

14. On the power of boundaries in our collective conscience, see generally Nedelsky 1990a.

15. However, the language of universal human rights does not transcend the forces of globalization; rather, Cheah 1997, p. 249, points to the "constitutive inscription" of rights "within the force field of global capital."

Chapter Two

1. For these purposes, the crucial provision is §1 of the Fourteenth Amendment 1868:

> All persons born or naturalized in the United States and subject to the jurisdiction thereof, are citizens of the United States and of the State wherein they reside. No State shall make or enforce any law which shall abridge the privileges or immunities of citizens of the United States; nor shall any State deprive any person of life, liberty, or property, without due process of law; nor deny to any person within its jurisdiction the equal protection of the laws.

2. Moreover, constitutional adjudication has been recognized as not simply reflecting national culture and identity, but as constitutive of that identity; see Teitel 1994.

3. However, this argument obscures the ways in which that ideology still informs national identity on a range of different levels. As Berlant 1991a, p. 113, and others have persuasively argued, the abstract constitutional identity of law remains implicitly white and male.

4. I have elsewhere elaborated on this point in the specific context of lesbian and gay expression; see Stychin 1996b.

5. Constitutional rights have also served as a basis for the mobilization of the propertied and advantaged throughout American history. For a good re-

view of deployments of rights rhetoric by the American right wing, see Pérez-Peña 1994.

6. For example, with respect to claims for equal rights by lesbians and gays, "the pursuit of nonprocreative sexual pleasure, both a failure and a threat to 'family values,' provides evidence of decadent, self-serving rejection of the nation's good," characterized by the "civil selflessness" of the heterosexual majority (Herrell 1996, p. 282).

7. Further evidence of the centrality of parades to national identity can be found in the fact that American constitutional law includes a substantial body of doctrine dealing directly with the right to march. For example, the Supreme Court's invalidation of attempts by local governments to block Nazi demonstrations could well be read as a statement of the centrality of dissenting speech to the American national identity. See *National Socialist Party v. Skokie* (1977), and see generally Yackle 1993, pp. 796–811.

8. The Civil Rights movement is replete with examples of cultural performance as a means to mobilize around rights. From "sit ins" to marches to sitting in a "whites only" section of a bus, these strategies highlight the importance of space, ritual, and movement in rights struggles; see Berlant 1996, p. 507. On the relationship of law, rights, and physical movement more generally, see Blomley 1994. However, Herrell 1992, p. 242, distinguishes between the political protest march and the community-creating parade based on his description of the latter as founded on an "ethnic model" of celebration. Although the former is much more strongly associated with rights struggles, I question whether such a sharp dichotomy is necessarily sustainable given that parades of celebration can carry with them demands for social and legal change.

9. This latter interpretation closely resembles Taylor's 1993, p. 132, conception of "deep diversity," which I consider in detail in chapter four.

10. For example, according to Herrell 1992, p. 232, nearly 25% of the entries in the 1987 Chicago Pride Parade were not self-identified as lesbian or gay.

11. For a more cautious account of the connections between anti-Semitism, anti-Communism, and anti-homosexuality, see Herman 1997.

12. These discourses are closely connected to the construction of AIDS in the American national imaginary, namely, as a foreign threat imported from abroad; see generally Yingling 1994. Interestingly, however, AIDS is often constructed elsewhere in the world as an American disease; see, e.g., Gilman 1992.

13. This theme of the constitution of some sexual identities as unnatural in terms of a national identity is one I shall return to at several points in different cultural contexts throughout this book.

14. GLIB also included self-described heterosexuals among its membership, a point that is largely obscured in the judicial reasoning.

15. On the history of the Boston parade and this controversy, see Yackle 1993, pp. 834–850.

16. On the history of the movement to include sexual orientation in this law, see generally Cicchino, Deming, and Nicholson 1995.

17. As Kearney 1997, p. 99, argues, an Irish identity is complex in its scope: "one refers not merely to the inhabitants of a state, but to an international group of expatriates and a subnational network of regional communities. This triple layered identity means that Irishness is no longer co-terminous with the geographical outlines of an island."

18. Irishness (unlike some other national identities within the U.S.) does not seem to be widely associated with terrorism in the American psyche, despite evidence of American connections to the Irish Republican Army.

19. In this regard, the parade underscores how, as Eisenstein 1996, p. 68, argues, "as ethnic, one's migrant identity is defined by one's past, by one's point of origin, rather than by the present. The statisticity of the construction preserves one's 'otherness' and limits the possibilities of a radically pluralized multicultural present."

20. Curiously, there is no particular tradition of St. Patrick's Day parades in the United Kingdom, despite the fact that the U.K. has the longest history of Irish immigration. This point suggests that some forms of the articulation of identity in diaspora within colonial settings are culturally foreclosed. It is further complicated by the association of terrorism and an Irish identity in the British national consciousness.

21. This decision of the Veterans Council provides further evidence of how national cultures in diaspora can become static. Lesbians and gays in the Republic of Ireland have made substantial legal and political progress in recent years in an increasingly secularized society, which I discuss in more detail in chapter five. In this regard, Beriss 1996, p. 194, astutely asks: "Does the debate over the sexuality of the Irish nation reflect on Ireland, or is it a product of American ideological confrontations? . . . Whose ideas about sexuality and gender are being deployed in this conflict?"

22. It has been argued that this was the crucial issue, and that it was wrongly decided by the lower courts; Van Ness 1996, pp. 650–651. The issue was not argued before the U.S. Supreme Court.

23. There are limits to the ability of law to control space. While the parade route may be privatized, sidewalks surrounding it can still provide a site for the articulation of other narratives of national identity, creating a more polyvocal performance.

24. See, more generally, Calhoun 1995, p. 247, arguing that "in varying degrees all public discourses are occasions for identity formation."

25. It has been suggested that the Supreme Court's reasoning may have interesting implications for the (in)famous "don't ask, don't tell" policy of the

American military. Zaleskas 1996, p. 549, questions the constitutional future of the policy given the Supreme Court's message in *Hurley* that "the assertion of one's sexual orientation constitutes an expressive act" that, by implication, should be "afforded the strictest protections of the First Amendment." Similarly, Currah 1997, p. 232, points to the importance of *Hurley* as a judicial recognition that "the act of identification is, at least in part, a public and potentially political process." I have elsewhere considered the relationship of sexual acts and identities as they are manifested in the military policy; see Stychin 1996c.

26. Van Ness 1996, p. 644, argues that the Veterans Council took deliberate steps to "privatize" the parade after 1992.

27. Such a description might be equally applicable to the "marching season" of the Orange Order in Northern Ireland today. These demonstrations are based on a claimed "inalienable" right to march (despite the absence of entrenched constitutional rights), and they symbolize territorial and spatial control through the exclusion of competing (non-British) identities.

28. On this point, see especially Eaton 1995, for a parallel argument in the context of homosexuality and an African American identity.

29. Despite this purported aim, lesbian and gay groups are now refused entry to the New York parade. In 1997, for example, demonstrators blocked the parade route, leading to arrests.

30. An exception might be made for groups that were subversive to the nation if they were, for example, attempting to deceive the public as to their true identity and motives. Ironically, that is precisely how homosexuals, as well as other groups in the United States, have been historically constructed within dominant discourses. But, given the centrality of dissenting speech to the American national identity, even that exception seems unsustainable.

31. This is what distinguishes the St. Patrick's Day Parade from the Pride Parade. Despite the diversity of participants in a Pride Parade, it remains possible to articulate a common endeavor that unites them. As a consequence, it is easier to justify excluding a group whose message is perceived as undermining that common project. At the same time, issues of exclusion give rise to fierce debates around the question of who enjoys the right to set conditions of group membership.

32. This explains why the legal regulation of "hate speech" proves a divisive issue. Hate speech might well be important for the constitution of group identities—bigoted, intolerant groups—but, in so doing, it clearly has an impact on the space of other groups in the series. On that basis, it would seem justifiable to exclude racist, sexist, or homophobic groups from participating in the parade. However, governmental attempts to regulate hate speech have been invalidated by courts on constitutional grounds; see *R.A.V. v. St. Paul* 1992 and also Butler 1997.

33. Van Ness 1996, p. 632, pointedly notes, in reply, that historically the Veterans Council's approach was to allow any group that asked to participate in the parade. This was the first time the council genuinely voted to revoke a parade registration made by a group (p. 640).

Chapter Three

1. The Constitution of the Republic of South Africa of 1993 (the Interim Constitution) is the product of the Multi-Party Negotiating Process, in which delegates representing a spectrum of political allegiances reached agreement on the constitutional principles that would come into effect following elections in April 1994. The final Constitution was drafted by the Constitutional Assembly in accordance with a series of "Constitutional Principles," and was accepted by the Assembly on May 8, 1996. It was then ratified, after some amendments were demanded, by the Constitutional Court. The assembly serves as the Parliament until elections in 1999. Both the Interim and final Constitutions include expansive bills of rights. Section 8(2) of the interim version, for example, states: "No person shall be unfairly discriminated against, directly or indirectly, and, without derogating from the generality of this provision, on one or more of the following grounds in particular: race, gender, sex, ethnic or social origin, colour, sexual orientation, age, disability, religion, conscience, belief, culture or language." Section 9(3) of the final Constitution declares: "the state may not unfairly discriminate directly or indirectly against anyone on one or more grounds, including race, gender, sex, pregnancy, marital status, ethnic or social origins, colour, sexual orientation, age, disability, religion, conscience, belief, culture, language, and birth." The history of the Interim Constitution, and the transition to democracy, is fascinating but beyond the scope of this work; see generally Corder 1994, Devenish 1996, Ellmann 1994, Govender 1996, Hatchard and Slinn 1995, Klug 1996, Thompson 1995.

2. The 34th Principle reads, in part:

> This Schedule and the recognition therein of the right of the South African people as a whole to self-determination, shall not be construed as precluding, within the framework of the said right, constitutional provision for a notion of the right to self-determination by any community sharing a common cultural and language heritage, whether in a territorial entity within the Republic or in any other recognised way.

3. I use the Winnie Mandela example with hesitation. Mandela is frequently constructed within racist and misogynist discourses as "the bad wife" (as opposed to "the good mother"). In many respects, I think she signifies white men's palpable fear of being governed by a black woman. My reluctance results from concern with further "demonizing" her. However, the trial, like

the Zimbabwean International Book Fair, is an event of particular discursive importance. Winnie Madikizela Mandela continues to be a controversial figure, as evidenced by her testimony before the Truth and Reconciliation Commission in November 1997, which concerned the events which preceded the 1991 trial.

4. Some Africanists would later rewrite that "tradition" as grounded within the heterosexual familial unit, a point upon which I shall elaborate shortly.

5. Male same-sex sodomy was illegal under the common law of South Africa. While female same-sex acts were not illegal under common law, in 1988 the higher age of consent was extended to acts between women and girls under the age of nineteen; see Cameron 1992, 1993.

6. Similarly, GASA (Gay Association of South Africa), formed in 1983, attempted to stay outside of the political fray.

7. In the process leading up to the adoption of the Interim Constitution,

four parties proposed bills of rights accepting that gays and lesbians required a measure of constitutional protection from discrimination: the African National Congress (ANC), the Democratic Party (DP), the Inkatha Freedom Party (IFP), and the National Party, which adopted the proposals of the Law Commission (a government-appointed body of lawyers and judges which considers law reform). (Cameron 1995b, p. 94)

8. I consider this constitutional struggle in detail elsewhere; see Stychin 1996a.

9. In 1997, a judge of the High Court of South Africa, Cape of Good Hope Provincial Division, ruled that the common law prohibition on male same-sex sodomy was a violation of the constitutional equality guarantee, on the basis of sexual orientation discrimination; see *State v. Kampher* 1997.

10. The four stated principles of the National Coalition for Gay and Lesbian Equality are: (1) "retaining the Sexual Orientation clause in the Constitution," (2) "decriminalizing same-sex conduct," (3) "constitutional litigation challenging discrimination against same-sex relationships," and (4) "training of representative and effective leaders within lesbian and gay organizations"; see Mtetwa 1995b, p. 1.

11. The appointment of gay rights advocate Edwin Cameron to the Supreme Court of South Africa provided an early indication of this new spirit of participation in national dialogue.

12. Interestingly, by the end of the process, the number of submissions favoring the inclusion of sexual orientation in the Constitution far outnumbered those against; see Dunton and Palmberg 1996, p. 29.

13. Within Afrikaner ideology, tradition and myth have played a central

role—the Great Trek across South Africa continues to resonate with many Afrikaners. See McClintock 1996; Thompson 1995, pp. 87–96.

14. Section 35(1) reads: "in interpreting the provisions of this Chapter a court of law shall promote the values which underlie an open and democratic society based on freedom and equality and shall, where applicable, have regard to public international law applicable to the protection of the rights entrenched in this Chapter, and may have regard to comparable foreign case law."

15. The concept of *ubuntu* is central to this construction of tradition. On the meaning and scope of *ubuntu* in constitutional interpretation, see especially the judgment of Justice Mokgoro in *S. v. Makwanyane* 1995, p. 308: "while it envelops the key values of group solidarity, compassion, respect, human dignity, conformity to basic norms and collective unity, in its fundamental sense it denotes humanity and morality. Its spirit emphasises respect for human dignity, marking a shift from confrontation to conciliation." On the Constitutional Court, see generally Mtshaulana and Thomas 1996.

Chapter Four

1. Translation: "In my opinion, the role of the state is not to institutionalize and exacerbate prejudice in permitting discrimination against minorities in society."

2. Translation: "We have the immense privilege of living and working in one of the most culturally rich, socially creative, politically dynamic societies in the entire world. That is our conviction."

3. Translation: "The Quebec of freedoms does not go back for centuries, but rather freedoms are created day to day."

4. Translation: "There is no comparable case in the West, nor in the world, of a society which has passed so quickly as Quebec, in a grown-up fashion, with so few negative aspects, from a closed, authoritarian, inward society, to one which is open, bold, and articulate."

5. In this way, Quebec exemplifies Weeks' 1995, pp. 119–120, argument that campaigns for lesbian and gay rights "try to force these societies to realize for self-defined sexual minorities what they claim to be the mobilizing ideals of the liberal polity."

6. There are two relevant limitations on the scope of the right to equality, however, which are pertinent to sexual orientation discrimination. First, §20 provides certain defenses to a complaint: "A distinction, exclusion or preference based on the aptitudes or qualifications required for an employment, or justified by the charitable, philanthropic, religious, political or educational nature of a non-profit institution or of an institution devoted exclusively to the well-being of an ethnic group, is deemed non-discriminatory." Second, §137 exempts insurance and benefits schemes from the antidiscrimination protec-

tion for distinctions drawn on the basis of age, sex, pregnancy, sexual orientation, and disability. On the sexual orientation equality provision and its scope and impact in law, see generally Girard 1986, pp. 268–273; Duplé 1984, pp. 826–841.

7. The most significant political development in recent years was the decision of the Quebec Human Rights Commission to initiate public consultations and to issue a report on violence and discrimination against lesbians and gays. The Consultation Committee made over forty recommendations dealing with Health and Social Services, relations with the police, and conformity of laws with the Quebec Charter. See Quebec Human Rights Commission 1994.

8. For example, from the age of eight, children are informed of their rights pursuant to the *Youth Protection Act,* including the right to resort to the state for assistance and protection without the intervention of a family member; Langlois et al. 1992, p. 249.

9. Section 15 of the Canadian Charter of Rights and Freedoms reads:

15(1). Every individual is equal before and under the law and has the right to the equal protection and equal benefit of the law without discrimination and, in particular, without discrimination based on race, national or ethnic origin, colour, religion, sex, age or mental or physical disability.

15(2). Subsection (1) does not preclude any law, program or activity that has as its object the amelioration of conditions of disadvantaged individuals or groups including those that are disadvantaged because of race, national or ethnic origin, colour, religion, sex, age or mental or physical disability.

The South African constitutional equality provisions were modeled on the Canadian Charter; see chapter three.

10. The implications of that Supreme Court decision may be relatively narrow. For example, a bare majority of the Court rejected the argument that the definition of "spouse" in federal Old Age Pension legislation—which included heterosexual common law partners—was discriminatory on the basis of sexual orientation; see Stychin 1995b.

11. However, the divorce metaphor, as it is employed to describe the relationship between Quebec and the ROC, might have interesting implications in this regard. If Quebec, the female partner, abandons her "husband" (ROC), could this imply that she has given up on the possibility of a satisfying heterosexual relationship?

12. By contrast, the United States is "a powerful attraction on the imagination of Québécois," a product in part of the more secure identity of Quebec vis-à-vis the U.S.; Langlois et al. 1992, p. 597.

13. The "threat to nation" discourse is also articulated within some gay texts. A fascinating example is the construction of Air Canada flight attendant Gaetan Dugas (the infamous so-called HIV "patient zero") in Shilts' *And The Band Played On* (1987). In the book, Dugas, with "his soft Québécois accent and his sensual magnetism" (p. 21) and "his voracious sexual appetite" (p. 22), spent his time "spreading the new [HI] virus from one end of the United States to the other" (p. 439), presumably on Air Canada (the national "carrier"). The book is also interesting in its construction of Quebec through Shilts' American eyes. The Québécois are described as "parochial" (because they do not speak English) (p. 78), and Dugas (because adopted) is the blonde outsider who never felt he could be part of this national culture (p. 196).

14. Interestingly, since 1981, women are obliged to use their "maiden names" in the exercise of civil rights, and children can carry the mother's or father's surname or both; Langlois et al. 1992, p. 249.

15. On this theme, pollsters have gathered data showing that young Québécois are more effective with the use of contraceptives than their contemporaries either in the ROC or the United States; Langlois et al. 1992, p. 249.

16. Schwartzwald 1992, p. 502, argues that recent productions of this work have underscored the problematic of authenticity and have focused instead on the *performativity* of all identities, a shift that is not surprising given the failure of the first Quebec referendum in 1980: "nationalist discourse has itself undergone profound mutations in its confrontation over the past two decades with feminism, theories of heterogeneity, and a political process which in the referendum defeat of May 1980, stubbornly refused to follow the 'logic of history.'"

17. The lesbian and gay movement has explicitly sought to construct itself within nationalist discourse. For example, in the early 1970s, Montreal francophone gays formed the Front de Libération Homosexuelle (FLH), "modeled after the Front de Libération du Québec (FLQ) [a terrorist separatist organization of the late 1960s] and the Gay Liberation Front in an attempt to combine gay liberation and Québécois nationalist consciousness"; Kinsman 1996, p. 291.

18. Probyn 1996, pp. 69–70, has discussed how the lesbian community (at least in Montreal) exhibits an extraordinary diversity, making any generalizations unwise.

19. It is significant that this "relationship" is not constructed in heterosexual terms with the federalist as the seductive woman. The *absence* of this characterization underscores how, whenever the relationship between Quebec and the ROC is heterosexualized, Quebec is invariably gendered female.

20. Schwartzwald 1991, pp. 179–180, notes that the term *pederaste* is not widely used in Quebec. Rather, *tapette* is more common. In this context,

the pun *federaste* reinforces the construction of homosexuality as a threat that is foreign to the nation. Former Canadian Prime Minister (and arch anti-nationalist) Pierre Trudeau was referred to as *tapette* in the manifestos of the Front de Libération du Québec in 1970 (p. 186).

21. It bears considering that numerous Canadian political theorists have been captivated by the question of how to hold the multinational, multicultural state together, while rarely inquiring whether it is a worthwhile project in the first place. For the sake of this discussion, I will accept the premise that there might well be benefits to such a state that warrant an inquiry into how to maintain its viability.

Chapter Five

1. The constitutional texts of the EU contain extensive rhetorical, but substantively unenforceable, language on the broader social and political objectives of the Union. For example, Article 2 of the Treaty on European Union states that one of the goals of the EU is the promotion of "a high level of employment and of social protection, the raising of the standard of living and quality of life, and economic and social cohesion and solidarity among member states." On the social policy elements of the European Constitution, see generally Shaw 1996b, chap. 2.

2. It has been forcefully argued, however, that these "progressive" legal gains are limited by both a false dichotomy of public/private spheres, and the deployment of a "sameness/difference" approach to equality within European law; see More 1993.

3. This characterization of Europe as a shared, common civilization, as I have already suggested, easily can be deployed to construct the uncivilized, barbaric foreigner, who then can be excluded from a Europe defined in terms of its cultural sameness.

4. However, in the current political climate of the European Union, many would argue that such an active, participatory citizenship is far from realistic. Rather, European citizenship is currently experienced as a passive identity, centering upon the problematic relationship between the individual and the institutions of the EU, not one in which the citizen is an active participant in a democratic polity; see Armstrong 1996.

5. For a particularly utopian account of this dynamic, see Meehan 1993, p. 185:

A new kind of citizenship is emerging that is neither national nor cosmopolitan but which is multiple in enabling the various identities that we all possess to be expressed, and our rights and duties exercised, through an increasingly complex configuration of common institutions, national and transnational interest groups and voluntary associations, local or provincial authorities, regions and alliances of regions.

But see also Aron 1974, p. 649, who has argued that the effect of this fragmentation of sovereignty is that "the ordinary citizen is less and less sure of the locus of decision-making."

6. The constitutional concept of "subsidiarity" included in the Maastricht Treaty is sometimes seen as emblematic of this reimagination. The principle of subsidiarity is enshrined in part as follows: "In areas which do not fall within its exclusive competence, the Community shall take action . . . only if and in so far as the objectives of the proposed action cannot be sufficiently achieved by the Member States."

7. Another example is the Court's finding "that failure to allow part-time workers access to occupational pension schemes may be indirect discrimination against women" (More 1996a, p. 278). But see also Shaw 1996, pp. 250–251, who notes that recent European Court of Justice jurisprudence suggests that "the Court can easily be persuaded by considerations of cost to equate equality with equalization," and to refuse socioeconomic claims in the field of pensions law.

8. It has been argued, however, that through political compromises, the Charter has been "reduced to a political document, containing rhetorical statements about the importance of social issues, but creating no legally binding social policy obligations on member states" (Ball 1996, p. 329).

9. But note that P. M. Twomey 1994, p. 124, argues that the reliance of the European Court of Justice on the common constitutional principles of member states and, in addition, upon human rights treaties adhered to by member states, has given rise to a situation in which the ECJ is prepared to draw upon international human rights law (usually in the form of the European Convention on Human Rights) "without explicitly linking it to the common constitutional traditions." However, that has resulted in a situation where "the Court has been accused of hijacking the fundamental rights discourse to facilitate its main priority of economic integration, resulting in the devaluation of fundamental rights" (p. 124).

10. See Lyons 1996, p. 96: "as member states have different methods of determining nationality it could mean, for example, that an Irish American may be able to avail herself of EU citizenship but a Turkish national who has lived all her life in Germany may not." There are approximately 10–15 million legally settled non-nationals in the EU (p. 96).

11. Thus, indigent persons "are not eligible to receive the benefits provided by a European social citizenship" (Ball 1996, pp. 362–363).

12. See Clapham and Weiler 1993, p. 13: "at the present stage of lesbian

and gay legal protection in Europe, classical rights discourse and mobilization seem to us the most promising."

13. The extent to which that subject position is now being imported into "Eastern" Europe, and whether such a "westernization" is a form of neocolonization, is an interesting question, but one that is beyond the scope of this work. In 1994, the Democracy Programme of the European Union, which supports political and economic reform in Eastern Europe, "funded an antidiscrimination project of the International Lesbian and Gay Association working with seven lesbian and gay organizations in Estonia, Latvia, Lithuania, and the Russian Federation" (Sanders 1996, p. 87).

14. Legal reform dealing with same-sex sexual relations between men also has occurred in *Northern* Ireland, again prompted by a case before the European Court of Human Rights (*Dudgeon v. U.K.* 1981); see also Rose 1994, pp. 38–39. However, broader social and legal changes have not significantly materialized. On this point, it has been argued that "the North has been particularly and actively repressive, partly due to loyalists such as the Democratic Unionist Party (DUP), who have promoted a particularly virulent form of homophobia" (p. 13). More generally, "the ongoing war has left little space for social movements such as the lesbian and gay movement to develop" (p. 13). On the marginalization of feminist struggles, see Roulston 1997.

15. Flynn 1997 argues, however, that an Irish identity not only repressed homosexuality, it sought to "manage" it in imaginative ways.

16. Such a rewriting of the past conveniently serves to mask the historical and continuing presence of homophobia, and the role of the Catholic Church in fostering it.

17. Interestingly, the struggle for abortion rights in Ireland also has relied upon the deployment of legal rights struggles before the European courts; see generally Spalin 1992.

18. But, in addition, as states from Eastern Europe seek admission to the Council of Europe (a prerequisite to EU membership), they are required to ratify the Convention. As a consequence, Lithuania in 1993 repealed its anti–same-sex laws and Romania has been called upon to do the same; Sanders 1996, p. 82. Romania's refusal to comply may well be a reaction against outsiders seeking to influence domestic affairs and is explainable by the role of religion in Romanian society.

19. This example underscores the extent to which *American* legal and political discourses are remarkably inward looking and insular, as demonstrated by the absence of references to international and comparative law in the Supreme Court's decision upholding the constitutionality of sodomy laws on privacy grounds in *Bowers v. Hardwick* 1986 (as well as in most subsequent commentary and jurisprudence).

20. On sexuality claims, "the Court of Human Rights has held that state

authorities, on issues raising questions of morality, are to be granted a wide margin of appreciation (or deference) in determining whether certain acts or conduct should be prescribed by law" (Ball 1996, p. 378). For example, the Court has upheld the prosecution and imprisonment in Britain of gay men for consensual sadomasochistic sexual activity (*Laskey, Jaggard, and Brown v. United Kingdom* 1997). For background to this case, see Stychin 1995a, chap. 7.

21. An interesting development *has* come from individual lesbians and gays entering into fraudulent marriages, thereby allowing non-EC nationals *rights* of residence within the Community.

22. The provisions governing sex discrimination in the workplace might provide the basis for a new European legal directive prohibiting discrimination based on sexual orientation in member states. In the 1997 Amsterdam Treaty, EU leaders agreed to a provision that empowers the Council of Ministers to "take appropriate action to combat discrimination based on sex, racial or ethnic origin, religion or belief, disability, age or sexual orientation." Whether that power will be acted upon remains to be seen.

23. Of interest, for similar reasons, is a challenge to the British ban on lesbians, gays, and bisexuals in the armed forces, which has been referred to the ECJ. The court must decide whether the ban constitutes sex discrimination and, if so, whether it is justifiable (*R. v. Secretary of State for Defence ex parte Perkins* 1997). The issue may also come before the European Court of Human Rights.

Chapter Six

1. At the time of the formation of the Commonwealth, the new citizens "saw themselves as British first, then as Victorians, South Australians and so only gradually became accustomed to being 'Australians'" (Eddy 1991, p. 26).

2. Castles, Kalantzis, Cope, and Morrissey 1988, p. 1, argue that the two major events of "world-historical significance" that have taken place in Australia are, first, "the severity of the conquest of the Aboriginal people" and, second, the extent of postwar immigration.

3. At the federal level, the Labor Party held power from 1983 to 1996, and this is the period in which issues surrounding national identity, and the role of the state in fostering that identity, have been central to public discourse.

4. For example, in the 1951 *Communist Party Case,* the High Court invalidated a federal government attempt to outlaw the Communist Party on federalism grounds; see Charlesworth 1994, p. 26. Opponents of an entrenched rights document point to how a similar case in the United States led to the opposite result, having been argued on the basis of individual freedoms under the Bill of Rights; see *Dennis v. U.S.* 1950.

5. As I have shown in other national contexts, homosexuality is frequently brought into the service of the national identity in these circumstances.

6. The High Court of Australia is the highest court in the jurisdiction, hearing appeals on both federal and state matters. Prior to 1975, appeals could be further launched to the Judicial Committee of the Privy Council in London (the "Law Lords" of the House of Lords), a colonial holdover. However, the High Court is appointed solely by the federal executive branch, exemplifying another departure from a classic federalism model and one that is increasingly coming in for criticism from state governments.

7. A consideration of this "Implied Bill of Rights" jurisprudence is beyond the scope of this chapter, but nevertheless remains a subject of considerable current controversy in Australia. See generally Zines 1994, Jones 1996.

8. The decision in *Mabo* 1992 was followed by the enactment of the *Native Title Act 1993* by the Labor government, which recognized native title and provided mechanisms for reparation. For a critique of the Act, see Povinelli 1994.

9. For background on the history of the lesbian and gay movements in Australia, see generally Altman 1987, 1988. On constructions of sexuality more generally, see Aldrich and Wotherspoon 1992; Aldrich 1994.

10. An interesting development in this regard is the enactment in the state of New South Wales of the *Anti-Discrimination (Homosexual Vilification) Act 1993*, which makes unlawful the "vilification" of gay men and lesbians.

11. For a critique of rights-based strategies around sexuality in the Australian context, on the basis that they give rise to a new system of regulation and normalization, see Fraser 1995.

12. Another example of interest is recent case law from the Australian Refugee Review Tribunal, which has shown a "receptive atmosphere to refugee claims based on sexual orientation"; Millbank 1995. But, for a more critical interpretation of the operation of refugee law with respect to sexual orientation, see Walker 1996.

13. Changes to the *Immigration Act* enacted by Parliament in 1997 illustrate the much more conservative climate in Australia today. The Act has been "exempted" from the operation of the *Sex Discrimination Act*, and it now requires those applying in the "Interdependency Visa Category" to have been cohabiting for a year previously; see Widdicombe 1997.

14. In 1984, the reservation was replaced by a federal "statement" having substantively the same effect; Opeskin and Rothwell 1995, p. 47. However, Article 50 of the ICCPR clearly states that "the provisions of the covenant shall extend to all parts of federal States without any limitations or exceptions."

15. Until 1997, the Tasmanian *Criminal Code* provided that:

§122. Any person who—

(a) has sexual intercourse with any person against the order of nature;

(b) has sexual intercourse with an animal;

(c) consents to a male person having sexual intercourse with him or her against the order of nature, is guilty of a crime.

§123. Any male person who, whether in public or private, commits any indecent assault upon, or other act of gross indecency with, another male person, or procures another male person to commit any act of gross indecency with himself or any other male person, is guilty of a crime.

The maximum penalty under these sections was imprisonment of twenty-one years. The precise scope of the provisions remained unclear. As Morgan 1994a, p. 742, argues, "although these provisions have a decided focus on (homo) male sex acts, §122 potentially also criminalises lesbian sex, though this has never been decided by Tasmanian law. In fact, the only form of sexual expression clearly not outlawed by §122 is heterosexual sex involving penetration of the vagina by the penis."

16. For a fascinating history of the gay law reform movement in Tasmania, see Morris 1995.

17. Article 17 provides that:

(1). No one shall be subject to arbitrary or unlawful interference with his privacy, family, home or correspondence, nor to unlawful attacks on his honour and reputation.

(2). Everyone has the right to the protection of the law against such interference or attacks.

Article 2(1) provides that:

Each State Party to the present Covenant undertakes to respect and to ensure to all individuals within its territory and subject to its jurisdiction the rights recognised in the present Covenant, without distinction of any kind, such as race, colour, sex, language, religion, political or other opinion, national or social origin, property, birth or other status.

18. Article 26 provides that:

All persons are equal before the law and are entitled without any discrimination to the equal protection of the law. In this respect, the law shall prohibit any discrimination and guarantee to all persons equal and effective protection against discrimination on any ground such as race, colour, sex, language, religion, political or other opinion, national or social origin, property, birth or other status.

19. An interesting argumentative turn is apparent here, as the law's explicit focus on sexual acts is translated into an argument based on the particular sexual identity of gay men. The complainant in *Toonen* 1994 argued that "in spite of the gender neutrality of Tasmanian laws against 'unnatural sexual intercourse,' this provision . . . has been enforced far more often against men engaged in homosexual activity" than others.

20. A separate opinion was delivered by the Swedish member of the Committee, Bertil Wennergren, who argued that sexual orientation was included within the equality rights provisions, and that the law discriminated on that basis. Controversially, he suggested that the justification for this finding was that "the common denominator for the grounds 'race, colour and sex' are biological or genetic factors" (and he implicitly analogized sexual orientation to those grounds); *Toonen* 1994.

21. See my discussion of Irish law reform in chapter five.

22. Under Article 2(3)(a) of the Covenant, the state is under a specific duty "to ensure to any person whose rights or freedoms as herein recognised, are violated shall have an effective remedy."

23. The sole substantive provisions of the law state:

§4(1). Sexual conduct involving only consenting adults acting in private is not to be subject, by or under any law of the Commonwealth, a State or a Territory, to any arbitrary interference with privacy within the meaning of Article 17 of the *International Covenant on Civil and Political Rights*.

(2). For the purposes of this section, an adult is a person who is 18 years old or more.

24. There might well be other legal implications. For example, Western Australia's age of consent law for male same-sex sexual activity presently stands at age 21; §4(2) of the *Human Rights (Sexual Conduct) Act 1994* presumably demands that it be rendered inoperative regarding sexual acts of 18- to 21-year-olds. On the legal implications of the Act, see generally Bronitt 1995a, 1995b.

25. For an academic elaboration of this position, see Mathew 1995, p. 178, arguing that "far from diminishing Australian sovereignty, the use of international human rights law enriches the notion of Australian nationhood."

26. The flaw in this analogy is that nation states *voluntarily* agree to the constraints of international law; see Burmester 1995, p. 132.

27. There is unintended irony in this statement, given the widespread construction of homosexuality as a Western, decadent import in much of that "Third World left wing ideology," as I have described in previous chapters.

28. However, as Burmester 1995, p. 130, argues, "Australian sovereignty and its legal independence remain relatively untrammelled by outside legislative or judicial bodies—in contrast to the position, for example, prevailing in the United Kingdom as a result of its membership of the European Union."

29. The debates are similar to those in other federal systems, such as the United States.

30. This argument reproduces Sawer's 1976, p. 152, claim that the language of autonomy in Australia is increasingly applied to individuals (or "minority" groups) rather than states.

31. A few opponents of federal intervention sought to answer this argument with the claim that the Tasmanian laws were not a gay rights issue, as they dealt with (dangerous) sexual practices, rather than persons; see, e.g., Senate 1994 (December 8), p. 4357, Senator Chapman.

32. The Tasmanian upper house historically has been heavily weighted in favor of rural voters and does not face the electorate in general elections. As Tenbensel 1996, p. 19, argues, "Australian state upper houses have their origins in attempts to curtail popular sovereignty vested in lower houses," allowing "plenty of room to contest arguments that its [the Tasmanian government's] stance reflects the wishes of the Tasmanian people."

33. See also Bronitt 1995b, p. 65, arguing that:

International human rights jurisprudence has developed a broader conception of privacy . . . beyond the *negative* conception of privacy as freedom from unwarranted state intrusion into one's private life, to include the *positive* right to establish, develop and fulfill one's emotional needs. By reconceptualising privacy in this way, the scope of "private" sexual conduct is redefined to include some types of "public" behaviour.

34. For a more critical appraisal of the politics of TGLRG, in terms of its own reification of the homo/hetero and gender dichotomies, see Dobber 1995.

35. TGLRG's campaign coordinator Croome 1995, p. 283, was critical of the way in which the Labor government kept much of its lesbian and gay (Labor supporting) constituency "on side" during its intervention: "Of all the Federal Government's cynical actions during the 1994 Tasmanian gay law reform debate nothing was as tragic as the ease with which it set gays and lesbians against each other in the pursuit of its own interests." According to Croome, "the ALP [Australian Labor Party] had pulled the strings of its Sydney based gay and AIDS client groups."

36. Another interesting example has been Parliament's enactment in 1997

of legislation to render inoperative the Northern Territory's voluntary euthanasia law: *Rights of the Terminally Ill Act*. The debates surrounding these legislative moves were articulated by all sides in the language of rights: right to die, right to life, and rights of states. See Windsor 1997, Ramsey and Hannon 1997.

37. The High Court ruled, as a preliminary matter, that Toonen and Croome had legal standing to bring the action, based on the continued existence of the law and the potential for criminal prosecution (*Croome v. Tasmania* 1997). The subsequent repeal of the sex laws in Tasmania rendered the case moot, and the High Court's decision may well have been instrumental in the Tasmanian government's decision to repeal the laws. The federal government denied a claim for legal aid to fight the case.

38. In this regard, Australia differs quite significantly from Canada and South Africa, where "full blown" rights documents have been implemented in recent times as a tool for nation building.

39. The government sought to foreclose this argument by including an explanatory memorandum to the legislation in an attempt to steer judicial interpretation towards a relatively narrow reading of the Act.

40. There are similarities here to the way in which the South African common law is constructed by conservative legal academics; see chapter three.

Chapter Seven

1. The "newness" of globalization may well be a distinctly Western phenomenon. In many parts of the world, the power of international economic forces to undermine the nation state has long been felt, and recent developments have simply exacerbated the situation.

2. I have developed this argument in more detail elsewhere; see Stychin 1996c.

References

Achmat, Z. 1993. "Apostles of Civilised Vice": "Immoral Practices" and "Unnatural Vice" in South African Prisons and Compounds, 1890–1920. *Social Dynamics,* 19:92.

———. 1995. Personal interview by author. Johannesburg, August 7.

Ackerman, B. 1995. The Next American Revolution. In *Identities, Politics, and Rights.* Edited by A. Sarat and T. R. Kearns. Ann Arbor: University of Michigan Press, 403.

Adam, B. D. 1995. *The Rise of a Gay and Lesbian Movement,* rev. ed. New York: Twayne.

Aldous, J. 1995. *The Human Rights Sexual Conduct Act: A Case Study in Changing the Law.* South Melbourne: VCTA Publishing.

Aldrich, R., ed. 1994. *Gay Perspectives II: More Essays in Australian Gay Culture.* Sydney: University of Sydney Department of Economic History and the Australian Centre for Gay and Lesbian Research.

Aldrich, R., and G. Wotherspoon, eds. 1992. *Gay Perspectives: Essays in Australian Gay Culture.* Sydney: University of Sydney Department of Economic History.

Alexander, M. J. 1991. Redrafting Morality: The Postcolonial State and the Sexual Offences Bill of Trinidad and Tobago. In *Third World Women and the Politics of Feminism.* Edited by C. T. Mohanty, A. Russo, and L. Torres. Bloomington: Indiana University Press, 133.

———. 1994. Not Just (Any)Body can be a Citizen: The Politics of Law, Sexuality and Postcoloniality in Trinidad and Tobago and the Bahamas. *Feminist Review,* 48:5.

Alfred, G. R. 1995. *Heeding the Voices of Our Ancestors.* Toronto: Oxford University Press.

Alston, P., ed. 1994a. An Australian Bill of Rights: By Design or Default? In *Towards an Australian Bill of Rights.* Canberra: Centre for International and Public Law, 1.

———, ed. 1994b. *Towards an Australian Bill of Rights.* Canberra: Centre for International and Public Law.

Altman, D. 1987. The Creation of Sexual Politics in Australia. *Journal of Australian Studies,* 20:76.

———. 1988. The Personal Is the Political: Social Movements and Cultural Change. In *Intellectual Movements and Australian Society*. Edited by B. Head and J. Walter. Melbourne: Oxford University Press, 308.

———. 1995. *The Comfort of Men*. Port Melbourne: Minerva.

Andermahr, S. 1992. Subjects or Citizens? Lesbians in The New Europe. In *Women and Citizenship in Europe*. Edited by A. Ward, J. Gregory, and N. Yuval-Davis. Stoke-on-Trent UK: Trentham Books, 111.

Anderson, B. 1991. *Imagined Communities*, rev. ed. London: Verso.

Armstrong, K. 1996. Citizenship of the Union? Lessons from *Carvel and The Guardian. Modern Law Review*, 59:582.

Armstrong, K. A. 1998. Legal Integration: Theorising the Legal Dimension of European Integration. *Journal of Common Market Studies*, 36, forthcoming.

Aron, R. 1974. Is Multinational Citizenship Possible? *Social Research*, 41:638.

Ashman, P. 1993. Introduction. In *Homosexuality: A European Community Issue*. Edited by K. Waaldijk and A. Clapham. Dordrecht Netherlands: Martinus Nijhoff, 1.

Backer, Larry C. 1997a. Harmonization, Subsidiarity and Cultural Difference: An Essay on the Dynamics of Opposition Within Federative and International Legal Systems. *Tulsa Journal of Comparative & International Law*, 4:185.

———. 1997b. Reading Entrails: *Romer, VMI* and the Art of Divining Equal Protection. *University of Tulsa Law Journal*, 32:361.

Bakan, J. C., and M. Smith. 1995. Rights, Nationalism and Social Movements in Canadian Constitutional Politics. *Social and Legal Studies*, 4:367.

Balakrishnan, G. 1996. The National Imagination. In *Mapping the Nation*. Edited by G. Balakrishnan. London: Verso, 198.

Balibar, E. 1991. Racism and Nationalism. In *Race, Nation, Class*. Edited by E. Balibar and I. Wallerstein. London: Verso, 37.

Ball, C. A. 1996. The Making of a Transnational Capitalist Society: The Court of Justice, Social Policy, and Individual Rights Under the European Community's Legal Order. *Harvard International Law Journal*, 37:307.

Bamforth, N. 1995. Sexuality and Law in the New Europe. *Modern Law Review*, 58:109.

Bankowski, Z. and A. Scott. 1996. The European Union? In *Constitutionalism, Democracy and Sovereignty: American and European Perspectives*. Edited by R. Bellamy. Aldershot UK: Avebury, 77.

Beckett, J. 1995. National and Transnational Perspectives on Multiculturalism: The View from Australia. *Identities*, 1:421.

Beer, S. H. 1995. Federalism and the Nation State: What Can Be Learned from the American Experience? In *Rethinking Federalism: Citizens, Markets, and Governments in a Changing World*. Edited by K. Knop, S. Ostry, R. Simeon, and K. Swinton. Vancouver: University of British Columbia Press, 224.

Beiner, R., ed. 1995. *Theorizing Citizenship.* Albany: State University of New York Press.

Bellamy, R. 1995. The Constitution of Europe: Rights or Democracy? In *Democracy and Constitutional Culture in the Union of Europe.* Edited by R. Bellamy, V. Bufacchi, and D. Castiglione. London: Lothian Foundation Press, 153.

Bennett, T., P. Buckridge, D. Carter, and C. Mercer, eds. 1992. *Celebrating the Nation: A Critical Study of Australia's Bicentenary.* Sydney: Allen and Unwin.

Beriss, D. 1996. Introduction: "If You're Gay and Irish, Your Parents Must Be English." *Identities.* Special issue: "The Nation/State and Its Sexual Dissidents." Edited by D. Murray and R. Handler, 2:189.

Berlant, L. 1991a. National Brands/National Body: *Imitation of Life.* In *Comparative American Identities: Race, Sex, and Nationality in the Modern Text.* Edited by H. Spillers. New York: Routledge, 110.

———. 1991b. *The Anatomy of National Fantasy: Hawthorne, Utopia, and Everyday Life.* Chicago: University of Chicago Press.

———. 1996. The Theory of Infantile Citizenship. In *Becoming National.* Edited by G. Eley and R. G. Suny. New York: Oxford University Press, 495.

Berlant, L., and E. Freeman. 1993. Queer Nationality. In *Fear of a Queer Planet.* Edited by M. Warner. Minneapolis: University of Minnesota Press, 193.

Bhabha, H. K. 1990. DissemiNation: Time, Narratives, and the Margins of the Modern Nation. In *Nation and Narration.* Edited by H. K. Bhabha. London: Routledge, 292.

Bhavnani, K.-K. 1993. Towards a Multicultural Europe?: "Race," Nation and Identity in 1992 and Beyond. *Feminist Review,* 45:30.

Blackwood, E. 1986. Breaking the Mirror: The Construction of Lesbianism and the Anthropological Discourse on Homosexuality. In *The Many Faces of Homosexuality: Anthropological Approaches to Homosexual Behavior.* Edited by E. Blackwood. New York: Harrington Park Press, 1.

Blasius, M. 1994. *Gay and Lesbian Politics.* Philadelphia: Temple University Press.

Bleys, R. 1996. *The Geography of Perversion.* London: Cassell.

Blomley, N. K. 1994. *Law, Space, and the Geographies of Power.* New York: Guilford Press.

Boch, C. 1993. The European Community and Sex Equality: Why and How? In *Sex Equality: Law and Economics.* Edited by H. L. MacQueen. Edinburgh: Edinburgh University Press, 1.

Bodnar, J. 1992. *Remaking America: Public Memory, Commemoration, and Patriotism in the Twentieth Century.* Princeton: Princeton University Press.

Botha, K. 1995. Personal interview by author. Johannesburg, July 28.

Bower, L. C. 1994. Queer Acts and the Politics of "Direct Address": Rethinking Law, Culture, and Community. *Law and Society Review,* 28:1009.

Bowers v. Hardwick 1986. *United States Reports,* 478:186.

Bowman, G. 1994. "A Country of Words": Conceiving the Palestinian Nation from the Position of Exile. In *The Making of Political Identities.* Edited by E. Laclau. London: Verso, 138.

Brody, J. D. 1995. Hyphen-Nations. In *Cruising the Performative.* Edited by S. E. Case, P. Brett, and S. L. Foster. Bloomington: Indiana University Press, 149.

Bronitt, S. 1995a. Legislation Comment: Protecting Sexual Privacy under the Criminal Law—Human Rights (Sexual Conduct) Act 1994 (Cth). *Criminal Law Journal,* 19:222.

———. 1995b. The Right to Sexual Privacy, Sado-masochism and the Human Rights (Sexual Conduct) Act 1994 (Cth). *Australian Journal of Human Rights,* 2:59.

Bronski, M. 1984. *Culture Clash: The Making of Gay Sensibility.* Boston: South End Press.

Brown, W. 1995. Rights and Identity in Late Modernity: Revisiting the "Jewish Question." In *Identities, Politics, and Rights.* Edited by A. Sarat and T. R. Kearns. Ann Arbor: University of Michigan Press, 85.

Bulbeck, C. 1996. "His and Hers Australias": National Genders. *Journal of Australian Studies,* 47:43.

Bull, M., S. Pinto, and P. R. Wilson. 1992. Homosexual Law Reform in Australia. In *Issues in Crime, Morality and Justice.* Edited by P. R. Wilson. Canberra: Australian Institute of Criminology, 177.

Burmester, H. 1995. National Sovereignty, Independence and the Impact of Treaties and International Standards. *Sydney Law Review,* 17:127.

Butler, J. 1990. *Gender Trouble.* New York: Routledge.

———. 1993. *Bodies That Matter.* New York: Routledge.

———. 1997. *Excitable Speech.* New York: Routledge.

Cairns, A., and C. Williams. 1985. Constitutionalism, Citizenship and Society in Canada: An Overview. In *Constitutionalism, Citizenship and Society in Canada.* Edited by A. Cairns and C. Williams. Toronto: University of Toronto Press, 1.

Calhoun, C. 1994. Nationalism and Civil Society: Democracy, Diversity, and Self-Determination. In *Social Theory and the Politics of Identity.* Edited by C. Calhoun. Oxford: Blackwell, 304.

———. 1995. *Critical Social Theory.* Oxford: Blackwell.

Cameron, E. 1992. Sexual Orientation and the Law. *South African Human Rights Yearbook,* 3:87.

———. 1993. Sexual Orientation and the Constitution: A Test Case for Human Rights. *South African Law Journal,* 110:450.

————. 1995a. Personal interview by author. Johannesburg, July 31.

————. 1995b. "Unapprehended Felons": Gays and Lesbians and the Law in South Africa. In *Defiant Desires: Gay and Lesbian Lives in South Africa*. Edited by M. Gevisser and E. Cameron. New York: Routledge, 89.

Castles, S., M. Kalantzis, B. Cope, and M. Morrissey, eds. *Mistaken Identity: Multiculturalism and the Demise of Nationalism in Australia*. Sydney: Pluto Press.

Chang, W. B. C. 1992. The "Wasteland" in the Western Exploitation of "Race" and the Environment. *University of Colorado Law Review*, 63:849.

Chanock, M. 1995. Race and Nation in South African Common Law. In *Nationalism, Racism and the Rule of Law*. Edited by P. Fitzpatrick. Aldershot UK: Dartmouth, 195.

Charlesworth, H. 1994. The Australian Reluctance About Rights. In *Towards an Australian Bill of Rights*. Edited by P. Alston. Canberra: Centre for International and Public Law, 21.

Chatterjee, P. 1996. Whose Imagined Community? In *Mapping the Nation*. Edited by G. Balakrishnan. London: Verso, 214.

Cheah, P. 1997. Posit(ion)ing Human Rights in the Current Global Conjuncture. *Public Culture*, 9:233.

Chetcuti, J. 1992. Relationships of Interdependency: Immigration for Same-Sex Partners. In *Gay Perspectives: Essays in Australian Gay Culture*. Edited by R. Aldrich and G. Wotherspoon. Sydney: University of Sydney Department of Economic History, 165.

Chetty, D. 1995. A Drag at Madame Costello's: Cape Moffie Life and the Popular Press in the 1950s and 1960s. In *Defiant Desires: Gay and Lesbian Lives in South Africa*. Edited by M. Gevisser and E. Cameron. New York: Routledge, 115.

Chow, R. 1993. *Writing Diaspora: Tactics of Intervention in Contemporary Cultural Studies*. Bloomington: Indiana University Press.

Cicchino, P. M., B. R. Deming, and K. M. Nicholson. 1995. Sex, Lies, and Civil Rights: A Critical History of the Massachusetts Gay Civil Rights Bill. In *Legal Inversions: Lesbians, Gay Men, and the Politics of Law*. Edited by D. Herman and C. Stychin. Philadelphia: Temple University Press, 141.

Clapham, A., and J. H. H. Weiler. 1993. Lesbians and Gay Men in the European Community Legal Order. In *Homosexuality: A European Community Issue*. Edited by K. Waaldijk and A. Clapham. Dordrecht Netherlands: Martinus Nijhoff, 7.

Clark, V. A. 1991. Developing Diaspora Literacy and *Marasa* Consciousness. In *Comparative American Identities: Race, Sex, and Nationality in the Modern Text*. Edited by H. Spillers. New York: Routledge, 40.

Closa, C. 1994. Citizenship of the Union and Nationality of Member States.

In *Legal Issues of the Maastricht Treaty*. Edited by D. O'Keeffe and P. M. Twomey. Chichester UK: Chancery Law Publishing, 109.

Cochrane, P., and D. Goodman. 1992. The Great Australian Journey: Cultural Logic and Nationalism in the Postmodern Era. In *Celebrating the Nation: A Critical Study of Australia's Bicentenary*. Edited by T. Bennett, P. Buckridge, D. Carter, and C. Mercer. Sydney: Allen and Unwin, 175.

Collins, H. 1985. Political Ideology in Australia: The Distinctiveness of a Benthamite Society. *Daedalus*, Winter: 147.

Comaroff, J. 1995. The Discourse of Rights in Colonial South Africa: Subjectivity, Sovereignty, Modernity. In *Identities, Politics, and Rights*. Edited by A. Sarat and T. R. Kearns. Ann Arbor: University of Michigan Press, 193.

Comaroff, J., and J. Comaroff. 1992. *Ethnography and the Historical Imagination*. Boulder: Westview Press.

Communist Party Case 1951. *Commonwealth Law Reports*, 83:1.

Coombe, R. J. 1993. Tactics of Appropriation and the Politics of Recognition in Late Modern Democracies. *Political Theory*, 21:411.

———. 1995. The Cultural Life of Things: Anthropological Approaches to Law and Society in Conditions of Globalization. *American University Journal of International Law and Policy*, 10:791.

Cooper, D. 1993. The Citizen's Charter and Radical Democracy: Empowerment and Exclusion Within Citizenship Discourse. *Social and Legal Studies*, 2:149.

———. 1995. *Power in Struggle*. Buckingham UK: Open University Press.

———. 1996. Talmudic Territory? Space, Law, and Modernist Discourse. *Journal of Law and Society*, 23:529.

Cooper, D., and D. Herman. 1995. Getting "The Family Right": Legislating Heterosexuality in Britain 1986–91. In *Legal Inversions: Lesbians, Gay Men, and the Politics of Law*. Edited by D. Herman and C. Stychin. Philadelphia: Temple University Press, 162.

Corder, H. 1994. Towards a South African Constitution. *Modern Law Review*, 57:491.

———. 1995. Personal interview by author. Cape Town, August 17.

Croome and Another v. The State of Tasmania 1997. Unreported.

Croome, R. 1995. Sexual (Mis)conduct. *Alternative Law Journal*, 20:282.

Currah, P. 1996. Securing the Rights of Sexual Minorities: Object Choice, Gender Expression, and the Future of Gay and Lesbian Identity Politics. Paper presented at the American Political Science Association Annual Meeting. San Francisco, California.

———. 1997. Politics, Practices, Publics: Identity and Queer Rights. In *Playing With Fire: Queer Politics, Queer Theories*. Edited by S. Phelan. New York: Routledge, 231.

d'Oliveira, H. U. J. 1994. European Citizenship: Its Meaning, Its Potential. In *Europe After Maastricht: An Ever Closer Union?* Edited by R. Dehousse. Munich: Law Books in Europe, 126.

Da Matta, R. 1984. Carnival in Multiple Planes. In *Rite, Drama, Festival, Spectacle.* Edited by J. J. MacAloon. Philadelphia: Institute for the Study of Human Issues, 208.

Darian-Smith, E. 1995a. Law in Place: Legal Mediations of National Identity and State Territory in Europe. In *Nationalism, Racism, and the Rule of Law.* Edited by P. Fitzpatrick. Aldershot UK: Dartmouth, 27.

———. 1995b. Rabies Rides the Fast Train: Transnational Interactions in Post-Colonial Times. *Law and Critique,* 6:75.

de Búrca, G. 1996. The Language of Rights and European Integration. In *New Legal Dynamics of European Union.* Edited by J. Shaw and G. More. Oxford: Clarendon Press, 29.

de Lange, R. 1995. Paradoxes of European Citizenship. In *Nationalism, Racism, and the Rule of Law.* Edited by P. Fitzpatrick. Aldershot UK: Dartmouth, 97.

de Sève, M. 1992. The Perspectives of Quebec Feminists. In *Challenging Times: The Women's Movement in Canada and the United States.* Edited by C. Backhouse and D. H. Flaherty. Montreal and Kingston: McGill–Queen's University Press, 110.

de Tocqueville, A. 1958. *Democracy in America.* Edited by P. Bradley. New York: Vintage, vol. 1.

de Vos, P. 1996. On the Legal Construction of Gay and Lesbian Identity and South Africa's Transitional Constitution. *South African Journal on Human Rights,* 12:265.

Delanty, G. 1995. *Inventing Europe: Idea, Identity, Reality.* London: Macmillan.

Dennis v. United States 1950. *United States Reports,* 341:494.

Derbyshire, P. 1994. A Measure of Queer. *Critical Quarterly,* 36:39.

Derrida, J. 1992. *The Other Heading: Reflections on Today's Europe.* Translated by P. A. Brault and M. Naas. Bloomington: Indiana University Press.

Devenish, G. E. 1996. Human Rights in a Divided Society. In *Understanding Human Rights.* Edited by C. Gearty and A. Tomkins. London: Mansell, 60.

Ditsie, B. 1995. What Unity? *Outright,* vol. 2, 8:14.

Dobber, M. 1995. SexCrime. *Alternative Law Journal,* 20:285.

Dubow, S. 1992. Afrikaner Nationalism, Apartheid and the Conceptualization of "Race." *Journal of African History,* 33:209.

———. 1994. Ethnic Euphemisms and Racial Echoes. *Journal of Southern African Studies,* 20:355.

Dudgeon v. United Kingdom 1981. *European Human Rights Reports,* 4:149.

Duggan, L. 1992. Making It Perfectly Queer. *Socialist Review,* 22:11.

———. 1994. Queering the State. *Social Text,* 39:1.

Duncan, D. G. 1996. Parading the First Amendment Through the Streets of South Boston. *New England Law Review,* 30:663.

Dunton, C., and M. Palmberg. 1996. *Human Rights and Homosexuality in Southern Africa.* Uppsala Sweden: Nordiska Afrikainstitutet.

Duplé, N. 1984. Homosexualité et droits à l'égalité dans les Chartes canadienne et québécoise. *Les Cahiers de Droit,* 25:801.

Eaton, M. 1994. Lesbians, Gays and the Struggle for Equality Rights: Reversing the Progressive Hypothesis. *Dalhousie Law Journal,* 17:130.

———. 1995. Homosexual Unmodified: Speculations on Law's Discourse, Race, and the Construction of Sexual Identity. In *Legal Inversions: Lesbians, Gay Men, and the Politics of Law.* Edited by D. Herman and C. Stychin. Philadelphia: Temple University Press, 46.

Eddy, J. 1991. What are the Origins of Australia's National Identity? In *Australia Compared: People, Policies and Politics.* Edited by F. G. Castles. Sydney: Allen and Unwin, 17.

Edelman, L. 1994. *Homographesis.* New York: Routledge.

Eisenstein, Z. 1996. *Hatreds: Racialized and Sexualized Conflicts in the 21st Century.* New York: Routledge.

Eley, G., and R. G. Suny, eds. 1996. Introduction. In *Becoming National: A Reader.* Oxford: Oxford University Press, 3.

Ellmann, S. 1994. The New South African Constitution and Ethnic Division. *Columbia Human Rights Law Review,* 26:5.

English, P. 1997. Heritage, Identity and Citizenship: A Single Past for the Single Market? Paper presented at the Critical Legal Conference. University College. Dublin Ireland.

Epstein, B. 1994. Anti-Communism, Homophobia, and the Construction of Masculinity in the Postwar U.S. *Critical Sociology,* vol. 20, 3:21.

Evans v. Romer 1996. *Supreme Court Reporter,* 116:1628.

Evans, D. T. 1993. *Sexual Citizenship.* London: Routledge.

Everson, M. 1996. The Legacy of the Market Citizen. In *New Legal Dynamics of European Union.* Edited by J. Shaw and G. More. Oxford: Clarendon Press, 73.

Fanon, F. 1967. *Black Skin, White Masks.* Translated by C. L. Markmann. New York: Grove Press.

Fine, D., and J. Nicol. 1995. The Lavender Lobby: Working for Lesbian and Gay Rights Within the Liberation Movement. In *Defiant Desires: Gay and Lesbian Lives in South Africa.* Edited by M. Gevisser and E. Cameron. New York: Routledge, 269.

Fitzpatrick, P. 1995. "We know what it is when you do not ask us": Nationalism as Racism. In *Nationalism, Racism and the Rule of Law.* Edited by P. Fitzpatrick. Aldershot UK: Dartmouth, 3.

References   231

———. 1997. New Europe, Old Story: Racism, Law and the European Community. In *The Critical Lawyers' Handbook 2*. Edited by P. Ireland and P. Laleng. London: Pluto, 86.

Fletcher, G. P. 1994. Constitutional Identity. In *Constitutionalism, Identity, Difference, and Legitimacy*. Edited by M. Rosenfeld. Durham: Duke University Press, 223.

Flynn, L. 1995. The Irish Supreme Court and the Constitution of Male Homosexuality. In *Legal Inversions: Lesbians, Gay Men, and the Politics of Law*. Edited by D. Herman and C. Stychin. Philadelphia: Temple University Press, 29.

———. 1996. The Internal Market and the European Union: Some Feminist Notes. In *Feminist Perspectives on the Foundational Subjects of Law*. Edited by A. Bottomley. London: Cavendish, 279.

———. 1997. "Cherishing All Her Children Equally": The Law and Politics of Irish Lesbian and Gay Citizenship. *Social and Legal Studies*, 6:493.

Fraser, D. 1995. Father Knows Best: Transgressive Sexualities (?) and the Rule of Law. *Current Issues in Criminal Justice*, 7:82.

Fuss, D. 1991. Inside/Out. In *Inside/Out*. Edited by D. Fuss. New York: Routledge, 1.

Fuss, D. 1995. *Identification Papers*. New York, Routledge.

Gagnon, L. 1996. Untitled. (Toronto) *Globe and Mail*. May 4, p. D3.

Galligan, B. 1994. Australia's Political Culture and Institutional Design. In *Towards an Australian Bill of Rights*. Edited by P. Alston. Canberra: Centre for International and Public Law, 55.

Galligan, B., R. Knopff, and J. Uhr. 1990. Australian Federalism and the Debate Over a Bill of Rights. *Publius: The Journal of Federalism*, 20:53.

Gamson, J. 1995. Must Identity Movements Self-Destruct? A Queer Dilemma. *Social Problems*, 42:390.

Gay, J. 1986. "Mummies and Babies" and Friends and Lovers in Lesotho. In *The Many Faces of Homosexuality: Anthropological Approaches to Homosexual Behavior*. Edited by E. Blackwood. New York: Harrington Park Press, 97.

Gevisser, M. 1995. A Different Fight for Freedom: A History of South African Lesbian and Gay Organisation from the 1950s to the 1990s. In *Defiant Desires: Gay and Lesbian Lives in South Africa*. Edited by M. Gevisser and E. Cameron. New York: Routledge, 14.

Gilman, S. 1992. Plague in Germany, 1939/1989: Cultural Images of Race, Space, and Disease. In *Nationalisms and Sexualities*. Edited by A. Parker, M. Russo, D. Sommer, and P. Yaeger. New York: Routledge, 175.

Girard, P. 1986. Sexual Orientation as a Human Rights Issue in Canada 1969–1985. *Dalhousie Law Journal*, 10:267.

Goldin, I. 1987. The Reconstitution of Coloured Identity in the Western

Cape. In *The Politics of Race, Class and Nationalism in Twentieth-Century South Africa*. Edited by S. Marks and S. Trapido. London: Longman, 156.

Goodman, D. 1992. Postscript 1991—Explicating Openness. In *Celebrating the Nation: A Critical Study of Australia's Bicentenary*. Edited by T. Bennett, P. Buckridge, D. Carter, and C. Mercer. Sydney: Allen and Unwin, 191.

Govender, K. 1996. Federal Features of the Interim Constitution. *Review of Constitutional Studies*, 3:76.

Grant, B. 1994. Australia Confronts an Identity Crisis. *New York Times*. March 20, p. D5.

Grant v. South-West Trains Ltd. 1998. Case C-249/96, unreported.

Green, L. (M.P.), 1995. Personal interview by author. Cape Town, August 16.

Grosz, E. 1993. Judaism and Exile: The Ethics of Otherness. In *Space and Place: Theories of Identity and Location*. Edited by E. Carter, J. Donald, and J. Squires. London: Lawrence and Wishart, 57.

Guiberneau, M. 1996. *Nationalisms: The Nation-State and Nationalism in the Twentieth Century*. Oxford: Polity.

Gunew, S. 1990. Denaturalizing Cultural Nationalisms: Multicultural Readings of "Australia." In *Nation and Narration*. Edited by H. K. Bhabha. London: Routledge, 99.

Haakonssen, K. 1991. From National Law to the Rights of Man: A European Perspective on American Debates. In *A Culture of Rights*. Edited by M. J. Lacey and K. Haakonssen. Cambridge UK: Cambridge University Press, 19.

Habermas, J. 1995. Citizenship and National Identity: Some Reflections on the Future of Europe. In *Theorizing Citizenship*. Edited by R. Beiner. Albany: State University of New York Press, 255.

Haig, T. 1994. Not Just Some Sexless Queen: A Note on "Kids in the Hall" and the Queerness of Canada. In *canadas*. Edited by J. Zinovich. New York: Semiotext(e), 227.

Halley, J. E. 1996. Introduction. Symposium: "Intersections: Sexuality, Cultural Tradition, and the Law." *Yale Journal of Law and the Humanities*, 8:93.

Halperin, D. M. 1995. *Saint Foucault: Towards a Gay Hagiography*. New York: Oxford University Press.

Hanafin, P. 1997. From "Queer Old Josser" to Equal Citizen? Reinterpreting Ga(y)elic Sexuality in Literary and Legal Discourse. Paper presented at the Socio-Legal Studies Association Conference. Cardiff, Wales.

Hansard (S.A.). 1995. Cape Town, Government of South Africa.

Harper, P. B. 1994. Private Affairs: Race, Sex, Property, and Persons. *GLQ*, 1:111.

Harries, P. 1990. Symbols and Sexuality: Culture and Identity on the Early Witwatersrand Gold Mines. *Gender and History*, 2:318.

Harris, A. P. 1996. Seductions of Modern Culture. *Yale Journal of Law and the Humanities*, 8:213.

Hart, J. 1992. A Cocktail of Alarm: Same-sex Couples and Migration to Australia 1985–90. In *Modern Homosexualities: Fragments of Lesbian and Gay Experience*. Edited by K. Plummer. London: Routledge, 121.

Hatchard, J., and P. Slinn. 1995. The Path Towards a New Order in South Africa. *International Relations*, vol. 12, 4:1.

Hays, M. 1996. My Own Private Partition. (Montreal) *Mirror*. March 21–28, p. 12.

Hennessy, R. 1995. Queer Visibility in Commodity Culture. In *Social Postmodernism*. Edited by L. J. Nicholson and S. Seidman. Cambridge UK: Cambridge University Press, 142.

Herdt, G. 1997. *Same Sex Different Cultures*. Boulder: Westview Press.

Herman, D. 1990. Are we Family? Lesbian Rights and Women's Liberation. *Osgoode Hall Law Journal*, 28:789.

———. 1994a. *Rights of Passage: Struggles for Lesbian and Gay Legal Equality*. Toronto: University of Toronto Press.

———. 1994b. The Good, the Bad, and the Smugly: Perspectives on the Canadian Charter of Rights and Freedoms. *Oxford Journal of Legal Studies*, 14:589.

———. 1997. *The Antigay Agenda: Orthodox Vision and the Christian Right*. Chicago: University of Chicago Press.

Herman, D., and D. Cooper. 1997. Anarchic Armadas, Brussels Bureaucrats, and the Valiant Maple Leaf: British Nationalism and the Canada-Spain Fish War. *Legal Studies*, 17:415.

Herrell, R. K. 1992. The Symbolic Strategies of Chicago's Gay and Lesbian Pride Day Parade. In *Gay Culture in America*. Edited by G. Herdt. Boston: Beacon Press, 225.

———. 1996. Sin, Sickness, Crime: Queer Desire and the American State. *Identities*, 2:273.

Hervey, T. K. 1996. Migrant Workers and their Families in the European Union: the pervasive market ideology of Community law. In *New Legal Dynamics of European Union*. Edited by J. Shaw and G. More. Oxford: Clarendon Press, 91.

Higgins, R., and L. Chamberland. 1992. Mixed Messages: Gays and Lesbians in Montreal Yellow Papers in the 1950s. In *The Challenge of Modernity: A Reader on Post-Confederation Canada*. Edited by I. McKay. Toronto: McGraw-Hill Ryerson, 422.

Hoffmann, S. 1982. Reflections on the Nation-State in Western Europe Today. *Journal of Common Market Studies*, 21:21.

Holiday, A. 1988. White Nationalism in South Africa as Movement and System. In *The National Question in South Africa*. Edited by M. van Diepen. London: Zed Books, 77.

Holmes, R. 1995. "White Rapists Made Coloureds (and Homosexuals)": The Winnie Mandela Trial and the Politics of Race and Sexuality. In *Defiant Desires: Gay and Lesbian Lives in South Africa*. Edited by M. Gevisser and E. Cameron. New York: Routledge, 284.

Hoskyns, C. 1996. *Integrating Gender: Women, Law and Politics in the European Union*. London: Verso.

House of Representatives (Australia). 1994. *Weekly Hansard*. Canberra: Parliament of the Commonwealth of Australia.

Howe, A. 1995. The Constitutional Centenary, Citizenship, the Republic and All That—Absent Feminist Conversationalists. *Melbourne University Law Review*, 20:218.

Hroch, M. 1996. From National Movement to the Fully-Formed Nation: The Nation-Building Process in Europe. In *Becoming National: A Reader*. Edited by G. Eley and R. G. Suny. Oxford: Oxford University Press, 60.

Human Rights and Equal Opportunities Commission, 1997. *Human Rights for Australia's Gays and Lesbians*. Sydney: Human Rights and Equal Opportunities Commission.

Hunter, N. D. 1995. Identity, Speech and Equality. In *Sex Wars: Sexual Dissent and Political Culture*. Edited by L. Duggan and N. D. Hunter. New York: Routledge, 123.

Hurley and South Boston Allied War Veterans Council v. Irish-American Gay, Lesbian and Bisexual Group of Boston 1995. *Supreme Court Reporter*, 115:2338.

Hutson, J. H. 1991. The Bill of Rights and the American Revolutionary Experience. In *A Culture of Rights*. Edited by M. J. Lacey and K. Haakonssen. Cambridge UK: Cambridge University Press, 62.

Huyssen, A. 1994. Nation, Race, and Immigration: German Identities After Unification. *Discourse*, vol. 16, 3:6.

Inglis, K. S. 1991. Multiculturalism and National Identity. In *Australian National Identity*. Edited by C. A. Price. Canberra: Academy of the Social Sciences in Australia, 13.

Irving, H. 1996. The Republic is a Feminist Issue. *Feminist Review*, 52:87.

Jackson, P., and J. Penrose, eds. 1994. Introduction: Placing "Race" and "Nation." *Constructions of Race, Place and Nation*. Minneapolis: University of Minnesota Press, 1.

Jensen, J. 1993. What's in a Name? Nationalist Movements and Public Discourse. In *Social Movements and Culture*. Edited by H. Johnston and B. Klandermans. London: UCL Press.

Jones, T. H. 1996. Fundamental Rights in Australia and Britain: Domestic and International Aspects. In *Understanding Human Rights*. Edited by C. Gearty and A. Tomkins. London: Mansell, 91.

Joseph, S. 1994. Gay Rights Under the ICCPR—Commentary on *Toonen v. Australia. University of Tasmania Law Review*, 13:392.

Journal des Débats (Assemblée Nationale) 1977. 31st legislature, 2d sess., vol. 19, pt. 121.

Kallen, E. 1996. Gay and Lesbian Rights Issues: A Comparative Analysis of Sydney, Australia and Toronto, Canada. *Human Rights Quarterly*, 18:206.

Kapferer, J. 1996. *Being All Equal: Identity, Difference and Australian Cultural Practice*. Oxford: Berg.

Kaplan, G. 1997. Feminism and Nationalism: The European Case. In *Feminist Nationalism*. Edited by L. A. West. New York: Routledge, 3.

Kaplan, W., ed. 1993. *Belonging: The Meaning and Future of Canadian Citizenship*. Montreal and Kingston: McGill–Queen's University Press.

Kearney, R. 1997. *Postnationalist Ireland*. London: Routledge.

Keller, B. 1994. Apartheid's Gone, and Anything Goes. *New York Times*, December 28.

Kinsman, G. 1996. *The Regulation of Desire*, rev. ed. Montreal: Black Rose Books.

Kirsch, G. 1995. The New Pluralism: Regionalism, Ethnicity, and Language in Western Europe. In *Rethinking Federalism: Citizens, Markets, and Governments in a Changing World*. Edited by K. Knop, S. Ostry, R. Simeon, and K. Swinton. Vancouver: University of British Columbia Press, 59.

Kiss, E. 1995. Is Nationalism Compatible with Human Rights? Reflections on East-Central Europe. In *Identities, Politics, and Rights*. Edited by A. Sarat and T. R. Kearns. Ann Arbor: University of Michigan Press, 367.

Klug, H. 1996. Participating in the Design: Constitution-making in South Africa. *Review of Constitutional Studies*, 3:18.

Kristeva, J. 1993. *Nations Without Nationalism*. Translated by L. S. Roudiez. New York: Columbia University Press.

Kymlicka, W. 1989. *Liberalism, Community and Culture*. Oxford: Clarendon Press.

Kymlicka, W. 1995. *Multicultural Citizenship*. Oxford: Oxford University Press.

Lacey, M. J., and K. Haakonssen, eds. 1991. History, Historicism, and the Culture of Rights. In *A Culture of Rights*. Cambridge UK: Cambridge University Press, 1.

Laclau, E., and C. Mouffe. 1985. *Hegemony and Socialist Strategy*. London: Verso.

Langlois, S., et al. 1992. *Recent Social Trends in Québec 1960–1990*. Frankfurt: Campus Verlag.

Laskey, Jaggard, and Brown v. United Kingdom 1997. *Human Rights Case Digest*, 8:319.

Lavarch, M. 1997. Personal interview by author. Brisbane, March 20.

Le Clerc, P., and L. A. West. 1997. Feminist Nationalist Movements in Québec:

Resolving Contradictions? In *Feminist Nationalism*. Edited by L. A. West. New York: Routledge, 220.

Lewis, J., and F. Loots. 1995. "Moffies en Manvroue": Gay and Lesbian Life Histories in Contemporary Cape Town. In *Defiant Desires: Gay and Lesbian Lives in South Africa*. Edited by M. Gevisser and E. Cameron. New York: Routledge, 140.

Luow, C. 1994. Former MI Man Behind New Party. (South Africa) *Mail and Guardian*. January 14.

Lynch, M. 1982. The end of the "human rights decade." In *Flaunting It! A Decade of Gay Journalism from The Body Politic*. Edited by E. Jackson and S. Persky. Vancouver: New Star Books, 244.

Lyons, C. 1996. Citizenship in the Constitution of the European Union: rhetoric or reality? In *Constitutionalism, Democracy and Sovereignty: American and European Perspectives*. Edited by R. Bellamy. Aldershot UK: Avebury, 96.

Mabo and Others v. The State of Queensland 1992. *Commonwealth Law Reports*, 175:1.

MacAloon, J. J. 1982. Sociation and Sociability in Political Celebrations. In *Celebration: Studies in Festivity and Ritual*. Edited by V. Turner. Washington DC: Smithsonian Institute Press, 255.

MacCormick, N. 1996. Liberalism, Nationalism and the Post-sovereign State. *Political Studies*, 44:553.

Manalansan, M. 1993. (Re)Locating the Gay Filipino: Resistance, Postcolonialism, and Identity. *Journal of Homosexuality*, vol. 26, 2/3:53.

Mangaliso, Z. A. 1997. Gender and Nation-Building in South Africa. In *Feminist Nationalism*. Edited by L. A. West. New York: Routledge, 130.

Marks, S., and S. Trapido. 1987. The Politics of Race, Class and Nationalism. In *The Politics of Race, Class and Nationalism in Twentieth-Century South Africa*. Edited by S. Marks and S. Trapido. London: Longman, 1.

Marshall, W. 1997. Paper presented at the Queering the Nation Conference, Warwick University. Coventry UK.

Martin, R. K. 1977. Two Days in Sodom. *The Body Politic*, July/August: 28.

———. 1994. Cheap Tricks in Montreal: Scott Symons's *Place d'Armes*. *Essays on Canadian Writing*, 54:198.

Mathew, P. 1995. International Law and the Protection of Human Rights in Australia: Recent Trends. *Sydney Law Review*, 17:177.

Maurer, B. 1995. Writing Law, Making a "Nation": History, Modernity, and Paradoxes of Self-Rule in the British Virgin Islands. *Law and Society Review*, 29:255.

McClintock, A. 1995. *Imperial Leather: Race, Gender and Sexuality in the Colonial Contest*. London: Routledge.

———. 1996. "No Longer in a Future Heaven": Nationalism, Gender, and

Race. In *Becoming National*. Edited by G. Eley and R. G. Suny. New York: Oxford University Press, 260.

McIntosh, M. 1993. Queer Theory and the War of the Sexes. In *Activating Theory: Lesbian, Gay, Bisexual Politics*. Edited by J. Bristow and A. Wilson. London: Lawrence and Wishart, 30.

McLean, H., and L. Ngcobo. 1995. Abangibhamayo Bathi Ngimnandi (Those who fuck me say I'm tasty): Gay Sexuality in Reef Townships. In *Defiant Desires: Gay and Lesbian Lives in South Africa*. Edited by M. Gevisser and E. Cameron. New York: Routledge, 158.

Meehan, E. 1993. Citizenship and the European Community. *Political Quarterly*, 64:172.

Megalogenis, G. 1997. Ministers Lash Hanson. *The Australian Online*, May 5.

Ménard, G. 1985. Du Berdache au *Berdache*: Lectures de l'homosexualité dans la culture québécoise. *Anthropologie et Sociétés*, vol. 9, 3:115.

Millbank, J. 1995. Fear of Persecution or Just a Queer Feeling? *Alternative Law Journal*, 20:261.

Milward, A. S. 1992. *The European Rescue of the Nation-State*. London: Routledge.

Minow, M. 1995. Rights and Cultural Difference. In *Identities, Politics, and Rights*. Edited by A. Sarat and T. R. Kearns. Ann Arbor: University of Michigan Press, 347.

Mohanty, C. T. 1995. Feminist Encounters: Locating the Politics of Experience. In *Social Postmodernism*. Edited by L. J. Nicholson and S. Seidman. Cambridge UK: Cambridge University Press, 68.

Mokgoro, Y. 1996. Traditional Authority and Democracy in the Interim South African Constitution. *Review of Constitutional Studies*, 3:60.

Montero, O. 1993. Before the Parade Passes By: Latino Queers and National Identity. *Radical America*, vol. 24, 4:15.

Montgomery, B. 1997. State to Dump Anti-Gay Laws. *The Australian*, March 27, p. 1.

Montgomery, B., and J. Hughes. 1997. Gay Law Battle Ends in Celebration. *The Australian Online*, May 3.

Moodie, T. D., with V. Ndatshe and B. Sibuyi. 1988. Migrancy and Male Sexuality on the South African Gold Mines. *Journal of Southern African Studies*, 14:228.

Moran, L. J. 1991. The Uses of Homosexuality: Homosexuality for National Security. *International Journal of the Sociology of Law*, 19:149.

More, G. C. 1993. "Equal Treatment" of the Sexes in European Community Law: What Does "Equal" Mean? *Feminist Legal Studies*, 1:45.

More, G. 1996a. Equality of Treatment in European Community Law: The Limits of Market Equality. In *Feminist Perspectives on the Foundational Subjects of Law*. Edited by A. Bottomley. London: Cavendish, 261.

More, G. 1996b. The Acquired Rights Directive: Frustrating or Facilitating Labour Market Flexibility. In *New Legal Dynamics of European Union*. Edited by J. Shaw and G. More. Oxford: Clarendon Press, 129.

Morgan, W. 1993. Sexuality and Human Rights: The First Communication by an Australian to the Human Rights Committee under the Optional Protocol to the International Covenant on Civil and Political Rights. *Australian Yearbook of International Law*, 14:277.

———. 1994a. Identifying Evil for What it is: Tasmania, Sexual Perversity and the United Nations. *Melbourne University Law Review*, 19:740.

———. 1994b. Protecting Rights or Just Passing the Buck? The Human Rights (Sexual Conduct) Bill 1994. *Australian Journal of Human Rights*, 1:409.

———. 1997. Personal correspondence with author, July 14.

Morris, M. 1995. *Pink Triangle*. Sydney: University of New South Wales Press.

Mosse, G. L. 1985. *Nationalism and Sexuality*. New York: Howard Fertig.

Mouffe, C. 1994. For a Politics of Nomadic Identity. In *Travellers' Tales: Narratives of Home and Displacement*. Edited by G. Robertson, et al. London: Routledge, 105.

Mtetwa, P. 1995a. Personal interview by author. Johannesburg, August 7.

———. 1995b. Defend the Equality Clause. *Equality: News and Views of the National Coalition for Gay and Lesbian Equality*, 1:1.

Mtshaulana, P., and M. Thomas. 1996. The Constitutional Court of South Africa: An Introduction. *Review of Constitutional Studies*, 3:98.

Murray, D. A. B. 1996. Homosexuality, Society, and the State: An Ethnography of Sublime Resistance in Martinique. *Identities*, 2:249.

National Association of Regulatory Utility Commissioners v. Federal Communications Commission 1976. *Federal Reporter*, 2nd series, 525:630.

National Coalition for Gay and Lesbian Equality 1995. *The Right to Equality*. Submission to Constitutional Assembly Theme Committee 4 on Fundamental Rights, unpublished.

National Socialist Party v. Skokie 1977. *United States Reports*, 432:43.

Ndatshe, V. 1993. Two Miners. In *The Invisible Ghetto: Lesbian and Gay Writing from South Africa*. Edited by M. Krouse. Johannesburg: COSAW Publishing, 45.

Nedelsky, J. 1990a. Law, Boundaries, and the Bounded Self. *Representations*, 30:162.

———. 1990b. *Private Property and the Limits of American Constitutionalism*. Chicago: University of Chicago Press.

Nkoli, S. 1995. Wardrobes: Coming Out as a Black Gay Activist in South Africa. In *Defiant Desires: Gay and Lesbian Lives in South Africa*. Edited by M. Gevisser and E. Cameron. New York: Routledge, 249.

Norris v. Attorney General 1984. *Irish Reports*, 1984:36.

Norval, A. J. 1994a. The Politics of Homecoming? Contending Identities in

Contemporary South Africa or Identité à Venir. *Angelaki*. Special issue: "Reconsidering the Political." Edited by D. Howarth and A. J. Norval, 1:157.

———. 1994b. Social Ambiguity and the Crisis of Apartheid. In *The Making of Political Identities*. Edited by E. Laclau. London: Verso, 115.

———. 1995. Decolonization, Demonization and Difference: The Difficult Constitution of a Nation. *Philosophy and Social Criticism*, vol. 21, 3:31.

Ohmae, K. 1995. *The End of the Nation State: The Rise of Regional Economies*. New York: The Free Press.

Opeskin, B. R., and D. R. Rothwell. 1995. The Impact of Treaties on Australian Federalism. *Case Western Reserve Journal of International Law*, 27:1.

Orford, A. 1996. The Uses of Sovereignty in the New Imperial Order. *Australian Feminist Law Journal*, 6:63.

Paliwala, A. 1995. Law and the Constitution of the "Immigrant" in Europe: A UK Policy Perspective. In *Nationalism, Racism, and the Rule of Law*. Edited by P. Fitzpatrick. Aldershot UK: Dartmouth, 77.

Pantazis, A. 1996. The Problematic Nature of Gay Identity. *South African Journal on Human Rights*, 12:291.

Parker, A. 1993. Grafting David Cronenberg: Monstrosity, AIDS Media, National/Sexual Difference. In *Media Spectacles*. Edited by M. Garber, J. Matlock, and R. L. Walkowitz. New York: Routledge, 209.

Passavant, P. A. 1996. A Moral Geography of Liberty: John Stuart Mill and American Free Speech Discourse. *Social and Legal Studies*, 5:301.

Patton, P. 1996. *Mabo*, Difference and the Body of the Law. In *Thinking Through the Body of the Law*. Edited by P. Cheah, D. Fraser, and J. Grbich. Sydney: Allen and Unwin, 43.

Pease, D. E. 1992. National Identities, Postmodern Artifacts and Postnational Narratives. *Boundary2*, 19:1.

Peller, G. 1990. Race Consciousness. *Duke Law Journal*, 1990:758.

Pérez-Peña, R. 1994. A Rights Movement that Emerges From the Right. *New York Times*, December 30, p. B6.

Phelan, S. 1989. *Identity Politics: Lesbian Feminism and the Limits of Community*. Philadelphia: Temple University Press.

———. 1994. *Getting Specific: Postmodern Lesbian Politics*. Minneapolis: University of Minnesota Press.

Phillips, O. 1997. Zimbabwean Law and the Production of a White Man's Disease. *Social and Legal Studies*, 6:471.

Phillips, T. L. 1996. Symbolic Boundaries and National Identity in Australia. *British Journal of Sociology*, 47:113.

Pieterse, J. N. 1991. Fictions of Europe. *Race & Class*, vol. 32, 3:3.

Pollard, R. 1997. IVF Battle. *Sydney Star Observer*, March 13, p. 1.

Pomeroy, W. 1988. What is the National Question in International Perspective? In *The National Question in South Africa.* Edited by M. van Diepen. London: Zed Books, 12.

Potgieter, J. M. 1991. The Role of the Law in a Period of Political Transition: The Need for Objectivity. *Journal of Contemporary Roman-Dutch Law,* 54: 800.

Povinelli, E. A. 1994. Sexual Savages/Sexual Sovereignty: Australian Colonial Texts and the Postcolonial Politics of Nationalism. *diacritics,* 24:122.

Pretorius, J. L. 1991. Minority Rights in Ideological Perspective: The Legacy of Ethno-Nationalism. *Journal of Juridical Science,* 16:1.

Preuss, U. K. 1994. Constitutional Powermaking of the New Polity: Some Deliberations on the Relations Between Constituent Power and the Constitution. In *Constitutionalism, Identity, Difference, and Legitimacy.* Edited by M. Rosenfeld. Durham: Duke University Press, 143.

———. 1995. Problems of a Concept of European Citizenship. *European Law Journal,* 1:267.

———. 1996. Two Challenges to European Citizenship. *Political Studies,* 44: 534.

Price, C. A., ed. 1991. *Australian National Identity.* Canberra: Academy of the Social Sciences in Australia.

Probyn, E. 1996. *Outside Belongings.* New York: Routledge.

Quebec Human Rights Commission. 1994. *From Illegality to Equality: Report on the Public Consultation on Violence and Discrimination Against Gays and Lesbians* (translated excerpts). Mont-Royal Quebec: Quebecor.

R. v. Secretary of State for Defence, ex parte Perkins 1997. No. CO 279–96, unreported.

R. A. V. v. St. Paul 1992. *United States Reports,* 505:377.

Rakove, J. N. 1991. Parchment Barriers and the Politics of Rights. In *A Culture of Rights.* Edited by M. J. Lacey and K. Haakonssen. Cambridge UK: Cambridge University Press, 98.

Ramsey, A., and E. Hannan. 1997. Premiers Condemn Assault on Rights. *The Australian,* March 26, p. 2.

Rattansi, A. 1995. Just Framing: Ethnicities and Racism in a Postmodern Framework. In *Social Postmodernism.* Edited by L. J. Nicholson and S. Seidman. Cambridge UK: Cambridge University Press, 250.

Rawlyk, G. 1995. Religion in Canada: A Historical Overview. *Annals of the American Academy of Political and Social Science,* 538:131.

Reid, J. P. 1986. *Constitutional History of the American Revolution,* Madison: Wisconsin University Press, vol. 1.

Retief, G. 1995. Keeping Sodom Out of the Laager: State Repression of Homosexuality in Apartheid South Africa. In *Defiant Desires: Gay and Lesbian Lives in South Africa.* Edited by M. Gevisser and E. Cameron. New York: Routledge, 99.

Reuters News Service, 1996. U.S. Senator Helms Blasts Allies on Cuba, May 21.

Richards, D. A. J. 1993. *Conscience and the Constitution*. Princeton: Princeton University Press.

———. 1994. Revolution and Constitutionalism in America. In *Constitutionalism, Identity, Difference, and Legitimacy*. Edited by M. Rosenfeld. Durham: Duke University Press, 85.

Rieder, I. 1992. Lesbianism in the house of Europe. In *Women and Citizenship in Europe*. Edited by A. Ward, J. Gregory, and N. Yuval-Davis. Stoke-on-Trent UK: Trentham Books, 107.

Robson, R. 1994. Resisting the Family: Repositioning Lesbians in Legal Theory. *Signs: Journal of Women in Culture and Society*, 19:975.

Roe v. Wade 1973. *United States Reports*, 410:113.

Rose, K. 1994. *Diverse Communities: The Evolution of Lesbian and Gay Politics in Ireland*. Cork Ireland: Cork University Press.

Rosenfeld, M. 1994. Modern Constitutionalism as Interplay Between Identity and Diversity. In *Constitutionalism, Identity, Difference, and Legitimacy*. Edited by M. Rosenfeld. Durham: Duke University Press, 3.

Rothwell, D. R., and B. Boer. 1995. From the Franklin to Berlin: The Internationalisation of Australian Environmental Law and Policy. *Sydney Law Review*, 17:242.

Roulston, C. 1997. Women on the Margin: The Women's Movements in Northern Ireland, 1973–1995. In *Feminist Nationalism*. Edited by L. A. West. New York: Routledge, 41.

Ryan, F. W. 1996. Sexual Orientation and Law Reform in the Republic of Ireland. Paper presented at the Critical Legal Conference, University of East London. Essex UK.

Ryan, M. 1989. The American Parade: Representations of the Nineteenth-Century Social Order. In *The New Cultural History*. Edited by L. Hunt. Berkeley, University of California Press, 131.

S. v. Makwanyane and Another 1995. *Butterworth's Constitutional Law Reports*, 6:665.

Sanders, D. 1996. Getting Lesbian and Gay Issues on the International Human Rights Agenda. *Human Rights Quarterly*, 18:67.

Satchwell, K. 1995. Personal interview by author. Johannesburg, July 31.

Saunders, C. 1995. Articles of Faith or Lucky Breaks?: The Constitutional Law of International Agreements in Australia. *Sydney Law Review*, 17:150.

Sawer, G. 1976, *Modern Federalism*. Carlton Australia: Pitman.

Sawer, M. 1991. Why has the Women's Movement had More Influence on Government in Australia than Elsewhere? In *Australia Compared: People, Policies and Politics*. Edited by F. G. Castles. Sydney: Allen and Unwin, 258.

Schwartzwald, R. 1990. an/other Canada. another Canada? other Canadas. *Massachusetts Review*, 31:9.

―――. 1991. Fear of Federasty: Quebec's Inverted Fictions. In *Comparative American Identities*. Edited by H. J. Spillers. New York: Routledge, 175.

―――. 1992. From Authenticity to Ambivalence: Michel Tremblay's *Hosanna*. *American Review of Canadian Studies*, 22:499.

―――. 1993. "Symbolic" Homosexuality, "False Feminine," and the Problematics of Identity in Quebec. In *Fear of a Queer Planet*. Edited by M. Warner. Minneapolis: University of Minnesota Press, 264.

Sedgwick, E. 1993. *Tendencies*. Durham: Duke University Press.

Senate (Australia) 1994. *Weekly Hansard*. Canberra: Parliament of the Commonwealth of Australia.

Senate Legal and Constitutional Legislation Committee (Australia) 1994. *Report: Human Rights (Sexual Conduct) Bill 1994*. Canberra: Parliament of the Commonwealth of Australia.

Shaw, J. 1996a. European Union Legal Studies in Crisis? Towards a New Dynamic. *Oxford Journal of Legal Studies*, 16:231.

―――. 1996b. *Law of the European Union*. Basingstoke UK: Macmillan.

Shaw, J., and G. More. 1996. *New Legal Dynamics of European Union*. Oxford: Clarendon Press.

Sheppard, C. 1997. The Promise and Practice of Protecting Human Rights: Reflections on The *Quebec Charter of Rights and Freedoms*. In *Mélanges Paul-André Crépeau*. Cowansville Quebec: Yvon Blais, 641.

Shiffrin, S. 1995. The First Amendment and the Meaning of America. In *Identities, Politics, and Rights*. Edited by A. Sarat and T. R. Kearns. Ann Arbor: University of Michigan Press, 307.

Shilts, R. 1987. *And the Band Played On*. New York: St. Martin's Press.

Shiose, Y., and L. Fontaine. 1995. La construction des figures de l'"autre": les Communautés culturelles au Québec. *Canadian Review of Sociology and Anthropology*, 32:91.

Shore, C., and A. Black. 1994. Citizens' Europe and the Construction of European Identity. In *The Anthropology of Europe*. Edited by V. A. Goddard, J. R. Llobera, and C. Shore. Oxford: Berg, 275.

Sieg, K. 1995. Deviance and Dissidence: Sexual Subjects of the Cold War. In *Cruising the Performative*. Edited by S.-E. Case, P. Brett, and S. L. Foster. Bloomington: Indiana University Press, 93.

Sinfield, A. 1996. Diaspora and Hybridity: Queer Identities and the Ethnicity Model. *Textual Practice*, 10:271.

Slaughter, M. M. 1994. The Multicultural Self: Questions of Subjectivity, Questions of Power. In *Constitutionalism, Identity, Difference, and Legitimacy*. Edited by M. Rosenfeld. Durham: Duke University Press, 369.

Smith, A. M. 1994. The Imaginary Inclusion of the Assimilable "Good Homosexual": The British New Right's Representation of Sexuality and Race. *diacritics*, vol. 24, 2/3:58.

Smolicz, J. J. 1995. The Emergence of Australia as a Multicultural Nation: An International Perspective. *Journal of International Studies,* 16:3.

Spalin, E. 1992. Abortion, Speech and the European Community. *Journal of Social Welfare and Family Law,* 1992:17.

State v. Kampher 1997. High Court of South Africa, No. 001377/97, Case No. 232/97, unreported.

Steedman, C. 1995. Inside, Outside, Other: Accounts of National Identity in the 19th Century. *History of the Human Sciences,* vol. 8, 4:59.

Stein, A., ed. 1993. *Sisters, Sexperts, Queers: Beyond the Lesbian Nation.* New York: Penguin.

Stolcke, V. 1995. Talking Culture: New Boundaries, New Rhetorics of Exclusion in Europe. *Current Anthropology,* 36:1.

Stychin, C. F. 1993. The Commentaries of Chancellor James Kent and the Development of an American Common Law. *American Journal of Legal History,* 37:440.

———. 1995a. *Law's Desire: Sexuality and the Limits of Justice.* London: Routledge.

———. 1995b. Novel Concepts: A Comment on *Egan and Nesbit v. The Queen. Constitutional Forum Constitutionnel,* 6:101.

———. 1996a. Constituting Sexuality: The Struggle for Sexual Orientation in the South African Bill of Rights. *Journal of Law and Society,* 23:455.

———. 1996b. Promoting a Sexuality: Law and Lesbian and Gay Visual Culture in America. In *Outlooks: Lesbian and Gay Visual Cultures.* Edited by R. Lewis and P. Horne. London: Routledge, 147.

———. 1996c. To Take Him "At His Word": Theorizing Law, Sexuality and the U.S. Military Exclusion Policy. *Social and Legal Studies,* 5:179.

Sunder, M. 1996. Authorship and Autonomy as Rites of Exclusion: The Intellectual Propertization of Free Speech in *Hurley v. Irish-American Gay, Lesbian and Bisexual Group of Boston. Stanford Law Review,* 49:143.

Sutherland v. United Kingdom 1997. Application 25186/84, unreported.

Swan, M. 1987. Ideology in Organised Indian Politics 1891–1948. In *The Politics of Race, Class and Nationalism in Twentieth-Century South Africa.* Edited by S. Marks and S. Trapido. London: Longman, 182.

Swinton, K., and C. Rogerson. 1988. *Competing Constitutional Visions: The Meech Lake Accord.* Toronto: Carswell.

Sydney Law Review 1995. Special Issue: "Internationalisation of Australian Law," 17:119–346.

Tanca, A. 1993. European Citizenship and the Rights of Lesbians and Gay Men. In *Homosexuality: A European Community Issue.* Edited by K. Waaldijk and A. Clapham. Dordrecht Netherlands: Martinus Nijhoff, 267.

Tasmanian Dam Case 1985. *Commonwealth Law Reports,* 158:1.

Tatchell, P. 1992. *Europe in the Pink.* London: GMP Publishers.

Taylor, C. 1993. *Reconciling Solitudes: Essays on Canadian Federalism and Nationalism.* Edited by G. Laforest. Montreal and Kingston: McGill–Queen's University Press.

Teitel, R. G. 1994. Reactionary Constitutional Identity. In *Constitutionalism, Identity, Difference, and Legitimacy.* Edited by M. Rosenfeld. Durham: Duke University Press, 233.

Tenbensel, T. 1996. International Human Rights Conventions and Australian Political Debates: Issues Raised by the "Toonen Case." *Australian Journal of Political Science,* 31:7.

Texas v. Johnson 1989. *United States Reports,* 491:397.

Thomas, K. 1993. Corpus Juris (Hetero)Sexualis: Doctrine, Discourse, and Desire in *Bowers v. Hardwick. GLQ,* 1:33.

Thompson, L. 1995. *A History of South Africa,* rev. ed. New Haven: Yale University Press.

Toonen v. Australia 1994. No. CCPR/C/50/D/488/1992, unreported.

Tremblay, M. 1974. *Hosanna.* Translated by J. Van Burek and B. Glassco. Vancouver: Talonbooks.

Turner Broadcasting System, Inc. v. Federal Communications Commission 1994. *United States Reports,* 512:622.

Turner, B. S. 1994. Postmodern Culture/Modern Citizens. In *The Condition of Citizenship.* Edited by B. van Steenbergen. London: Sage, 153.

Twomey, A. 1994. *Strange Bedfellows: The UN Human Rights Committee and the Tasmanian Parliament.* Canberra: Parliament of the Commonwealth of Australia.

Twomey, P. M. 1994. The European Union: Three Pillars without a Human Rights Foundation. In *Legal Issues of the Maastricht Treaty.* Edited by D. O'Keeffe and P. M. Twomey. Chichester UK: Chancery Law Publishing, 121.

United States v. Eichman 1990. *United States Reports,* 496:310.

Van Ness, G. 1996. Parades and Prejudice: The Incredible True Story of Boston's St. Patrick's Day Parade and the United States Supreme Court. *New England Law Review,* 30:625.

Vipond, R. C. 1993. Constitution-making in Canada: Writing a National Identity or Preparing for National Disintegration? In *Writing a National Identity: Political, Economic, and Cultural Perspectives on the Written Constitution.* Edited by V. Hart and S. C. Stimson. Manchester: Manchester University Press, 231.

Visser, P. J., and J. M. Potgieter. 1994. Some Critical Comments on South Africa's Bill of Fundamental Human Rights. *Journal of Contemporary Roman-Dutch Law,* 57:493.

wa Sibuyi, M. 1993. Tinkoncana Etimayinini: "The Wives of the Mines" An Interview with "Philemon." In *The Invisible Ghetto: Lesbian and Gay Writ-*

ing from South Africa. Edited by M. Krouse. Johannesburg: COSAW Publishing, 52.

Waaldijk, K. 1993. The Legal Situation in the Member States. In *Homosexuality: A European Community Issue.* Edited by K. Waaldijk and A. Clapham. Dordrecht Netherlands: Martinus Nijhoff, 71.

Waaldijk, K., and A. Clapham, eds. 1993. *Homosexuality: A European Community Issue.* Dordrecht Netherlands: Martinus Nijhoff.

Wald, P. 1995. *Constituting Americans: Cultural Anxiety and Narrative Form.* Durham: Duke University Press.

Waldstreicher, D. 1995. Rites of Rebellion, Rites of Assent: Celebrations, Print Culture, and the Origins of American Nationalism. *Journal of American History,* 82:37.

Walker, B. 1998. Social Movements as Nationalisms. *Canadian Journal of Philosophy.* Supplementary volume: "Nationalism," 22:505.

Walker, K. 1994. The Participation of the Law in the Construction of (Homo)-Sexuality. *Law in Context,* 12:52.

———. 1996. The Importance of Being Out: Sexuality and Refugee Status. *Sydney Law Review,* 18:568.

Walshe, E. 1996. Sexing the Shamrock. *Critical Survey,* 8:159.

———. 1997. Paper presented at the Queering the Nation Conference, Warwick University. Coventry, UK.

Ward, I. 1994. In Search of a European Identity. *Modern Law Review,* 57:315.

———. 1996a. Identifying the Eurosceptic. *Res Publica,* 2:87.

———. 1996b. Identity and Difference: The European Union and Postmodernism. In *New Legal Dynamics of the European Union.* Edited by J. Shaw and G. More. Oxford: Clarendon Press, 15.

Warner, M., ed. 1993. *Fear of a Queer Planet.* Minneapolis: University of Minnesota Press.

Weeks, J. 1995. *Invented Moralities: Sexual Values in an Age of Uncertainty.* Cambridge UK: Polity.

Weiler, J. H. H. 1994. Fin-de-Siècle Europe. In *Europe After Maastricht: An Ever Closer Union?* Edited by R. Dehousse. Munich: Law Books in Europe, 203.

———. 1995. Does Europe Need a Constitution? Demos, Telos and the German Maastricht Decision. *European Law Journal,* 1:219.

Weiler, J. H. H. 1996. European Neo-constitutionalism: in Search of Foundations for the European Constitutional Order. *Political Studies,* 44:517.

West, L. A., ed. 1997. *Feminist Nationalism.* New York: Routledge.

Wetherell, I. 1995. Mugabe Cracks Down on Gay Rights. (South Africa) *Mail and Guardian.* August 4, p. 15.

White, R. 1981. *Inventing Australia.* Sydney: Allen and Unwin.

Widdicombe, B. 1997. Immigration Gets Tougher. *Sydney Star Observer,* March 13, p. 4.

Wik Peoples v. The State of Queensland and Others 1996. *Australian Law Reports,* 134:637.

Windsor, G. 1997. Euthanasia Contravenes Basic Human Rights, Says Andrews. *The Australian,* March 17, p. 4.

Wintemute, R. 1995. *Sexual Orientation and Human Rights.* Oxford: Clarendon Press.

Wotherspoon, G. 1991. From Sub-culture to Mainstream Culture: Some Impacts of Homosexual and Gay Sub-cultures in Australia. *Journal of Australian Studies,* 28:56.

Yack, B. 1995. Reconciling Liberalism and Nationalism. *Political Theory,* 23:166.

Yackle, L. W. 1993. Parading Ourselves: Freedom of Speech at the Feast of St. Patrick. *Boston University Law Review,* 73:791.

Yalda, C. 1997. Walking the Straight and Narrow: Performative Sexuality and the First Amendment After *Hurley.* Paper presented at the American Law and Society Association Annual Conference. St. Louis, Missouri.

Yeatman, A. 1994. *Postmodern Revisionings of the Political.* New York: Routledge.

Yingling, T. 1994. Wittgenstein's Tumour: AIDS and the National Body. *Textual Practice,* 8:97.

Young, I. M. 1990. *Justice and the Politics of Difference.* Princeton: Princeton University Press.

———. 1995. Gender as Seriality: Thinking About Women as a Social Collective. In *Social Postmodernism.* Edited by L. Nicholson and S. Seidman. Cambridge UK: Cambridge University Press, 187.

Yuval-Davis, N. 1997. *Gender and Nation.* London: Sage.

Zaleskas, K. M. 1996. Pride, Prejudice or Political Correctness? An Analysis of *Hurley v. Irish-American Gay, Lesbian and Bisexual Group of Boston. Columbia Journal of Law and Social Problems,* 29:507.

Zines, L. 1994. A Judicially Created Bill of Rights? *Sydney Law Review,* 16:166.

Index